Oral Bible Translation and Biblical Performance in Southern Siberia

Oral Bible Translation and Biblical Performance in Southern Siberia

A Design for a Performance-Based Oral Bible Translation in the Southern Altai Language (Siberia)

by
BRONWEN CLEAVER

Foreword by James A. Maxey

WIPF & STOCK · Eugene, Oregon

ORAL BIBLE TRANSLATION AND BIBLICAL PERFORMANCE IN SOUTHERN SIBERIA
A Design for a Performance-Based Oral Bible Translation in the Southern Altai Language (Siberia)

Copyright © 2025 Bronwen Cleaver. All rights reserved. Except for brief quotations in critical publications or reviews, no part of this book may be reproduced in any manner without prior written permission from the publisher. Write: Permissions, Wipf and Stock Publishers, 199 W. 8th Ave., Suite 3, Eugene, OR 97401.

Wipf & Stock
An Imprint of Wipf and Stock Publishers
199 W. 8th Ave., Suite 3
Eugene, OR 97401

www.wipfandstock.com

PAPERBACK ISBN: 979-8-3852-3638-1
HARDCOVER ISBN: 979-8-3852-3639-8
EBOOK ISBN: 979-8-3852-3640-4

VERSION NUMBER 07/30/25

Scripture quotations marked (NASB) are taken from the (NASB®) New American Standard Bible®, Copyright © 1960, 1971, 1977, 1995, 2020 by The Lockman Foundation. Used by permission. All rights reserved. www.lockman.org

Scripture quotations marked (NIV84) are taken from the Holy Bible, New International Version®, NIV®. Copyright © 1984, by Biblica, Inc.™ Used by permission of Zondervan. All rights reserved worldwide. www.zondervan.com The "NIV" and "New International Version" are trademarks registered in the United States Patent and Trademark Office by Biblica, Inc.™

Contents

List of Tables | vii
List of Figures | viii
List of Abbreviations | ix
Foreword by James A. Maxey | xi
Acknowledgments | xiii

1. Introduction | 1
2. Theoretical Framework | 15
3. Oral Bible Translation | 64
4. Biblical Performance Criticism | 103
5. The Poetic Features of Judges 4 and 5 for Oral Translation and Performance | 115
6. The Poetic Features of Psalms 1, 100, and 133 for Oral Translation and Performance | 135
7. Altai Epics and *Ochy-Bala* | 152
8. Translating the Texts into Altai | 185
9. Altai Performances | 203
10. Conclusions | 228

Appendix 1—Story chart for Judges 4 | 239
Appendix 2—Translators' oral notes for Judges 4 | 241
Appendix 3—Story chart for Judges 5 | 254
Appendix 4—Translators' oral notes for Judges 5 | 255
Appendix 5—Story Chart for Psalm 1 | 272
Appendix 6—Translators' Oral Notes for Psalm 1 | 273
Appendix 7—Story chart for Psalm 100 | 280
Appendix 8—Translators' Oral Notes for Psalm 100 | 281

Appendix 9—Story chart for Psalm 133 | 284
Appendix 10—Translators' Oral Notes for Psalm 133 | 285
Appendix 11—Illustrations of Judges 4 for internalization | 287
Appendix 12—Illustrations of Judges 4 by the Altai team | 291

Bibliography | 293

List of Tables

Table 1: Summary of the internalization process used | 84
Table 2: Summary of preferences for different methods of internalization | 85
Table 3: Translators' oral notes for Judges 4 | 243
Table 4: Translators' oral notes for Judges 5 | 257
Table 5: Translators' oral notes for Psalm 1 | 276
Table 6: Translators' oral notes for Psalm 100 | 283
Table 7: Translators' oral notes for Psalm 133 | 287

List of Figures

Figure 1: Story chart for Judges 4 | 242
Figure 2: Story chart for Judges 5 | 256
Figure 3: Story chart for Psalm 1 | 274
Figure 4: Story chart for Psalm 100 | 282
Figure 5: Story chart for Psalm 100 | 286
Figure 6: Illustrations of Judges 4 for internalization | 290
Figure 7: Illustrations of Judges 4 by the Altai team | 291

List of Abbreviations

ANE	Ancient Near East
BPC	Biblical Performance Criticism
BSR	Bible Society of Russia
BT	Bible Translation
CRV2	Contemporary Russian Version, 2nd edition
EGIDS	The Expanded Graded Intergenerational Disruption Scale
EMDC	The Eurasia Media and Distribution Consultation
EPA	Embodied Performance Analysis
FCBH	Faith Comes by Hearing
IBT	Institute for Bible Translation
LWC	Language of Wider Communication
MIT	Most Important Thing
MTT	mother-tongue translator
NASB	New American Standard Bible
NIV84	New International Version 1984
NLT	New Living Translation
NT	New Testament
OBS	Oral Bible Storying
OBT	Oral Bible Translation
OT	Old Testament
RL	Receptor Language
RT	Receptor Text
SL	Source Language
ST	Source Text
TA	Translation Advisor

Foreword

Biblical Performance Criticism (BPC) has blossomed into a multifaceted discipline where biblical studies remains a significant but not exclusive part. An increasingly integral additional element to BPC is Bible translation (BT). This book is a significant contribution to such growth and demonstrates the value of anthropological studies in appreciating how host communities shape how the Bible is translated, not only in content but form and medium.

The book contains abundant material for others to benefit from in terms of research methodologies and data collection. The author provides a methodology, based on extensive interviews and field research, to demonstrate her approach to Oral Bible Translation (OBT). Cleaver reveals the questions posed to OBT teams and trainers, Altai performers, translators, and poets. In turn, these research methods inform her careful pursuit of the functions of genres and performative features to be translated. The pedagogical value of this work is evident, as it proposes designing a performance-based translation. Her modeling of these steps moves the proposed methodology beyond theoretical assertions to practical implementation.

OBT has become a more common method in BT in the past couple of decades. Hundreds if not thousands of language communities now have the opportunity to hear the Bible in their own language. This book contributes to the methodology of OBT while demonstrating the inherent value of cultural preferences of a community to communicate the Bible. We have learned from BPC that it's more than hearing; this methodology understands how we experience the Bible in multisensory, performative ways.

Perhaps the most significant offer that OBT in general and this book in particular contribute to BPC is the extended discussions of internalization and emotion. While BPC had discussed social memory and assumed some type of memorization, the actual methodology for internalizing large swaths of biblical material was left under-described. Cleaver provides a well-supported internalization approach that is pedagogical in its scope for

OBT scalability. A relatively new aspect of the performance of biblical material is the emergence of emotive studies. Insights from such studies provide important contributions to both the exegetical analysis of the source material as well as how to intentionally perform emotion.

This book breaks new ground by presenting OBT in Siberia, a relatively unknown part of the world for many of us doing BT. The author demonstrates her knowledge of this region and her experiences with the Altai language community. It is fascinating to read how a distinct mode of communication is explored to express the translated Bible. Also significant: whereas there are ample examples by others of OBT in the translation of narratives, the author selects biblical poetry as the genre to demonstrate her OBT methodology. By signaling the poetic features of the biblical compositions, she is able to challenge us to consider translation beyond words to rhythms, alliterations, and other prosodic features of the Altai language.

Bible translation is asserted in this book as part of the larger discipline of Translation Studies (TS). Cleaver demonstrates her comprehension of TS by articulating her functional approach to translation while exploring complexity theory's potential for BT. Additionally, Cleaver examines the semiotic multimodal nature of translation, especially with OBT. This approach requires equal attention to the source text and its performative features, as well as the local context with its genres of performance and how functionality is pursued to link the source and local performances.

BT has expanded exponentially over the past decade with the number of translations begun in smaller language communities around the world—especially with OBT. Cleaver contributes to this expansion with a sophisticated design-oriented approach that demonstrates her close attention to theory while providing pedagogical steps for others to follow. Practitioners, trainers, and theoreticians of Bible translation will find ample material to inspire and challenge them as they look to the next generation of global Bible translation studies.

James Maxey, PhD
Director for Translation Quality Development at Seed Company

Acknowledgments

This book would not have been possible without the help and support of my excellent PhD supervisors, Professor Jacobus Naudé and Professor Cynthia Miller-Naudé at the University of the Free State (Bloemfontein, South Africa). I am happy to be appointed as a research fellow at the university. I am extremely grateful to my proofreaders, Dr. Vitaly Voinov and Dr. Teija Greed, who read through my drafts with patience and thoroughness. In addition to proofreading, Charlie Law, a friend from the US, helped Americanise—I mean, Americanize—the text to conform to my publisher's requirements. I am thankful to Brian Kelly, who encouraged me from the beginning of this process, and to SIL Global, which provided the majority of the funding to complete this research. Of course, this endeavor would not have been possible without the unending support and help of my faithful husband, Colin Cleaver, and from my children, Emily and Jon, who encouraged me along the way and let me spend many hours in the basement. I am always grateful to my parents for their investment in my education and upbringing and their never-ending assistance in all my endeavors. Finally, I would like to thank my best friend, Yulia Notkina, for her continual prayers, friendship, and humor throughout this long process.

1

Introduction

BACKGROUND

I was involved from June 2019 to June 2024 as a translation advisor (TA) in an oral Bible translation (OBT) project in the Southern Altai language in the Republic of Altai (Russian Federation). The Republic of Altai covers an area of 92,600 sq km in Siberia, bordering China, Mongolia, and Kazakhstan.

According to the *Ethnologue*, the ethnic Altai population is 74,200.[1] Of this number, approximately 57,400 people identified themselves as speakers of the Turkic language Altai (alt) in data from the 2010 Russian census. The vitality of the Altai language is considered high. It has been assigned by the *Ethnologue* a language status of Level 2 on the Expanded Graded Intergenerational Disruption Scale (EGIDS), indicating use in "education, work, mass media and government at the national level."[2]

The New Testament (NT) is available in Southern Altai (Institute for Bible Translation 2003, 2017), and the Old Testament (OT), translated by the Bible Society of Russia (BSR), is currently being combined with a revised NT to produce a full Altai Bible. I serve as an exegete with the Institute for Bible Translation (IBT) for the Altai Bible and have been the TA for a separate OBT project in the Southern Altai language. I am also involved in Scripture engagement work in the Republic of Altai and speak the Altai language at a conversational level.

1. *Ethnologue*.
2. *Ethnologue*.

The OBT Altai translation team has orally translated Genesis, Ruth, Jonah, and Exodus, as well as fifteen Psalms, translated as songs, and a selection of Proverbs organized according to themes. The available texts can be found at http://www.altai-obt.ru/?page_id=24 and on a mobile phone application, available at https://play.google.com/store/apps/details?id=ru.wycliffe.alt.obt. While working with this team, I began comparing translations of the same biblical text into Altai produced by the oral method and by the written method.[3] This was possible because the same biblical text was being translated using both methods. My 2020 pilot research on the translations of Jonah chapter 1 revealed that the text created by the oral method was perceived as more natural and comprehensible by the Altai community, which has a strong preference for orality in general.

At the same time, the translation team and I also began experimenting with using local genres such as epic stories to contextualize the oral translations and render them more accessible and understandable to a local audience. One of the main indicators of oral-preference on the part of the Altai people is their love of heroic epic stories. The Altai epics are renowned oral masterpieces that have been conveyed from one generation to the next. One of the pioneers in the field of Altai epic poetry and folklore was Radlov (1837–1918), who compiled an extensive collection of this oral material, which included ten epic oral texts that were published in St. Petersburg. The late Surazakov (1925–80) was the founder of the series Altaj Baatyrlar, "Altai Heroes," and a renowned researcher and collector of Altai epics. To date, fifteen volumes have been published, containing more than eighty epic texts.[4] Like other Turkic peoples, the Altai have a rich heritage of such epics, in which the mighty deeds of heroic warriors are celebrated. Together with the translation team, I began to investigate whether some of the features of the Altai oral epic stories could be utilized in an oral performance of a biblical text, in order for the biblical text to become more familiar and understandable to an Altai audience.

DESIGNING A PERFORMANCE

I became increasingly interested in developing ways to design a performance based on an oral Bible translation in Altai and to find out if using the method of OBT, adapted and contextualized for culturally relevant performances, would give oral-preference learners in the Republic of Altai the best possible access to Scripture.

---

3. Cleaver, "Comparison of Listeners' Responses."
4. Surazakov and Shinzhin, *Altai Baatyrlar*.

My interest in finding ways to optimize access to Scripture for the Altai people came at a time when the field of Biblical Performance Criticism (BPC) had been growing. This expanding field of BPC reinterprets the ancient biblical texts in the light of the oral and scribal cultures of Judaism and early Christianity and then constructs culturally relevant modern performances. Proponents of BPC, which is discussed in more detail in chapter 4, assert that certain biblical authors, rather like some musical composers, did not initially write down their speeches or stories but instead composed them orally.[5] Their art was not primarily literary but dramatic.[6] Many biblical texts were intended to be enacted before a gathered audience. These oral compositions were then transmitted orally, although there were also scrolls that provided a written record of the performance.

To date, most BPC scholarship has focused on the NT, with the result that there is only limited research on how BPC can construct modern performances of OT texts. Doan and Giles have applied BPC principles to the Hebrew Bible, looking at Song of Songs and prophetic texts such as Jonah and Ruth.[7] Work on the prophetic books in BPC has been continued by Mathews.[8] More recently, Cousins's PhD dissertation used a performance-critical methodology as the basis of a theological interpretation of the Psalms of Ascent, assessing multiple performances of the psalms for different audiences in Australia.[9] I decided to expand this research on constructing performances of OT texts in the Altai context.

In the process of translating and constructing modern performances of biblical texts, choices for performance can even influence and change the translation itself. Exegesis becomes a more interactive process, through the impact of the oral translation on the listeners and engagement with the audience. I proposed, in consultation with the Altai Bible translation team, to translate the narrative prose and narrative poetic passages of Judges chapters 4 and 5 using the oral translation approach. The reasons for the choice of this text are as follows. First of all, to my knowledge, there has been no significant research on the performance of these chapters from Judges in the field of BPC. Secondly, these chapters present the same story, in chapter 4 in prose and in chapter 5 in poetry, providing the opportunity to compare and analyze the oral translation and performance of both prose and poetry. Finally, the text of Judg 5 is one of the oldest poetic passages in the Hebrew

---

5. Rhoads, *Mark as Story*, 26.
6. West, "Art of Biblical," 10.
7. Doan and Giles, *Prophets and Performance* and *Story of Naomi*.
8. Mathews, *Performing Habakkuk*.
9. Cousins, "Pilgrim Theology."

Bible. It is a dense poem which includes repetition, parallelism, word pairs, alliteration, paronomasia, formulaic constructions, multiple verb phrases, and chiastic structures. It has the marks of typical Hebrew poetry in a song format.[10] The large and varied number of oral literary devices used in this text allows the Altai team to creatively investigate how the different features in the Altai language can serve the same function as the features of orality in the biblical text.

The Altai translation team also decided to translate Pss 1, 100, and 133. Psalm 1, probably together with Ps 2, forms the introduction or prologue to the book of Psalms.[11] The collectors of the psalms probably considered Ps 1 an especially characteristic psalm, suitable as an introductory psalm to commence the collection.[12] As one of the best-known passages in the Hebrew Bible, Ps 1 is a wisdom psalm which instructs the listeners to dedicate themselves to the study of God's law and warns them of the consequences if they do not. Seow argues that Ps 1 is not just poetry but is "exquisite poetry."[13] It features parallelism, chiasm, contrast, ambiguity, assonance, a formulaic introduction, an *inclusio*, and familiar imagery that is typical of the psalms in general.[14] Such poetry invites the audience to a dialogue, as they have to negotiate multiple meanings and seemingly ambiguous interpretations. The Altai translation team decided to experiment to see if it would be possible to orally translate this psalm poetically and to set it to traditional Altai music.

Psalm 100 is a typical praise psalm which may have been used as a doxology at the end of the collection of Pss 95–100. Brueggemann refers to this psalm as one of the "best-known and best-loved in the entire repertoire of the Psalter."[15] Mays says of the poetry in Ps 100 that the words "are not used casually, but in a careful precision that aims at maximum significance crafted into chiseled brevity."[16] St. Augustine said of Ps 100, "The verses are few, but big with great subjects."[17]

Finally, Ps 133 was chosen because its subject is unity and its communicative purpose is to inspire and motivate the listeners toward a common goal. It was decided that this would be an apt psalm to set to an Altai melody that signifies harmony. Melodies themselves and even the instruments have

10. Block, *Judges/Ruth*, 212.
11. Bratcher and Rayburn, *Handbook*.
12. Alter, *Art of Biblical Poetry*, 142.
13. Seow, *Exquisitely Poetic*, 275.
14. Segal, *New Psalm*, 59–61.
15. Brueggemann, "Psalm 100," 65.
16. Mays, "World, Worship," 318.
17. Schaff, *St. Augustine*, loc. 23449.

a semiotic significance apart from the lyrics; this is discussed in more detail in chapter 7.

After an analysis of local Altai genres, the Altai translation team decided to adapt and contextualize these biblical passages using features of Altai local genres, including the oral epic genre, to create live performances to be shown around Altai to local audiences. These culturally relevant performances would then be assessed by local audiences as to whether this approach gave them the best possible access to Scripture, with feedback from the performances to be incorporated into the translation process by the translation team.

SUB-QUESTIONS

Using an integrated approach informed by the complex interplay of discussions about orality in the world today, orality and literacy in the Bible, and also performance criticism, I propose a design model for performing orally translated texts that takes into account traditional local genres. This model, founded on the functional theory of translation and drawing on aspects of complexity theory, multimodality, and hospitality theory, highlights principles that are most relevant for other OBT teams seeking to orally translate and perform biblical passages.

My main research question is the following: how can one design a performance based on the oral translation of biblical texts into the Altai language, taking into account traditional Altai cultural genres? In my work, this main research question was supplemented by addressing the following sub-questions:

1. How does the process of internalization influence the method of OBT, distinguishing it from written Bible translation (BT)?
2. How can the method of OBT be used to translate genres other than narrative?
3. How and when should the process of extralinguistic exegesis take place during the OBT process?
4. How can the oral features of local poetry be incorporated into an oral poetic translation of a biblical text?
5. What is the most useful way to create notes for the oral performance of an orally translated text, including extralinguistic and paralinguistic features?

6. How can the response to the oral performance be incorporated back into the oral translation process and thereby become part of the process of translation?

THEORETICAL FRAMEWORK

Presenting a model for a performance-based OBT in the Altai language requires a multidisciplinary approach that incorporates an understanding of current research on orality, orality and literacy in the Bible, and, of course, of BPC itself. In terms of translation studies, I use principles of the functional approach, informed by complexity theory, multi-modality, and hospitality theory. In chapters 2 and 4, I explain this theoretical framework used in more detail, but I present a summary here.

This book is written in the context of the growing emphasis on orality in the world, with particular interest in how this is influencing BT. The theory of orality was most notably developed by Ong, who proposed that, in comparison to highly literate societies, oral societies think, learn, and communicate differently about the world around them.[18] I have defined an oral-preference community as one with a reliance on oral communication rather than written modes of communication. This is a fast-growing category among the world's population, even in ostensibly literate societies. As the Republic of Altai is an oral-preference community, this language group is an ideal candidate for an OBT approach. The topic of orality is discussed in more detail in chapter 2.

Another important area of research providing part of the theoretical framework for this book is the study of orality and literacy in the Bible. Although the past one hundred and fifty years have been marked by a textual bias in OT scholarship,[19] there has been a steadily growing interest in oral aspects of Scripture. For example, Kelber was one of the first to examine the Bible in the light of the characteristics of orality put forward by Ong and others.[20] More recently, the field of BPC has produced research affirming that both ancient Israel and the early church were mainly oral cultures. This research demonstrates that both oral transmission and scribal activity played essential roles in the composition of the Bible.[21] De Vries concludes that the Hebrew Bible is a product of a specific oral-written interface.[22] As

---

18. Ong, *Orality and Literacy*, 36.
19. West, "Art of Biblical," 7.
20. Kelber, *Oral*.
21. Naudé and Miller-Naudé, "Translation of Biblion," 1.
22. De Vries, "Local Oral-Written," 73.

such, it is not the product of an essentially oral culture but an integration of the oral, written, and memorization-enculturation dimensions. Each of these aspects made a specific contribution to the preservation, transmission, and performance of the Scriptures.

The history of media culture demonstrates how the biblical text has changed from oral to scribal, to print, and finally to electronic forms. Walton and Sandy's research has elucidated the concept of dominance within oral and literate practices by distinguishing between hearing-dominant cultures (traditions transmitted orally across generations) and text-dominant cultures (traditions conveyed through scribally produced texts).[23] Makutoane, Miller-Naudé, and Naudé describe the media history of the Bible in the following stages: hearing-dominant (oral/aural communication followed by handwritten manuscript communication) and text-dominant (print communication followed by electronic/media communication).[24] Often this evolution has been associated with technical innovation, as when the invention of the printing press made possible the mass production of translations of the Bible. This in turn led to widespread silent individual reading, as memorization of texts became less common.

The majority of people within ancient Israel and within ancient Near Eastern (ANE) cultures more generally would not have read biblical texts written on papyrus or parchment but would instead have experienced them orally.[25] Texts were still utilized but for a more limited purpose than in an environment where culture and traditions are predominantly relayed via texts written by scribes. Steffen demonstrates through numerous historical examples that the oral methods of storytelling and drama were common practice in early Christianity.[26] Naudé and Miller-Naudé comment that visuality also played an integral role in this hearing-dominant culture and has also been present during all stages of the history of media culture.[27] Visual media is now playing an increasingly prominent role in the digital age.

My research demonstrates that throughout this media history, both oral and written communication have been extremely significant and always interlinked. The biblical texts chosen for this research (Judg 4–5 and Pss 1, 100, and 133) were almost certainly originally composed and heard orally. The topic of orality and literacy in the Bible is discussed in more detail in chapter 2 and BPC in chapter 4.

23. Walton and Sandy, *Lost World*, 18.
24. Makutoane et al., "Similarity and Alterity," 3.
25. Wendland, *Finding*, 6.
26. Steffen, *Worldview-Based Storying*.
27. Naudé and Miller-Naudé, "Translation of Biblion," 4.

As the main theoretical framework for this research, I am using the functional theory of translation. According to this theory, translating is described as a "purposeful activity."[28] Proponents of functionalist approaches view translation as an act of purposeful communication and argue that the *purpose* of the receptor text (RT) is the most important constraint on the translator's action.[29] A translation is viewed as adequate if the translation meets the targeted communicative objectives of the RT in a relevant context.[30] The purpose (Greek: *skopos*) of a particular translation is normally agreed upon by the various people who play some role in the translation process. This agreed-upon purpose then guides the translators in determining what approach and strategies to use during translating.

Linguistic translation models have viewed translation as a code-switching linear activity.[31] Equivalence was the standard for translation evaluation, which focused always on the source text (ST) and the preservation of its features in the RT. In contrast, in a functionalist approach, texts are seen as acts of communication, influenced by their situational context as well as cultural customs and norms. Translation is viewed as a circular process looping back on itself, rather than as a linear process. Functionalism recognizes that equivalence alone can never be the standard for translation because translation is determined by function. The status of the ST is lower in functionalism than in equivalence-based theories, yet the principle of loyalty preserves the relationship between the ST and the RT. The translation process is only complete when the text is accepted by the target audience. Functional theory is an important basis for this research, with its emphasis on the role of the target audience in the translation process.

As well as functional theory, I also use some aspects of complexity theory. Complexity theory has recently emerged as a new paradigm to study complex systems such as translation.[32] This theory maintains that translation is a complex adaptive system which relates to the environment and to the larger socio-cultural reality of which it is a part. There is both dynamic interaction between the various elements and the agents active in the process of translation. It cannot be reduced to any of its constituent parts but rather emerges from an interaction of language, literature, culture, ideology, and sociology.[33] Complex adaptive systems are open and are characterized

---

28. Nord, *Translating*.
29. Nord, "Text Analysis," 39.
30. Naudé, "Translation Studies," 2015.
31. Nord, *Translating*, loc. 300.
32. Marais, *Translation Theory*; Shreve, "Translation as a Complex," 69–87.
33. Marais, *Translation Theory*, 32.

by both stability and change.³⁴ Change can come from within the system or from outside the system, as the system interacts with its environment. Marais emphasizes the idea of agency in translation, as the translators themselves influence change and are being influenced by their social and cultural contexts.³⁵

Marais also challenges the idea that translation is a linear process, rather describing it as a unique creative process where there is a complex, dynamic interplay of all the factors which affect translation.³⁶ Translations can be very different, even when based on the same ST, because each translation context is unique, and the initial conditions are always different. Longa also rejects reductionist tendencies among translation theories, arguing that translation is a nonlinear process affected by many factors.³⁷ The text emerges from the dynamic interaction of all these factors. As a result of this, Tymoczko emphasizes that translation training should coach translators in strategies to creatively respond to unique situations by taking into account all the relevant factors.³⁸ Marais calls these factors "constraints" and "attractors," which influence the process of translating.³⁹ Within Marais's view of complexity as applied to translation studies, instead of employing the terms ST and RT, he proposes using "incipient sign system" (or "incipient text") and "subsequent sign system" (or "subsequent text"). Naudé and Miller-Naudé have applied Marais's terminology to BT, but I have decided to employ the traditional terms ST and RT, as is conventional within the BT community. Shreve (2021) also develops this idea of translation as a complex adaptive system within the framework of cognitive translatology.⁴⁰ For my research, I am particularly interested in the nonlinear approach of complexity theory, the ability of this theory to allow for the dynamic interaction of multiple factors, its non-reductionist character, and its conception of translation as a collaborative process.

I also draw on several concepts from the field of multimodality because the final performance presented to the Altai audiences uses local styles of music with ethnic instruments, national costumes, dance, nature photography of the Altai landscape, contextualized pictures drawn by an Altai artist, and artifacts from Altai history and culture. Multimodality, a

34. Marais, *Translation Theory*, 27.
35. Marais, *Translation Theory*, 89.
36. Marais, *Translation Theory*, 59.
37. Longa, "Nonlinear Approach," 210.
38. Tymoczko, "Translation as Organized Complexity," 250.
39. Marais, "Effects Causing Effects," 61.
40. Shreve, "Translation as a Complex," 69–87.

concept mainly developed over the last twenty years, refers to use of multiple media in communication to express social meaning.[41] The discipline assumes that all communication is multimodal, that language analysis alone cannot account for meaning, and that modes occur together and relate together for the purpose of making meaning. Societies have developed modes such as gestures, sounds, image, color, and layout to make meaning, which effectively enhance meaning when they accompany text or language. This is discussed in more detail in chapter 2.

Finally, I briefly examine hospitality theory as applied to translation by Maxey.[42] This theory is particularly appropriate for biblical performance, with its emphasis on relationships, negotiation, and the role of the audience.

METHODOLOGY

The first part of this book offers a review of the relevant literature on orality, orality and literacy in the Bible, performance criticism, functional translation and aspects of complexity theory, multimodality, and hospitality theory.

The second part focuses on the method of OBT, and, in particular, includes an examination of the process of internalization and how this process influences the translation of the text. This is accomplished via interviews with nine OBT teams and one trainer who are currently using the method of internalization. Answers are collected through written interviews and during live interviews by videoconference. Conclusions drawn from those interviews are used in the preparation of the Altai translation team's process of OBT and internalization.

My research on Altai epic poetry draws on personal interviews with noted singers of the Altai epics and musicians in the Republic of Altai. The selections includes both younger and older performers, including one woman, all experienced in the retelling of Altai epic poetry. Conclusions drawn from the interviews are used in the preparation and performance of the biblical narrative in the Altai epic song genre.

The final stage of the research is the creation of an oral performance, using the Altai epic story genre. After the preparation and performance of the concert, responses to the oral performance are evaluated through unstructured informal interviews. Some of these responses are incorporated back into the oral translation process in such a way that the performance therefore becomes part of the process of translation.

---

41. Adami, "Multimodality," 1.
42. Maxey, "Alternative Evaluative Concepts."

UNIQUE CONTRIBUTION

The examination of the method of OBT includes a more detailed study of the crucial internalization step, including a review of the current research on internalization and a summary of interviews with OBT teams around the world. This unique research is used to help the Altai OBT team and, in the future, other OBT teams, better understand the process of internalization and how to carry it out most effectively.

Secondly, I discuss how to translate other, non-narrative genres using OBT. To date, the method of OBT has mainly been used to translate narrative biblical passages. Some teams have experimented with the NT Pauline letters, but few OBT teams have attempted to use this method to translate poetry, except for Jonah 2 and Gen 49. I investigate possible ways of using internalization to translate poetry orally, and based on the field interviews, I compare the experience of OBT teams around the world who have attempted to translate poetry orally. A major contribution of this research is that I make recommendations for those OBT teams which plan to translate biblical poetry orally in the future.

Another distinctive feature of the OBT process is its use of an approach to extralinguistic exegesis that could be referred to as emotional exegesis. This approach typically involves a discussion, often during the internalization stage, about the kinds of emotions that the characters in the Bible passages may have been experiencing and expressing. The importance of this component of OBT is becoming increasingly evident as OBT and sign language translation projects proliferate in various parts of the world. As with recorded audio and video presentations, Scripture performances produced without first identifying the emotional aspects of a passage and without attempting to incorporate these emotional aspects into the finished product will fail to convey the full meaning of the passage. For this reason, TAs and consultants should be prepared to offer guidance on emotional exegesis. My research discusses how to create extralinguistic exegetical notes preparatory to constructing a performance which incorporate extralinguistic and paralinguistic features. It is hoped that these will be a useful tool for future OBT teams.

Fourthly, this research examines how to design a performance based on an orally translated text in the context of a local culture. The process leading to this performance begins with me, as the TA, doing a detailed study of the original Hebrew text of Judg 4–5 and Pss 1, 100, and 133, focusing on the features of orality in these passages. After the detailed exegetical study, the process continues with my translation of these passages from Hebrew into English, during which I strive to internalize the passages to engage with them as deeply as possible and perform the passages so as to communicate their meaning as fully as I am able. I then investigate and observe the use of Altai oral epics within the context of the history and culture of the Altai people, finally deciding which poetic features of the Altai epic poems can perform the same function as the features of orality in the biblical text. The Altai translation team then creates the performance in their own way, making full use of appropriate multimodal methods of presentation.

Finally, as part of the translation cycle, or loop, to be described in more detail below, I review and analyze feedback from performance with a view to incorporating it as the process continues. Meaning is not solely found in the original text but also in the performance, as multiple meanings may be negotiated by the audience. Performance, therefore, is part of a cyclical model, so that even after a performance, and during other post-performance discussion, the translators can review, analyze, and incorporate the insights brought to light in the course of the process up to that point. Currently in OBT practice, feedback on the translation is provided via the stages of peer review and community review, but there are few teams which have experimented with the idea of using performance itself as a way of getting additional community feedback.

LIMITATIONS

One limitation of my research is that it is specific to the local situation in the Altai Republic. I was able to focus on only one particular speech community and their oral genres. However, the results from this study are certainly relevant to OBT work in other oral-preference communities, despite differences in context. Each situation in which BT is performed is unique, so the usefulness of this research depends on the measure to which it is contextualized in the local setting. It is hoped that the results of this research will inspire others to use the performance model presented in this book in their own local, unique translation contexts. This model should be particularly useful to other OBT teams in oral-preference communities who would like to use features of local genres to help make biblical texts more accessible to the receptor audience.

Another limitation of this research is that I was not able to visit OBT teams around the world, as originally planned, in order to observe their process of internalization. Instead, it was possible only to conduct long-distance interviews, either by videoconference or by written communication, with OBT teams working in other places and contexts.

STRUCTURE

Beginning in the second chapter, this account of my research includes a theoretical examination of the functional translation approach so as to evaluate how it is applied in OBT. This also includes a discussion of ideas from complexity theory, multimodality, and hospitality theory, which help contribute to my theoretical approach. Key ideas discussed include the idea of the text as a communicative act which is only finally completed by the receiver; an examination of how meaning emerges relationally through the audience's response to performance; and consideration of the use of extralinguistic, paralinguistic, and visual features as metatext. The conclusions from this assessment are then used to develop a model of poetic translation for OBT to guide translators, upon which a performance can be based. The model for OBT translation and performance is then developed in the light of this functional theoretical translation model.

The third chapter commences with an examination of the process of internalization and how, in OBT, this process uniquely influences the translation of the text. This is followed by a study of how the method of OBT can be used to translate different genres, including poetry. Finally, there is a discussion of when and how extralinguistic exegesis should take place during OBT and how future OBT teams can be assisted with this process.

Chapter 4 is a theoretical examination of the field of Biblical Performance Criticism (BPC). This includes a short history of this field, practical examples of BPC, an overview of the benefits of BPC for the translation process, and, finally, a discussion of Embodied Performance Analysis. Among the key matters considered are ways which nonverbal features of performance contribute to communication, the importance of the audience in performance, and the uniqueness of each performance. At this point, I draw conclusions for the preparation of the Altai performances.

Chapters 5 and 6 present a study of the features of orality in the original Hebrew text of Judg 4–5 and Pss 1, 100, and 133. This includes tables showing the oral and performance features of these passages as well as story charts of these passages.

Chapter 7 discusses the oral features of Altai epic poetry and how the different features in the Altai language can fulfill the same functions as the features of orality in the biblical text. As part of this discussion, the use of Altai oral epics in the history and culture of the Altai people is investigated. This is accomplished by describing and analyzing the features of the poetic devices in the Altai epic poems and by identifying their functions and special structures. I focus in particular on the Altai epic *Ochy-Bala*, which is the story of a heroine who kills an enemy attacking the land and people of

Altai. This research isolates key features of the Altai epics, and, in particular, of the epic *Ochy-Bala*, which the Altai OBT team then uses in the creation of their Altai epic version of Judg 4–5. This chapter continues with a review of other Altai local genres, highlighting *jangar* singing and the style of an Altai song, and a discussion of why these genres have been chosen for Pss 1, 100, and 133.

Chapter 8 begins with a description of the methods of internalization that I personally used to retell these passages and to produce my own embodied performance in English. This is followed by a discussion on translating psalms as songs. The chapter concludes with a description of the process of translating the texts into Altai by the method of OBT.

Finally, in chapter 9 there is a description of the creation of an oral performance using the Altai epic story genre. This includes detailing the process of making notes for the performance with extralinguistic and paralinguistic features highlighted, intended in part as a tool for future OBT teams. The oral performance was then performed before different audiences throughout the Republic of Altai and was evaluated with field research through unstructured, informal interviews with twelve different audiences. The evaluation was intended to gauge the audiences' reactions to the performance, including their assessment of the artistry, aurality, and acceptability of the performance.

Chapter 10 is a summary of my research and conclusions, and I make suggestions for further research and application in the area of orality and performance in BT.

2

Theoretical Framework

INTRODUCTION

This chapter discusses research developments in the fields of orality, literacy and orality in the Bible, functional translation, and complexity theory and assesses how they influence oral Bible translation (OBT). As a theoretical framework for this research, I present a functional approach informed by supplementary ideas drawn from complexity theory, multimodality, and a hospitality theory of translation. Principles drawn from this framework assist the Altai translation team in the translation and performance process.

RESEARCH BACKGROUND—ORALITY

This book is written in the context of the growing awareness of the significance of orality in the world and how this awareness is influencing Bible translation. As the background to this book, it is important to understand previous research on orality, how oral communication differs from written communication, what the interface is between the oral and the written, and how orality has impacted translation and missiology.

A definition of orality

In the past, orality was generally viewed negatively, as the absence of literacy, equating it with illiteracy. More recent characterizations of orality show a shift in perception. Madinger, for example, has described orality as a form of communication conducted without print or with a preference over it.[1] Similarly, Lovejoy writes that orality is a reliance on oral communication over written communication.[2] Box refers to oral communicators as those "who respond primarily to oral messages and to the people and events within their society."[3]

The Gutenberg Parenthesis

Maxey argues that orality has always been the predominant mode of communication in the world and that literacy is a more recent development in human history.[4] Pettitt goes further, labeling the modern era the "Gutenberg Parenthesis."[5] This is defined as the textual period between the orality of the past and a future in which technology will allow people to be no longer print- or text-dependent. It has been argued that the Western humanities have moved from a preference for orality to a preference for written text and, more recently, back again to orality in their communication methods.[6] Foley asserts that for most of the existence of our species, cultural literacy did not involve reading or writing but instead depended on oral tradition.[7]

Literacy and orality in the world today

Lovejoy estimates that over 80 percent of the world's population, or about 5.7 billion people, are oral-preference communicators.[8] According to Konstanski, an oral-preference communicator has the ability to read and write but prefers to learn orally.[9] He estimates that two-thirds of the world's

---

1. Madinger, "Literate's Guide," 15.
2. Lovejoy, "Extent of Orality," 12.
3. Box, *Don't Throw*, loc. 226.
4. Maxey, *From Orality to Orality*, loc. 1868.
5. Pettitt, "Before the Gutenberg," 3.
6. Swarr et al., *Master Storyteller*, xix.
7. Foley, *How to Read*, 48.
8. Lovejoy, "Extent of Orality," 17–22.
9. Konstanski, "Digital Orality," 17.

population are oral-preference learners. In today's highly literate societies, many choose to learn orally, even though they are able to read. Within the International Orality Network, an orality advocacy affiliation of agencies and organizations which grew out of the 2004 Lausanne Forum for World Evangelism, the phrase "Orality by Choice" is used to describe this group or oral-preference learners. Ott asserts that oral learners are those who learn aurally (with the exception of people who are hearing-impaired), and that perhaps even in literate societies, only 5 percent turn to reading as their preferred way to learn.[10]

Sundersingh writes about the growing number of non-literate people, highlighting in particular India and South Asia more broadly.[11] He also emphasizes that even among the functionally literate, there has been a reduction in the habit of reading, which he attributes to globalization and entertainment media. The Lausanne Occasional Paper No. 54, "Making Disciples of Oral Learners," asserts that approximately two-thirds of the world's population live by orality, which means that despite being literate, they still prefer to learn by oral means.[12]

Primary and secondary orality

In his classic work *Orality and Literacy*, Ong distinguishes two kinds of orality: primary and secondary.[13] Primary orality, now rare, is found in communities that have no written language with no reliance on written communication. Secondary orality is becoming increasingly common as people communicate orally through television, radio, and mobile phones. More recently, Armstrong, observing the prevalence of secondary orality in Europe, has written on the influence of orality on theological education in Romania and beyond.[14]

Conclusion

My definition of orality is a preference or reliance on oral communication over written communication. This represents a large proportion of the world's population, even in literate societies.

10. Ott, "Rationale," 61.
11. Sundersingh, *Audio-Based Translation*, loc. 49.
12. Lausanne, Making Disciples, 11.
13. Ong, *Orality and Literacy*, 10–13, 132–134.
14. Armstrong, "Orality Reality," 21.

An overview of the recent scholarly debate on orality and literacy

Gunkel

With regards to orality, Gunkel was one of the first to argue that oral traditions are behind the biblical literary text.[15] Gunkel concluded that oral folklore was the origin of Israel's epic stories. The topic of orality then began to be taken seriously in scholarly circles by Parry and Lord, working in the field of classical literature. Their oral-formulaic theory suggested that Homer was in fact a semiliterate master poet who was extremely skilled at linking together multiple oral legends into epic poems like *The Odyssey* and *The Iliad*.[16] They both concluded that the authors of Homer's source material had composed in a special formulaic language, so that each recital of the oral text was original but with formulaic and thematic consistency.

Ong

The theory of orality was then most notably developed by Ong, who proposed that oral societies think, learn, and communicate differently about the world around them than highly literate societies.[17] Ong maintained that as people become literate, their culture changes, features of oral speech begin to disappear, and people start to lose the ability to memorize long stories. Reading becomes a more solitary and private activity, and analytic modes of thinking become more dominant.[18] Ong's definitions of primary and secondary orality, mentioned above, marked a starting point for modern orality discussions.[19]

Ong's work, which has been widely accepted, provides insights into orality and textuality which are helpful for understanding the Israelite cultural context of the Hebrew Bible.[20] According to Ong, an oral culture and its reality are created and maintained by uttered words or sounds.[21] Communication is therefore relational. He also contends that oral cultures perceive time differently, not as a linear progression, with the past being complete

---

15. Gunkel, *Psalms*.
16. Parry, *Making*; Lord, *Singer*.
17. Ong, *Orality and Literacy*, 36.
18. Ong, *Orality and Literacy*, 68.
19. Ong, *Orality and Literacy*, 10–12.
20. West, "Art of Biblical," 11.
21. Ong, *Orality and Literacy*, 71.

and unreachable, but rather as something that exists within the present, actively influencing life today.[22] In like fashion, the people of ancient Israel also felt a deep connection between their past history and their present experiences, as exemplified in the genealogies of the Hebrew Bible.[23]

Characteristics of oral-preference cultures

Using Ong's research, Brown summarized some general differences between print and oral communication.[24] Oral-preference communicators prefer narrative forms, such as stories, and they may rely more on memory; learn from real-life, people-orientated events; and value dialogue and drama. Ott says, "Oral learners can handle any thought, idea, concept, principle or teaching that a literate can handle, if it is properly clothed/communicated within a story."[25] Box summarizes characteristic features of oral communicators as the following: group orientation (in contrast to individualism), event orientation (rather than time orientation), the acquisition and preservation of knowledge by oral rather than literate means, and the attribution of power to the spoken word.[26] Sundersingh also isolates characteristics of orality, such as a reliance on mnemonic devices (formula, proverb, or rhyme) to assist memory, a closeness to the real world, and the presence of audience.[27] He describes non-literate audiences as active, participatory, and interactive, as well as being potentially louder and more assertive than literate audiences.[28] In primary oral cultures, memory is important, and perception is global, contextual, and simultaneous, tending towards an insider or participatory view. There is extended and frequent intense interaction between the community members. Often there is the use of communicative devices such as poetry, rhythm, dance, and music to reinforce the message.

In their book, *The Return of Oral Hermeneutics*, Steffer and Bjoraker also highlight what they consider to be the central components of orality: spoken words have power and are able to create, bless, or curse; orality focuses on the concrete rather than the abstract; orality highlights community relationships and face-to-face dialogue; orality focuses on the whole, the global, and the big picture; orality prefers nonlinear processing,

22. Ong, *Orality and Literacy*, 97.
23. West, "Art of Biblical," 13.
24. Brown, "Communicating God's Message," 27.
25. Ott, "Literate Mind-Set," 10.
26. Box, *Don't Throw*, loc. 291–44.
27. Sundersingh, *Audio-Based Translation*, loc. 2928–3016.
28. Sundersingh, *Audio-Based Translation*, loc. 3083–3132.

using association, echoes, or circular thinking; orality emphasizes learning through apprenticeship and personal mentoring, using observation and imitation; orality relies on experiential and active learning; orality makes use of repeated stories, symbols, and rituals to reinforce what society regards as significant; orality uses imagination, emotion, images, metaphors, stories, and ambiguity; oral communities have respect for rhythm and rhyme, poetry, song, visuals, and gestures; and orality is expressed locally and generationally.[29]

Bartsch also compared characteristics of oral versus written style.[30] Although discourse features are language-specific, some of the common characteristics of oral style identified by Bartsch are the following: substantial repetition; less organization, because speakers attempt to connect thoughts in their minds as they speak; less variety of vocabulary and fewer abstract terms; more emotive words; and more frequent authorial intrusions (explanations or comments that are not part of the story line). In addition to these, Bartsch says, "Another feature of communication is prosody (intonation, stress, tone of voice, and other paralinguistic signals), which provides information that in written material is signaled by punctuation and description."[31]

Oral versus literate

Gunkel's work operates under the implicit assumption that orality and literacy are incompatible and cannot coexist.[32] However, the dichotomy between oral and written communication as initially described by Gunkel and Ong has since been largely rejected.[33] In its place there is a more recent consensus that cultures are not best characterized as being either oral or not oral. Instead, orality in any culture is on a continuum of varying degrees.[34] Pushing beyond even the idea of a continuum is de Vries, who describes localized interaction of oral and written tendencies.[35] De Vries gives a frank critique of Ong's work, demonstrating that the dichotomy of oral versus literate cultures is false.[36] Based on his research in Papua New Guinea, de

29. Steffen and Bjoraker, *Return of Oral*, 67.
30. Bartsch, "Oral Style," 42–44.
31. Bartsch, "Oral Style," 41.
32. Gunkel, *Psalms*.
33. Naudé and Miller-Naudé, "Translation of Biblion," 3.
34. Reynolds, "Shape," 1.
35. De Vries, "Views of Orality," 24.
36. De Vries, "Local Oral-Written," 69.

Vries maintains that there is no proof for absolute differences between literate and oral societies "in terms of mode of thinking or type of discourse."[37] He observes that primary orality is very rare in today's modern world and that orality and literacy are almost always linked. Even cultures that appear to be primarily oral in nature are engaged in an interface between oral and written communication. Similarly, Biber studied oral and written language in a corpus of texts and found no absolute universal differences between written and oral texts.[38] His findings concluded that the mode of communication, either oral or written, is merely one element of a genre, and whether the text is spoken or written is less significant than the combined influence of other elements of its genre. For example, a shopping list is written but has all the properties of being oral.

Local Oralities

Oral Bible translation must begin with a deep understanding of what could be called "local oralities." Features of orality are locally determined and may even vary within a single culture with respect to time, place, and genre. People use both textuality and orality in a variety of contexts and can be oral or literate in different domains. Different cultures employ both literacy and orality in diverse ways.[39]

Accordingly, we should expect to find uniquely local aspects of the ways people from either oral or literary cultures think, learn, and communicate. People from an oral-preference culture, such as that of the Republic of Altai, will appreciate a translation and performance paradigm that is connected to their history, that is community-based, and that is locally expressed using communicative devices such as dance, poetry, and music, and that includes dialogue, story, and drama.

Orality and translation

Orality in Bible translation

With regards to the influence of orality on Bible translation, Klem, already in 1982, wrote about the rich oral art of Nigeria, including proverbs, folk

---

37. De Vries, "Bible Translation," 101.
38. Biber, *Variation Across Speech*.
39. Maxey, *From Orality to Orality*, loc. 1916.

songs, storytelling, singing, and dancing during key cultural events.[40] He noted that there was extensive audience participation and response. Klem suggested starting translation in such contexts orally, using indigenous media like song or drama as a stepping-stone to the written text and literacy. Several years later, Kilham was one of the first to emphasize that Bible translation should not be solely focused on literacy.[41] She maintained that oral approaches are not only stepping stones to literacy but are valid in themselves. Kilham recommended that translation should be available in a variety of media, giving accessibility to different kinds of people.

In the 1990s, Sundersingh conducted field research in India to find out if rural audiences preferred an orally translated Bible text to an oral reading of a text translated using written Bible translation methods.[42] His method of incarnational translation is receptor-oriented, aiming to produce narrative oral Scriptures that are relevant and appropriate for his audience, while remaining faithful to the Scriptures. His research demonstrated that the audiences preferred the orally translated Bible texts. Sundersingh also investigated which format of oral recordings the listeners preferred, with the choice of straight reading, storytelling, or dramatized reading using multiple voices. He found that a large majority of people preferring the storytelling version.

There has recently been more research on audience preferences for oral Scripture materials as opposed to written texts and on the kinds of format audiences preferred. In 2020 I completed an MA research project comparing texts translated by means of a written process and by means of an oral process.[43] The core of this project is an analysis of listeners' responses to two texts produced in the Southern Altai language. The project is a presentation and analysis of field research, comparing people's response to the written and oral translations. The conclusion is that the listeners preferred the text translated through the oral process.

Maxey presents an even more radical audience oriented approach to translation. He disagrees with dynamic equivalence theory that separates form and meaning, arguing for Relevance Theory, which, he contends, is more audience-oriented.[44] Maxey uses research on ethnopoetics and Biblical Performance Criticism (BPC) to conclude that translation should be seen as a performative act. This means that translators act as performers

40. Klem, *Oral Communication*.
41. Kilham, "Written Style," 9.
42. Sundersingh, *Audio-Based Translation*.
43. Cleaver, *Comparison of Listeners' Responses*."
44. Maxey, *From Orality to Orality*, loc. 2288.

who interpret a text, considering its cultural, social, and emotional dimensions. The translator's choices reflect not only linguistic accuracy but also the nuances of the original work, engaging the audience in a way that can be seen as a live performance. Translations are also for performance, meaning that translations are often crafted not just for literal understanding but also for their impact on an audience. Later, Maxey argues for a move beyond orality to embrace the interface of multimedia.[45] He asserts that the complexity of today's modern multimedia culture means that not only the oral medium should be taken into account in Bible translation. He maintains that performance as a complex media interface is necessary for Bible translation to address the felt needs of communities today.

Kroneman, observing that oral and written methods of Bible translation have been practiced side-by-side throughout the history of the Bible and the church, contends that achieving a balance between oral and written methods in Bible translation is essential.[46] He argues against maintaining a strict dichotomy between orality and literacy in Bible translation. According to him, orality has always played an important role in Bible translation projects, for example when native speakers read a translation aloud to improve naturalness. However, he asserts that orality has recently taken on a more central role. He highlights three areas where orality is now playing a more prominent role in Bible translation: orality as a means of internalizing a story, orality as performance, and orality as a method of translation.[47]

Conclusion

Orality has always had a role in the translation of the Bible. In the past, oral drafting has successfully been used as a part of the written translation process, to leverage the participation of non-literate mother tongue speakers. An oral component in drafting helps achieve a natural translation. Klem and Kilham,[48] as pioneers in the field, laid the groundwork for more extensive research, which was continued by Sundersingh and culminated in Maxey's influential work.[49] Although most Bible translation projects currently being undertaken are still using the textual Bible translation method, orality is playing an increasing role in most translation efforts, and gradually oral and

---

45. Maxey, "Beyond Print/Oral," 5–6.
46. Kroneman, "Translation, Literacy," 43–47.
47. Kroneman, "Translation, Literacy," 48.
48. Klem, *Oral Communication*; Kilham, *Written Style*.
49. Sundersing, *Audio-Based Translation*; Maxey, *From Orality to Orality*.

performance Bible translation is becoming more widespread, particularly in parts of South America, Africa, and Indonesia.

Orality and missiology

Orality's influence on missiology

At the 2004 Forum for World Evangelization hosted by the Lausanne Committee for World Evangelization, it became apparent that advances in the understanding of orality were beginning to have a significant impact on missiology. At the forum, the Lausanne Committee recommended choosing strategies for the communication of God's word which meet the needs of oral-preference communicators and which oral learners can themselves reproduce.[50] They recommended the development of an oral Bible through chronological storytelling as an effective strategy for enabling oral-preference communicators to learn and reproduce Scripture.[51] As a result of this, many oral Bible storying organizations and partnerships were formed, and oral storying began playing an increasingly significant role in the implementation of orality strategies in Bible translation.

In keeping with these recommendations, Green (2007) proposed an oral Bible for oral communities as an effective translation strategy. She suggested six goals for a translation project: a translation should be faithful, clear, understandable, natural, accessible, reproducible, and complete.[52] Green challenged the Bible translation community to give oral-preference communicators access to Scripture without a dependence on literacy strategies.[53] In 2009, Dye published an extremely significant paper on the eight conditions of Scripture engagement. This paper included accessibility as one of those eight conditions, highlighting the point that, where a community is not literate, providing Scripture in print form will not be adequate.[54] A new interest in oral Bible translation work was also marked by development of the software program Render, specifically designed for OBT by workers at Faith Comes by Hearing (FCBH), Pioneer Bible Translators, and partner organizations. Render is a tremendously vital instrument in OBT, allowing translators and exegetes to maintain a focus on the oral nature of translation.

---

50. Lausanne, *Making Disciples*, 28.
51. Lausanne, *Making Disciples*, 33.
52. Green, "Orality Strategy," 67–77.
53. Green, "Orality Strategy," 13.
54. Dye, "Eight Conditions," 93.

Oral Bible translation began in many parts of the world in the early 2010s using Render or other recording software.

Conclusion

In the last fifteen years, the missions movement has manifested an increasing focus on orality and, more recently, on multimedia. The Bible translation movement has been choosing to produce Scripture materials which are accessible for oral learners in the context of both primary and secondary orality. Initially, there was an emphasis on chronological Bible storying, then on oral Bible translation itself, with now a trend towards performance translation. As Maxey argues, it is necessary to go beyond orality, towards a multimedia and performance approach to translation.[55]

ORALITY AND LITERACY IN THE BIBLE AND IN ANCIENT HEBREW CULTURE

This section provides a review of recent research on orality and literacy in the Bible and in the early church. It is important to understand the interplay of orality and literacy throughout Israelite and early church history in order to rediscover the oral features of the original biblical texts.

Kelber

Kelber, a NT scholar, was one of the initial researchers to analyze the Bible in the context of the features of oral style identified by Gunkel, Ong, and others.[56] He concluded that the Gospel of Mark was written after the stories and teachings of Christ had been repeated orally for many years and that the writing of Mark reflects the oral style of that tradition.

Foley

Foley's work helped biblical studies move away from a strict dichotomy between oral and literate cultures, acknowledging the relationship between orality and textuality.[57] Foley pioneered the field of oral tradition as a distinct

---

55. Maxey, "Beyond Print/Oral," 18.
56. Kelber, *Oral*.
57. Foley, *Immanent Art*, 15.

discipline. He refers to the fact that oral traditions have been composed and transmitted among all peoples of all times and are in fact more widespread, adaptable, and durable than written traditions.[58] Foley points out that some communication strategies are oral, and some are written, but most are a complex interaction of both.[59] In his work *Singer of Tales in Performance*, Foley concludes that "word-power derives from the enabling act of performance and the enabling referent of tradition."[60] Words are much more significant than the text into which performances can be reduced, and it is the context of the performance, the assumptions of the audience about the event based on previous tradition, and the reactions of the audience to the performance that contribute towards the wholeness of the event. Grosser, in her study of biblical poetry, says that ancient Israelite poems would have been heard as lines, rather than read, meaning that "the listener was (and the reader still must be) an active partner in this process; without the active mental processing of the listener, lines cannot be perceived as interrelated, organized or patterned."[61]

Oral and written interface of the Hebrew Bible

Although the origins of the Scriptures were both oral and written, a large part of Scripture was first spoken before being written, in both the OT and the NT. Oral traditions were preserved, collected, and written down, at first only partially as memory aids. Later, compilers and editors continued to work on the text. Other parts of the OT were composed in writing, either by scribes like Baruch, or the prophets who wrote 1 and 2 Samuel. Ezra began the oral tradition in Judaism, as is written in Neh 8:8, "translating to give the sense so that they understood the reading" (NASB). The scribes interpreted the meaning so that people could apply it to their daily lives.[62] Russell says, "The method they use in their teaching was in the nature of a running commentary on the words of Scripture."[63] The question then arose in the community about the authority of what was now written and the oral commentary on the written, which lead to the emergence of the oral Torah that included a mass of interpretation alongside the written Torah. Russell says, "And so there emerged the all-important belief that the Torah

58. Foley, *How to Read*, 24.
59. Foley, *How to Read*, 26.
60. Foley, *Singer*, 208.
61. Grosser, "What Symmetry," 178–79.
62. Russell, *Between the Testaments*, 64.
63. Russell, *Between the Testaments*, 64.

was more than simply the written word of Scripture, but included the traditions which had been handed down from generation to generation."[64] The Pharisees believed that the oral law held the same authority as the written Torah, whereas the Sadducees asserted that the written Torah was superior to any new traditions.[65]

One of the earliest examples of oral Bible translation was the Targums, from approximately 100 BC to AD 100. These were the oral interpretations or translations of the Hebrew Bible into the Aramaic language. Metzger describes the Targums as the interpretive renderings of the Hebrew Scriptures into Aramaic, which were needed when Hebrew ceased to be the main language used among the Jews.[66] In the services in the synagogues, Hebrew Scripture was read first, followed by a translation into Aramaic. Initially, the oral Targum was comparable to an Aramaic paraphrase, but it gradually began to add more explanatory information into the Hebrew source text. Although the writing down of the Targums was initially prohibited as to protect the authority of the written Hebrew text, from the mid-second century AD, the Targums were eventually recorded in written form to render them more authoritative.[67]

Miller argues that many ancient societies produced oral and written literature simultaneously.[68] Writing supported oral tradition and vice versa. For example, the culture of ancient Egypt shows the interdependence of oral and written literatures. In ancient Egypt, written works were often composed for performance and intended for live audiences rather than single readers.[69] In Mesopotamia, although written texts began to appear in stabilized form in about 1200 BC, orality continued well beyond this date. Miller cites three specific cases as examples of oral-written interaction and overlapping that provide the best ethnographic analogies to the biblical material: Homer's text, Icelandic sagas, and Arabic epic poetry.[70] These traditions are made up of modules, which Miller calls "gobbets." He describes them as deliberately crafted memory helps that assist with narration construction, functioning as markers in the text, such as story patterns, character sketches, structural

---

64. Russell, *Between the Testaments*, 63.
65. Russell, *Between the Testaments*, 50.
66. Metzger, "Important Early Translations," 35.
67. Floor, "Reflections on the Authority," 2.
68. Miller, *Oral Tradition*, 30–32.
69. Miller, *Oral Tradition*, 30–32.
70. Miller, *Oral Tradition*, 12.

pathways, images of situations, or traditional phraseology.[71] However, these are culturally and historically specific.

Miller searches for orally derived features in the OT, finding them for example in Gen 49, specifically in Jacob's final blessing. According to Miller, the insertion of a poem into the narrative here, including as it does abundant parallelism, punning, and euphemisms, identify this part of Gen 49 as an orally derived text.[72] Miller also attempts to reconstruct the Bible's own presentation of oral performance.[73] He proposes that often a lyre may have accompanied narrative recitation at feasts. Post-battle celebrations seemed to include a commemoration in song, such as a ballad, probably accompanied by a particular dance, for example in Judg 5, where the heroic song is paired with a prose description of the same event.[74] Miller suggests that in Israel there was probably a wealth of songs, myths, poems, cultic laws, etc., out of which flowed "streams of traditions," both oral and written.[75]

Miller maintains that ancient Israel was always both an oral and a literate culture but that literacy was quite restricted in the ancient Near East.[76] There may have been scribal schools and scribal education for a minority, but the great majority of the people of biblical Israel before and after the exile received the message of the text aurally. This was circulated in spoken form by recitation, probably with several oral versions in use.

Walton and Sandy describe Ancient Near Eastern (ANE) societies as hearing-dominant, in contrast to the text-dominant culture of today's West.[77] ANE societies were equipped to process information differently than today. In ANE times, there was nothing comparable to the authors and books of today's world. Hearing-dominant means that information was disseminated orally, and so traditions were passed on by word of mouth from generation to generation. The ability to read and write was not essential to be a functioning member of society, and literacy was not part of the basic education process. In the ancient world the scribes represented the elite minority. In an ancient hearing-dominant society, document-writing served a different purpose than today. Documents in the ancient world were written for archives, for libraries, or as school texts, to be read aloud, and as symbolic expressions of power. Copies of texts were reference points for

71. Miller, *Oral Tradition*, 48.
72. Miller, *Oral Tradition*, 96.
73. Miller, *Oral Tradition*, 116.
74. Miller, *Oral Tradition*, 120.
75. Miller, *Oral Tradition*, 47–48.
76. Miller, *Oral Tradition*, 63–65.
77. Walton and Sandy, *Lost World*, 17.

recitation and memorization. The focus was on keeping the culture's most important traditions in the people's minds and hearts.[78]

Textual transmission, storage, and revision in ancient Israel

When the Bible first mentions Israel, it was a society with a strong emphasis on oral tradition, just like most other ancient cultures at the time. However, there were some members of the elite who did possess certain literary skills.[79] Slowly over the course of the monarchy period, Israelite society became increasingly literate, and the role of texts and literary production became more important. Still, oral dominance continued through the Greco-Roman period. Evidence that Israel was hearing-dominant is found in the Bible itself, with frequent references to the words being spoken and people hearing (Gen 3:8–13; Exod 3:1–6; Exod 19:5–6; Deut 6:4; Prov 1:8). However, written documents also played a role in the Bible. In the ancient world, there were authorities, scribes, and documents, rather than authors and books. Authorities were the individuals and institutions that generated information, the foremost of which was the king, followed by the local government and temple personnel. Documents were recorded on wax tablets, papyrus, parchment, clay tablets, or stone and therefore tended to be brief and simple rather than complex. They were designed for storage and consultation in archives, not for circulation. When tales were told or wisdom conveyed, these documents were not referred to, but rather such information was mentally stored in the oral traditions of the culture. Authority was not connected to the document but rather to the person of authority behind the document or the tradition itself. Writing was done by scribes who were trained to produce documents and maintain archives for the court and the temple.

Expansions and revisions of documents were possible as documents were copied generation after generation and eventually compiled into literary works.[80] Oral traditions, on the other hand, were more fluid. The speaker of an oral tradition may have had some flexibility depending on audience, artistry, and time, and each speaker would have presented the information differently. Carr (2005) argues that it is writing which brings more conservatism.[81] Initially a well-known tradition may have been preserved in a document multiple times in multiples cities and in multiple versions. The

78. Carr, *Writing on the Tablet*, loc. 1427.
79. Walton and Sandy, *Lost World*, 23–26.
80. Walton and Sandy, *Lost World*, 30.
81. Carr, *Writing on the Tablet*, loc. 8.

document carried no authority regarding the tradition, as it was not the original version but had a secondary status.

As an important document deteriorated, scribes probably then made a new copy and may have added some careful revision of that document.[82] If the oral tradition had permitted adaptation, newer revisions of the document would be brought into line with the current form of the oral tradition. Also, language itself may have changed, as well as geographical references, and the scribe would accordingly update the language and the place names. A scribe might have added brief explanatory glosses for a contemporary audience, added sections, updated formulations, and integrated revision to address a new audience. This was an activity undertaken by the scribes that was probably approved by the community, within certain limits, and was even considered legitimate and advantageous. While invention was doubtless an evolving role for scribes, probably exercised only by the most prestigious among them, the scribe may have taken on more of the role of an editor as time went on, doing both compilation and integration. Occasionally scribes may have expanded the text or even interpreted it for a new audience, such as, for example, expanding collections of psalms and proverbs.

Carr also discusses textual transmission, storage, and revision in ancient Israel, and he emphasizes that scribes could copy texts, but they did not need the texts to be physically in front of them because of the process of memorization.[83] "Long duration" Israelite texts, i.e., those transmitted from generation to generation, like contemporary texts from Mesopotamia, Egypt, and Greece, were transmitted not only in written media but first and foremost in the minds of those who internalized and orally vocalized them. Up until the tenth century BC, traditions would have been oral and fluid, likely poetic and musical. That was probably the time of the first textualization of poems such as the song of Deborah, early psalms, parts of proverbs, and early forms of the creation and flood narratives and patriarchal narratives. Carr also introduces the idea of variations in ancient Israelite texts due to memory variants or slips of the mind. These were the kinds of textual changes which occur when a textual tradition is stored by memory and then reproduced.[84] These include synonym substitutions, rearrangement of poetic lines, and variation in minor particles. Carr proposes adding memory

---

82. Walton and Sandy, *Lost World*, 31.

83. Carr, *Writing on the Tablet*, 721.

84. Carr, *Writing on the Tablet*, 166.

to the already accepted dimensions of orality and literacy, memory being intertwined with both.[85]

Hebrew theology

In their book *The Return of Oral Hermeneutics*, Steffen and Bjoraker discuss Hebrew hermeneutics.[86] Hermeneutics refers to the theory and methodology of interpretation of texts and, in this context, theological texts. They describe Israel as a hearing-dominant society in which repetition, story, symbol, and ritual were a vital part of teaching and learning. This meant that oral traditions were memorized and then transmitted orally over generations. Story was very significant in the biblical and later Jewish traditions, and stories were annually retold at feasts such as Passover. Steffen and Bjoraker describe knowledge as being gained and preserved through the means of story rather than through propositional truths and Hebrew language and thought as being concrete, experiential, and relational. The Hebrews were narrative theologians, and they used poetry, songs, and music to help them remember events and internalize them. Wisdom was found in proverbs, stories, parables, and other creative literature arising from evaluative logic (assessing a matter based on the knowledge at hand and experience).

Visuality

Naudé and Miller-Naudé note that visuality also played a crucial role in the hearing-dominant culture associated with Scripture and has likewise been evident during all stages of media history.[87] In the digital age, visuals have not taken the place of words but instead have become more prevalent as a means of supplying context to text.[88] Gravelle, who refers to "visual literacy as a new area of study," discusses the possibility of producing meaning through visuals and images and interpreting that meaning.[89] Visuality always played an integral role in biblical oral texts through the appearance, movement, and gestures of performers in oral performances. The visuality of the performance and their movements provided an iconic link to the biblical text, giving additional information, or "metatext," to guide the

---

85. Carr, *Writing on the Tablet*, 172.
86. Steffen and Bjoraker, *Return of Oral*, 135.
87. Naudé and Miller-Naudé, "Translation of Biblion," 4.
88. Makutoane et al., "What Do We Actually?"
89. Gravelle, "Meaning Making", 3.

hearers and the performers. Also, visuality fulfilled a variety of functions in manuscript Bibles, of which Naudé and Miller-Naudé give four examples.[90] First of all, the shapes of letters and arrangements of letters, words, and phrases in writing all played a communicative role. Secondly, the stichography (white space in the arrangement of texts in columns) in biblical texts from Qumran was used to convey features of an oral performance of a text. Miller notes that stichography illustrates the interface between speech, writing, and memory.[91] He writes, "Stichography demonstrates that the ancient Jewish scribe is a special kind of speaking performer who incorporates his understanding of the oral register of language into a written copy."[92] The role of voice in ancient Judaism was intertwined with textual elements because speaking and reading were viewed as interconnected.[93] Miller concludes, "The primary existence of stichography lies neither in academic taxonomy nor in written scrolls, but rather in the memory and performance of ancient readers and scribes who spoke these compositions."[94] Tov points to thirty such Qumran manuscripts structured by stichometry, the majority of which contain the poetic books of the Bible and some songs, including the Song of Deborah and the Song of the Sea.[95] Tov comments that this may suggest a performative function for these manuscripts. Davis also concludes that specific poetic collections of texts from the Qumran were sometimes formatted into narrow columns in a stichometric arrangement.[96]

Thirdly, the work of the Masoretes in the Middle Ages represented both the received written text and the oral text together in parallel, as seen, for example, in the kəṯîḇ/qərê traditions.[97] Finally, the tradition of illuminated codices with illustrations incorporated aspects of performance into the biblical text, and the visual layout assisted in reading the text aloud.[98] In the earliest printed Bibles, the visuality of the text continued as a key aspect in many ways, such as in the Geneva Bible of 1560, which had twenty-six woodcuts alongside the text and a table of the pronunciation of proper names at the end of the Bible to assist reading aloud.[99] Other visual aspects

90. Naudé and Miller-Naudé, "Translation of Biblion," 4.
91. Miller, "Oral-Written Textuality," 163.
92. Miller, "Oral-Written Textuality," 163.
93. Miller, "Oral-Written Textuality," 134.
94. Miller, "Multiformity of Stichographic," 244.
95. Tov, *Scribal Practices*, 166–67.
96. Davis, "Structure, Stichometry," 162.
97. Naudé and Miller-Naudé, "Translation of Biblion," 4.
98. Naudé and Miller-Naudé, "Translation of Biblion," 4.
99. Naudé and Miller-Naudé, "Translation of Biblion," 4.

in modern printed Bibles include red-letter editions for the words of Christ, the column format imitating the columns of handwritten manuscripts, the formatting of chapters and verses, and visual adjustments made to the Bible for Muslim and Muslim-background readers.[100] In modern digital media culture, the Bible is often presented in electronic formats with combined oral-written-visual interfaces, for example, in video formats, where the visual mediates between the oral and the written.

Conclusion

The biblical text exhibits a complex interface of both oral and literary features, reflecting the close interaction between the oral and literary in the ANE and ancient Israelite cultures. Visuality has also been evident as metatext (additional information) alongside the oral-written text of the Bible in every era. Therefore, a greater emphasis on orality and visuality in Bible translation today is in keeping with the origin and transmission of the early biblical texts and of the early church culture more broadly. In this research, the original biblical texts are examined for their features of orality, the texts are translated using the method of oral Bible translation, and the created oral and visual performance reflects oral features of the culture of the Altai Republic.

FUNCTIONAL TRANSLATION

This section initially examines the functional approach to translation, exploring its historical roots together with the theoretical and conceptual aspects of the approach. The features of the functionalist approach are compared to other, sometimes more purely linguistic theories of translation. It is also intended to demonstrate how the functionalist approach attempted to solve the problem of equivalence and why it is found to be the most useful theoretical approach for this oral Bible translation and performance project.

Linguistic translation theories

Translation studies

In work appearing as early as 1972, Holmes proposed the designation "translation studies" for the discipline of translation, giving it a framework

---

100. Naudé and Miller-Naudé, "Theology and Ideology," 294.

and dividing it into two fields: pure translation studies and applied translation.[101] The pure-science field includes translation theory, the principles to describe and explain translation, and the descriptive science of translation, describing the translation according to product, process, and function.[102] The applied branch deals with applications to the practice of translation, such as translation training and translation aids.

From the 1980s translation studies have become multidisciplinary, using methodologies derived from psychology, literary theory, anthropology, philosophy, the theory of communication, and cultural studies.[103] Around the first decade of the 2000s, translation studies became an independent discipline.[104] In 2007, van Doorslaer's visual map for the Benjamins *Translation Studies Bibliography* distinguished between translation and translation studies.[105] Translation includes lingual categories such as interlingual and intralingual; media (printed, audio-visual, electronic); mode (covert/overt, direct/indirect); and field (religious, literary, etc.). Translation studies involves approaches, theories, research methods, and applied translation research. Translation studies is now a multidisciplinary and established international academic discipline.[106]

Equivalence

Linguistic-based theories of translation have traditionally focused on the concept of equivalence, introduced by Jakobson.[107] Nida and Taber added the dimensions of formal and dynamic equivalence.[108] Formal equivalence strives to produce a faithful reproduction of the source text (ST) in both the form and the content, while dynamic equivalence aims at complete naturalness. The criterion to judge the translation is equivalence to the ST. Nida also emphasized the roles of the translators and of the receivers of the texts, the purpose of the translation, and the cultural and worldview aspects of the translation process.[109] One identifying mark of dynamic equivalence is that the recipient's response to the translated message should be similar to the

---

101. Holmes, "Name and Nature," 70–71.
102. Maust and Naudé, "Translation Studies," 5.
103. Naudé, "Overview," 46.
104. Maust and Naudé, "Translation Studies," 5.
105. Van Doorslaer, "Risking Conceptual Maps," 223.
106. Naudé, "Overview," 45.
107. Jakobson, "On Linguistic Aspects."
108. Nida and Taber, *Theory and Practice*, 159.
109. Nida, "Framework," 64.

way the original recipients may have reacted to the message (although the original recipients' response cannot be known for certain).[110]

However, translations can never be fully equivalent or an exact image of the ST, because the sociocultural environment in which the ST was produced differs from that in which the receptor text (RT) functions.[111] Pym describes the equivalence paradigm as "naïve or limited in scope."[112] The concepts of accuracy, naturalness, and clarity,[113] which were key criteria associated with equivalency, have, according to Maxey, also started to become untenable.[114] Nord concludes that the idea of equivalence is ultimately imprecise and unclear.[115] Naudé agrees that a receptor text "can never fully resemble its ST in every respect linguistically and culturally" because the translation text will be both similar and divergent in relation to the original text.[116]

Text linguistics and sociolinguistics

Despite this, the normative and prescriptive approach of weighing a translation against its equivalence to its ST continued until the 1980s.[117] Gradually there were attempts to redefine the term equivalence, using text linguistics and sociolinguistics. The text analysis-oriented model developed the idea of a text being a communication system and translation occurring through a top-down approach. In this approach, the entire text becomes the unit of translation, and equivalence is found not at the sentence and lexical level but at the textual and communicative level.[118] The sociolinguistic approach emphasized how linguistic structures function in communication and as part of their social context.[119] These linguistic approaches were also limited and revealed yet more problems with the concept of equivalence. Due to the extensive linguistic and culture differences in languages, translations can never fully be equivalent.

---

110. Nida and Taber, *Theory and Practice*, 1.
111. Naudé, "Overview," 47.
112. Pym, *Exploring Translation Theories*, 7.
113. Beekman and Callow, *Translating the Word*; Barnwell, *Bible Translation*; Larson, *Meaning-Based Translation*.
114. Maxey, "Alternative Evaluative Concepts," 59.
115. Nord, "Function and Loyalty," 567.
116. Naudé, "Equivalence," 422.
117. Naudé, "Narrative Frame Analysis," 256.
118. Naudé, "Overview of Recent," 48.
119. Naudé, "Narrative Frame Analysis," 256.

Functionalism

Reiss and Vermeer

The idea of purpose (*skopos*) was first introduced to translation by Reiss.[120] Still using equivalence as her basis, Reiss, as early as 1971, proposed an objective model of translation criticism founded upon the functional relationship between the ST and RTs, asserting that the optimal translation would be one "in which the aim in the RL (receptor language) is equivalence as regards the conceptual content, linguistic form and communicative function of a SL (source-language) text."[121] For Reiss, the method of translation correlated to the text type, which she classed as informative (texts communicating content) and expressive (communicating artistic content).[122] Reiss then discussed certain exceptions to equivalence, when the RT is designed to meet a different purpose than the original, suggesting these would be referred to as "renderings."[123]

Vermeer then developed the *skopos* theory, bridging the gap between theory and practice. Vermeer wrote, "To translate means to produce a text in a target setting for a target purpose and target addressees in target circumstances."[124] Vermeer broke with traditional linguistic translation theory, pointing out that translation cannot be a simple one-to-one transfer between languages and that a theory of culture is also necessary.[125] The main concept of *skopos* theory was that the primary factor in translation should not be a translation's equivalence to the ST but the fulfilment of its function. In Reiss's book co-authored with Vermeer, her model is presented as a specific theory within Vermeer's general *skopos* approach.[126] They wrote, "We shall define translating as a specific type of translational action in which the complete ST and RT and all parts thereof remain accessible to the translator in such a way that the process as well as its result can be corrected at any time."[127]

---

120. Reiss, *Translation Criticism*.
121. Nord, *Translating*, loc. 9.
122. Reiss, "Type, Kind and Individuality," 171.
123. Reiss, *Translation Criticism*, 92.
124. Vermeer, "What Does It Mean," 29.
125. Nord, *Translating*, loc. 375, 399.
126. Reiss and Vermeer, *Towards a General Theory*.
127. Reiss and Vermeer, *Towards a General Theory*, 9.

Holz-Mänttäri

Holz-Mänttäri, a Finnish translation scholar, formulated the theory of translatorial action and the idea of a message carrier. Translation is defined as "a complex action designed to achieve a particular purpose."[128] Holz-Mänttäri sets aside traditional concepts associated with the word "translation" and instead uses the theories of communication and action to highlight the idea of intercultural transfer. She speaks of "message transmitters," produced by agents (the translator), consisting of texts combined with other media, which can then be used by other agents in their communications.[129] According to Holz-Mänttäri, the primary aim of translatorial action is to enable effective communication between individuals from different cultures.

Nord

Purpose (the intended communicative function) is the key point in this functional translation theory. Translating is described as a "purposeful activity."[130] Nord argues that functionalism has always been recognized to some extent in translation, even as early as Jerome (348–420 AD).[131] For example, Jerome acknowledged that in some cases the translator should reproduce the word order of the ST, but in other cases the translator should emphasize the sense, therefore adapting the form of the text to the requirements of the receptor audience.[132]

THE COMMUNICATIVE PURPOSE OF THE TEXT

In functionalism, the expectations and needs of the recipient audience influence the translation itself.[133] The translation *skopos* is the intended or demanded function (function here referring to how it works) of the RT, and translation is the production of that RT according to this *skopos*. There may be many different ways to represent the ST in the receptor language (RL). The *skopos* may be to produce a dynamic equivalent translation in which many features of the ST are domesticated to the RL or to produce a translation in which as many features of the ST as possible are represented

---

128. Holz-Mänttäri and Vermeer, "Entwurf für einen," 4.
129. Holz-Mänttäri and Vermeer, "Entwurf für einen," 17.
130. Nord, *Translating*.
131. Nord, "Functionalist Approaches," 131.
132. Jerome, "Pammachius," 21–30.
133. Nord, *Text Analysis*, 12.

in the RT. The functionality of the text (how it works) is determined by the recipient audience at the point of reception.[134] The communicative purpose or intention of the text producer or sender (who may be different) may be incongruous with the function determined by the receiver. If the source and recipient cultures are separated by a large cultural gap, the sender's intention and the effect intended by the original author may be different from the function of the text for the recipient audience.

Translation Brief

It therefore follows that in functional translation the translator needs as much information as possible about the purpose for which the text is intended.[135] The translation brief is the document which provides the translator with this necessary information. The translation purpose, which determines the choice of translation strategy and method, is reflected in this translation brief. There may be as many different translations of a ST as there are purposes in the recipient culture. The *skopos* may require a faithful or a free translation or anything between these two extremes.[136] Hence the need for a detailed and clear translation brief.

Culture

Skopos theory helped translation studies to see texts as occurrences of communication, influenced by their situational context and cultural customs and norms.[137] Translating is a communicative intercultural action which employs both verbal and nonverbal signs. The communicative act is completed only when the text is received by the recipient audience.[138] The reception of the translated text depends on the expectations of the receivers, their worldview, their social background, and their needs. Hatim and Mason also acknowledge that translation strategy is closely linked to cultural views, values, and assumptions.[139] Both the ST and the RT are culturally bound; therefore, their communicative function is determined by the sociocultural

---

134. Nord, "Function and Loyalty," 570.
135. Nord, *Translating*, loc. 763.
136. Nord, *Translating*, loc. 736.
137. Nord, "Functionalist Approaches," 127.
138. Nord "Function and Loyalty," 570.
139. Hatim and Mason, *Discourse and the Translator*, 143.

Theoretical Framework 39

situation in which they are grounded.[140] Translating, therefore, involves a comparison of cultures.[141]

THE LOOPING MODEL

Nord describes a looping inductive model for translation, in contrast to the linear movement from ST to RT normally involving only two or three phases.[142] The looping model begins with the analysis of the RT *skopos*, followed by the analysis of the ST. Then the ST features relevant for the translation are identified and matched with the corresponding RL features suitable for the determined *skopos* or function of the RT. The circle is closed with the final structuring of the RT, in accordance with the RT *skopos*. This circular translation process also includes many smaller recurring loops, meaning that at each step forward the translator looks back and uses the information discovered in further analysis.

Van Rooyen and Naudé found that this looping model, developed by Nord, is more useful and closer to the reality of professional translation in a media situation, such as in relating news.[143] The first step is the interpretation of the implicit translation brief and the editor's translation *skopos*. The bulletin producer/translator then analyzes the news texts written for print (ST analysis) to determine what needs to be adapted, what translation problems there might be, and ways to solve them. The final step is the production of the RT for radio listeners.

INTERTEXTUAL AND INTRATEXTUAL COHERENCE

The translator should produce a text which is coherent, both intratextually and intertextually.[144] Intratextual coherence means that the recipient audience should be able to make sense of the text, and intertextual coherence ensures that the RT has a suitable relationship with the ST. The extent of this similarity between the RT and the ST will depend on the translation brief. It may be a very close resemblance, or it may be an adaptation in form. The

---

140. Nord, *Text Analysis*, 8.
141. Nord, *Translating*, loc. 843.
142. Nord, *Text Analysis*, 37–39.
143. Van Rooyen and Naudé, "Media and Translation," 252–54.
144. Nord, "Functionalist Approaches," 122.

skopos rule is the main priority, followed by the intratextual coherence, and then in final place is the importance of intertextual coherence.[145]

Loyalty

Nord introduced the concept of loyalty, going together with functionality, in order to solve the problem that, in a functionalist approach, the ST no longer has priority.[146] Loyalty is described as an interpersonal category, i.e., a social relationship between two parties.[147] In adhering to the concept of loyalty, the translators are responsible to their partners in the activity of translation with regard to the possible range of translation purposes for the ST. Consequently, a translation brief which calls for them to be disloyal either to the author or to the recipient audience is unacceptable. The function decided by the recipient audience should not be contradictory or otherwise incompatible with the author's original communicative intent, thereby ensuring a coherent intertextual relationship between the ST and the RT.

Equivalence in Functionalism

In functionalism, therefore, it is not the ST that sets the standard for translation evaluation but, rather, the functionality of the translated text, which depends on the translation brief in any particular situation and culture.[148] However, the ST is still extremely important. Intertextual coherence between the ST and the RT is ensured by Nord's loyalty principle, and so equivalence is not entirely abandoned in *skopos* theory.[149] Reiss uses the concept of adequacy, developed by Nord to refer to the qualities of the RT according to the requirements of the translation brief.[150] It is a dynamic concept arising from the goal-orientated process of translation, rather than being a static concept requiring equivalence between two texts.

---

145. Nord, *Translating*, loc. 815.
146. Nord, "Function and Loyalty," 570.
147. Nord, "Functionalist Approaches," 126.
148. Nord, "Function and Loyalty," 570.
149. Nord, *Translating*, loc. 865.
150. Reiss, "Adequacy and Equivalence."

Applying functional theory to Bible translation

The linguistic models viewed translation as a linear, code-switching activity.[151] Equivalence was the standard for translation evaluation, which always focused on the ST and the preservation of its features in the RT. In comparison, in functionalism, texts are seen as acts of communication, influenced by their situational context and cultural customs and norms. Translation is viewed as an inductive process looping back on itself, rather than a linear process. Functionalism recognizes that equivalence can never be the standard for translation, as that is determined by function. The status of the ST is lower in functionalism than in equivalence-based theories, yet the principle of loyalty preserves the relationship between the ST and the RT. The translation process is complete only when the text is finally accepted by the recipient audience.

Himes points out that *skopos* theory in Bible translation affects the choice of ST used, the methodology and style of the translation, and its designation for a particular audience.[152] In his dissertation on *skopos* theory in Bible translation, Cheung writes, "The reason why Bible translation is well suited to *skopos* theory is that multiple functions for Bibles exist. Or, to put it another way, a single translation cannot satisfy all the needs that exist for all receivers, because of the varying functions for which a text is used."[153] In Bible translation, there is not only a large cultural gap between the text-producers and the recipient audience, but there are also many varying text types (narratives, parables, letters, prayers, hymns, theological doctrine, songs, etc.), which were intended for different functions in their source cultures.

Conclusions for OBT and performance

This discussion of functionalism highlights the need in oral Bible translation for a clear and detailed translation brief, based on the *skopos* of the translation project. The translation brief should be developed together with the stakeholders (those with an interest or concern in the project, such as community and church representatives) and is intended to provide the translators with information as to the translation purpose, with the result that all parties are better prepared to accept the final product. In the case of the Altai project, the team began by writing a detailed translation brief,

---

151. Nord, *Translating*, loc. 300.
152. Himes, "Reaching the Goal," 5.
153. Cheung, "Functionalism and Foreignisation," 160.

which was discussed and adjusted at the beginning and throughout the duration of the project, working together with the project stakeholders.

Functionalism also emphasizes the role of the recipient audience in the translation process. Communication is considered finished only when the text or performance is understood and accepted by this recipient audience. Though not as strictly literal as formal equivalence, the dynamic-equivalence model is still not sufficiently sophisticated when it is applied to a performance-orientated translation. This is because it is not only words but also paralinguistic and extralinguistic features that contribute to the communication process. As a result, performance by its nature is in opposition to any model of communication which separates form from meaning and does not incorporate the role of the recipient audience. Meaning is not solely found in the original text, but instead multiple meanings may be negotiated by the audience. I recommend that performance be added to the looping model, so that even after a performance and post-performance discussion, the translators can look back and use the information discovered by this process in further analysis. In the Altai project, response and feedback by the audience to initial performances is fed back into the translation loop in this fashion.

COMPLEXITY THEORY

In this section I provide an overview of complexity theory, as explained by Marais and Shreve.[154] In addition, I outline some conceptual tools from complexity theory which inform the functional practice of this research.

Introduction to complexity theory

Complexity theory has recently emerged as a new paradigm to study complex systems such as translation. Complexity theory is essentially a systems theory, where reality is seen as consisting of a myriad of complex open systems that interact with other systems.[155] These systems are dynamic, adaptive, and emerging with their own self-organizing, non-linear behavior, changing and evolving over time. Complexity theory emphasizes that systems are open and interconnected, with context playing a fundamental role in their dynamics. It involves two-way interactions between the systems and

---

154. Marais, *Translation Theory*; Marais, *(Bio)Semiotic Theory*; Marais, "Translation as Organized"; Shreve, "Translation as a Complex."

155. Larsen-Freeman and Cameron, *Complex Systems*, 12.

their surroundings, and it accommodates substantial, unforeseen changes that can arise from the periphery or external factors.

Pym notes that complexity theory has developed out of an increasing dissatisfaction with equivalence.[156] However, it does not intend to replace previous translation paradigms but instead seeks to remove biases and oversimplifying tendencies.[157] Western science has been built on a model in which reductionism functions as the main operating principle, focusing on order, structure, and predictable relationships. This approach reduces the complexity of reality to simplified and fragmented phenomena, positing that complex phenomena can be explained by a number of simple causes and that one law can explain many phenomena.[158] In fact, the opposite can be the case, with complex causes leading to simple phenomena.[159] Although complexity does not necessarily mean complicated or difficult, Marais argues that reality cannot be completely understood simply by knowing all the parts. The focus is rather on processes and the movement of things, and relationships between parts, and between the parts and the whole.

Complexity theory offers a complex and hierarchical view of reality, which allows for paradox. Complexity theory overcomes dualism by focusing on adaptation and emergence.[160] Adaptation refers to the fact that systems continually adjust to changes in their environment. Emergence is the process of how new unknown phenomena result from existing, already known phenomena, which could not have been known from a knowledge of the parts.[161] For example, literature emerges out of language, but it cannot be reduced to language.[162] The emergent behavior of a dynamic system is often nonlinear.[163] In complexity theory, all parts of this open system interact to create effects, which, interacting again with other parts, cause more effects. However, certain effects cannot be realized, as they are constrained by conditions.[164]

---

156. Pym, *Exploring Translation Theories*, 104.
157. Marais, "Effects Causing Effects," 2.
158. Longa, "Nonlinear Approach," and Turner and Baker, "Complexity Theory," 17–18.
159. Marais, *Translation Theory*, 2–3.
160. Sammut-Bonnici, "Complex Adaptive Systems," 1.
161. Larsen-Freeman and Cameron, *Complex Systems*, 2.
162. Marais, *Translation Theory*, 4.
163. Sammut-Bonnici, "Complex Adaptive Systems," 2.
164. Marais, "Effects Causing Effects," 61.

Complexity theory as applied to translation

Viewing translation in terms of complexity theory means focusing on the dynamic processes and relevant environments involved in the entire phenomenon of translation. In this section, I outline some of the major features of complexity approaches to translation, especially those put forward by Tymoczko and Marais[165], emphasizing the most relevant to my research process.

Tymoczko describes translation as organized complexity, which is "the result of non-random, correlated interactions among the parts."[166] She avoids a reductionist definition, describing translation as a cluster or family concept which emphasizes the multi-layers of skill, knowledge, theory, and cultural particularity that make up translation.[167] Tymoczko labels translation as a "complex cross-cultural concept."[168] Tymoczko talks about expanding translation theory to include non-Western experience and bias. She points out that Western translation theory is based on monolingualism, a written text excluding orality, literacy as the primary way of learning, equivalence rather than difference, and an understanding of genre based on the Greco-Roman tradition.[169] Tymoczko highlights globalization as one process that has added significantly to the complexity of translation.

Marais and Shreve view translation in terms of complex adaptive systems. Marais argues that seeing translation as a complex adaptive system focuses on "the complex nature of these systems as well as their historicity and their open, process-related nature."[170] Translation studies must therefore also be transdisciplinary and recognized as part of a larger social reality.[171] Complexity theory argues against linear causality, maintaining that effects cannot always be predicted in advance because of the interaction of a myriad of relevant factors.[172] It encourages the study of relationships, processes, and change and the interaction between them, rather than focusing on substance. Complex behavior may emerge from the interaction of all

---

165. Tymoczko, "Reconceptualizing Translation Theory"; Tymoczko, *Enlarging Translation*; Tymoczko, "Translation as Organized Complexity"; Marais, *Translation Theory*; Marais, *(Bio)Semiotic Theory*; Marais, "Effects Causing Effects"; Tymoczko, "Translation as Organized"; Marais and Meylaerts, *Complexity Thinking*.

166. Tymoczko, "Translation as Organized," 240.

167. Tymoczko, *Enlarging Translation*, 84.

168. Tymoczko, *Enlarging Translation*, 84.

169. Tymoczko, "Translation as Organized."

170. Marais, *Translation Theory*, 27.

171. Marais, *Translation Theory*, 31, 97.

172. Longa, "Nonlinear Approach," 204.

the individual parts.[173] Translation is an imaginative endeavor, and every situation, as well as the initial parameters of a translation assignment, are distinctive. According to Marais and Meylaerts, "This should prevent translation studies from understanding too superficially the function and effect of various translation strategies."[174] Any ST can result in different translation trajectories and results.[175] This is evident even in translations based on the same ST. Marais explains this difference with what he calls "constraints" and "attractors" (points which give a tendency to stabilize), which play a role in the process of translating.[176] Meaning emerges during the course of the interpretive process, constrained by constraints, attractors, and the initial conditions of the project, and is not contained in itself in any part of the translation process.[177] These constraints have causal effects on the translation process and explain the fact of different translations.

Complexity theory undermines traditional binary reductionist translation oppositions such as universal/particular, local/global, and monolingualism/multilingualism.[178] Complexity theory understands that these sets of two opposing logics are dependent on each other and use each other. Traditional boundaries between the ST and RTs, and between literature and culture, become more unstable and fuzzier.

Marais calls the ST an "incipient sign system" and refers to the RT as the "subsequent sign system," both of which are part of a fluid historical process containing many streams of meaning.[179] This avoids assuming a stable formalized meaning in the ST. Instead, meaning is a continual process of creating relationships between meanings. These terms highlight the fact that translation is first and foremost a recursive process. Meaning is not given by somebody or found in something but instead emerges historically and relationally. These terms also account for the collaborative production processes in translation, levels of uncertainty and ambiguity, and many other contextual factors.[180]

Shreve similarly suggests that translation can be understood as emerging from an organized complex system of interacting components.[181]

---

173. Longa, "Nonlinear Approach," 205.
174. Marais and Meylaerts, *Complexity Thinking*, 4.
175. Longa, "Nonlinear Approach," 209.
176. Marais, "Effects Causing Effects", 61.
177. Marais, "Translation Complex," 49.
178. Marais, *(Bio)Semiotic Theory*, 8–10.
179. Marais, *(Bio)Semiotic Theory*, 123.
180. Marais, *(Bio)Semiotic Theory*, 2.
181. Shreve, "Levels of Explanation," 97.

Shreve also applies this complex adaptive systems framework to cognitive translatology.[182] Transfer, as a metaphor for translation, is a convenient label for a nonlinear pattern that emerges dynamically during the course of a translation.[183] Shreve emphasizes the dynamic interaction during translation of all the following factors: translation is complex, communicative, and interactive; translation involves multiple agents; translation is cognitive, adaptive, and continuously developing; translation is goal oriented; translation is both ordered and disordered, but patterns emerge; translation is multi-scale and hierarchical; translation involves response to the environment; and translation can be understood empirically with proper methods.[184]

Shreve emphasizes that translation processes are cognitive activities involved in transferring information, which are seen as the active responses of a group of agents to their environmental conditions.[185] This dynamism is, in part, a result of the unpredictable relationship between system outcomes and changes in initial conditions. The dynamics of translation systems indicate that the interactions among elements influence all the other variables within the system.[186] These intricate systems constantly interact, maintaining a balance between order and chaos. The behavior of complex adaptive systems is characterized by non-linear dynamics. A modification in any individual component may result in minimal impact on the entire system, a significant effect, or potentially no effect at all.

The ST provides some of the initial conditions to direct a translation event in a local setting.[187] However, it is impossible to predict the outcome of that system to a high degree of precision because the rules of language alone are not sufficient. There is some predictability but there is also, quite necessarily, creativity and divergence. It is important to study the processes that have explanatory relevance in order to demonstrate which processes are active and have some demonstrable influence on the overall process. Previous configurations of the complex system, due to their being preserved for a period of time, may have an effect on how the system behaves going forward. Thus, the history of a complex system becomes another critical factor in its future behavior.[188]

---

182. Shreve, "Translation as a Complex," 69.
183. Shreve, "Translation as a Complex," 84.
184. Shreve, "Translation as a Complex," 71.
185. Shreve, "Translation as a Complex," 72.
186. Shreve, "Translation as a Complex," 73.
187. Shreve, "Translation as a Complex," 75.
188. Shreve, "Translation as a Complex," 80.

Language is also a complex adaptive system.[189] Texts (source and receptor) are emergent structures arising from the interaction of biological, cognitive, and social systems. The active social system provides a social context, with the intents, purposes, desires, and needs of a group of social actors exerting influence on the translation. Source texts are artifacts, external material representations of a creator's thought process and intent. They have been captured either in writing or digitally and to some extent frozen when the time course of an active translational system ends. They will persist in influencing others and be of value in achieving future goals.

Naudé also suggests considering translation as a complex holistic phenomenon, rather than looking at it in terms of successive paradigm shifts over periods of time.[190] This means that reductionism and prescriptivism are avoided and that there will be multiple interacting and emergent ways to solve problems.[191]

Other implications of complexity theory for translation

Translators as agents

One of Marais's conclusions from understanding translation through complexity theory is that translators become agents of multilingual human interaction in a complex society.[192] Language and interlingual translation play an important part in how society emerges, and translators have an influential role as agents in this process. Naudé and Miller-Naudé, in an article about translating biblical proverbs, also emphasize that the translator is an agent of cultural mediation, choosing between different strategies, for example, foreignization or indigenization.[193]

Translation of sacred texts

Naudé and Miller-Naudé apply complexity theory to the translation of sacred writings, which belong to a culture completely separate from the recipient readers in both time and space.[194] After examining the three oral-dominant religious traditions—Hindu, Buddhist, and Taoist—Naudé

189. Shreve "Translation as a Complex," 81.
190. Maust and Naudé, "Translation Studies," 7.
191. Maust and Naudé, "Translation Studies," 18.
192. Marais, *Translation Theory*, 10–11.
193. Naudé and Miller-Naudé, "Translator as an Agent," 306–8.
194. Naudé and Miller-Naudé, "Sacred Writings," 27.

comes to the conclusion that oral transmission supersedes written traditions in each case.[195] The majority of translations that have been completed are by outsiders for outsiders, and none of these three religions encourage the translation of their holy texts. However, the majority of religious communities have known their sacred texts through translation, and their maintenance of that religious tradition is also often the result of translation.[196] The terms *incipient text* and *subsequent text* explain well the translations of sacred texts. The readers must understand these texts, but the texts cannot fulfill exactly the same communicative functions in modern society as those for which they were intended in their original setting. This means that equivalence is not the most important standard for translation. The translator has a role like a narrator, telling the readers about the ST but inevitably hiding other parts of it, as it is impossible to relate everything. Naudé and Miller-Naudé describe the strategies needed by the translator as including transference, indigenization/domestication, cultural substitution, generalization, specification (intensification/explication), and mutation (deletion and addition).[197]

Bible translation, as a complex system, fits within the category of translation of sacred writings carried out with religious motivation. Religion itself is a complex phenomenon, consisting of four aspects of complexity: an individual or psychological aspect, a sociological and cultural aspect, the chronological dimension of religion as a changing phenomenon over time, and finally the oral-written interface realized in religion with respect to sacred writings.[198] These sacred writings as translations become incipient STs and are translated for other religious groups. For many religious groups, the only contact they have with these sacred writings is through translation. Therefore, complexity theory is useful for explaining this complexity of the translation of religious texts.

The use of metatext

Complexity theory as applied to translation can respect the alterity (otherness) of the source culture at the same time as ensuring that the translation is intelligible to the receptor readers.[199] This can be done by using metatexts, which explain key cultural terms and concepts, to help guide the reader's

---

195. Naudé, "Religious Texts," 196.
196. Maust and Naudé, "Translation Studies," 4.
197. Naudé and Miller-Naudé, "Sacred Writings," 29.
198. Naudé and Miller-Naudé, "Alterity, Orality and Performance."
199. Naudé and Miller-Naudé, "Theology and Ideology," 4–5.

interpretation of the text. In this way, a paradox develops, as allowed by complexity theory, where the otherness of the ST and that of the RT are both respected. The distance between the two texts is highlighted but is also simultaneously bridged.[200]

In an analysis of the translational aspects of the Book of Ben Sira in the Septuagint, Naudé and Miller-Naudé, applying complexity theory to translation, propose that the strategies of foreignization and indigenization can be employed simultaneously.[201] This involves retaining the otherness of the ST, while also making the translation understandable for the reader, using metatext to help make the material accessible. In this way, it is possible to maintain the paradoxical, complex relationship between the emergent source and RTs.

Conclusions for OBT and performance

Complexity theory is intended to complement rather than replace earlier and differing approaches to translation. It adds a different focus rather than another perspective, emphasizing the connections between the different parts and the interrelatedness of the resultant emerging whole. Therefore, in this research, I am applying some aspects of complexity theory to complement a functional view of translation.

The cyclical nature of this research (a performance in a local genre based on the oral translation of a narrative and poetic text) is by necessity a complex process. The cause-and-effect processes are nonlinear and constantly interacting. The performance influences the translation, and the translation influences the performance. The oral text and the visual elements within the performance also influence each other. Complexity theory helps in understanding this process as a complex process, where A does not automatically lead to B (linear causality) but could instead lead to multiple results. Similar changes do not necessarily lead to the same results, and the outcome cannot be predicted in advance. Complexity theory offers a relational approach, meaning that the outcome is normally more than the sum total of these parts.

The translational approach in this research is also multifactorial and works with several modes of production. Complexity theory helps consider these multiple factors, such as language, genre of the ST, genre of local texts, the performance, and the audience, each of which influences the others. In each case these factors add constraints to the translation process, which is

200. Naudé and Miller-Naudé, "Theology and Ideology," 28.
201. Naudé and Miller-Naudé, "Sacred Writings," 181, 202.

constrained by the ST, by the genre of the ST, by the interpretation of that genre, by the translators themselves, by the receptor genre, by the audience, and by the performance. Complexity theory here offers a complex mode of working, taking into account the different factors that contribute to this process of translation and performance. It is non-reductionist, avoiding reducing the process to only the language or the text or the performance but instead acknowledging the existence of multiple factors and their complex interaction.

Shreve's adaptation of complex adaption systems to translatology allows for multiple situational translation practices, each described on its own terms. It brings context fully into the process, focusing on connections and interactions among various factors, allowing for both stability and change. It views translation as an emerging phenomenon or process, helps to organize and manage the many factors relevant to translating, assists in appreciating and understanding different translational outputs, acknowledges that trajectories emerge from unique circumstances and processes, and allows for the paradoxical relationship between the agent of translation and the system itself. Shreve maintains that the functionality of translation does align with complex system theory. However, functionality, used here as the main model for the translation process in the current project, does not always answer the practical questions that the translators ask. Viewing translation as a complex adaptive system helps translation teams see translation from different angles and understand it as a collaborative process.

The task of the translation of sacred texts is particularly complex, as will be evident in my account of this research. The translators of these sacred texts should be recognized as agents for change and transformation in every translation choice that is made. The translator chooses deliberately and consistently which features of the ST should be given greater prominence in the RT. Metatexts can be used in the translation of sacred texts; they allow the translation team to respect the otherness of the incipient text while bridging the gap to the RT.

INTERSEMIOTIC TRANSLATION

As a theoretical framework for this research, I am using a functional approach, incorporating some aspects of complexity theory. Additional insights can be gleaned from semiotics, which is the study of signs and symbols and how meaning is created. A sign is any motion, gesture, image, sound, pattern, or event that conveys meaning. My research involves interacting with different media and can also be described as intersemiotic (the interpretation of verbal signs by means of nonverbal signs, or translation other than print) or multimodal translation. I, therefore, also use some concepts from the developing field of multimodality.

Introduction to multimodality

Multimodality refers to the use of multiple forms of media in communication to convey meaning.[202] Kress and Leeuwen define multimodality as the operation of semiotic principles in and across different modes of communication.[203] It is "the use of several semiotic modes in the design of a semiotic product or event, together with the particular way these modes are combined."[204] Multimodality as a concept has been introduced and developed over the last twenty years. The discipline assumes that all communication is multimodal, that language analysis alone cannot account for meaning, and that modes occur together and relate together for making meaning. Societies have developed modes such as gestures, sounds, images, color, or layout to make meaning. When they accompany text or language, they add to the meaning. Previously, the written text was considered the primary mode of conveying meaning, and visuals were included to enhance the text.[205] Today multimodality adds meaning to the text through images and design features, so people are now "no longer simple readers of a text, but also viewers of a text."[206] Multimodality is an important concept in today's digital society. Gravelle says that "translation is currently experiencing major upheaval in the digital age."[207] Van Rooyen and Naudé draw attention to the fact that due to globalization and new information technology, translation now takes place between different media and different media cultures.[208] Media translation involves multiple sign systems, and so translation from one medium to another will involve giving more detailed attention to explicit and implicit cultural implications in translation. An image will not communicate if it is not an image connected with the local culture with which it is associated.[209]

---

202. Adami, "Multimodality," 1.
203. Kress and Leeuwen, *Multimodal Discourse*, 2.
204. Kress and Leeuwen, *Multimodal Discourse*, 20.
205. Gravelle, "Meaning Making," 2.
206. Gravelle, "Meaning Making," 2.
207. Gravelle, "Meaning Making," 1.
208. Van Rooyen and Naudé, "Media and Translation," 586, 590.
209. Gravelle, "Meaning Making," 1.

Kress and Leeuwen list four strata or domains that contribute to how meaning is made: discourse, which they define as "knowledge of reality"; design, the expression of discourse; production, the expression in material form; and distribution.[210] They point out that the production is the expression in material form of the semiotic product of the event, giving form to the design and also adding meaning.[211] For example, when a voice reads out or sings what has already been designed, the performer's bodily articulation communicates directly to the audience and may transfer meaning that was not designed.[212] In the case of the Altai performance, the multimodal performance of Judg 4–5 and Pss 1, 100, and 133 includes some traditional Altai dances and other expressions of local genre as part of the medium of communication of the text. These chosen modalities such as the genre of throat singing, the playing of ethnic instruments, photos of Altai nature scenes, contextualized drawings, and the use of objects all contribute to a socially shaped meaning. Kress and Van Leeuwen comment that signs are constantly imported from other contexts into new contexts to signify ideas and values which are associated with that other context.[213] In the case of the Altai production, the medium of throat singing is imported from the context of the telling of epic tales into a new context, that of telling a story from the Bible. This helps signify to the audience the worldview and values which accompany the Altai epic tales and applies them to the biblical story.

Some of Marais's analysis of complexity theory is based on Aguiar and Querioz's approach to intersemiotic translation, which is founded on the premises that translation is fundamentally a semiotic process (semiosis) and that semiosis is a multi-layered process.[214] A semiotic process is a process in which something functions as a sign to an organism, leading to meaning-making. They emphasize that this process is not a binary relation between the ST and the RT but is instead a multi-hierarchical process between different layers of descriptions which have mutual constraints. Interlingual translation selects relevant aspects from the ST and recreates them in the RT, creating new materials and processes, such as translating literature into dance.

---

210. Kress and Leeuwen, *Multimodal Discourse*, 4.
211. Kress and Leeuwen, *Multimodal Discourse*, 21.
212. Kress and Leeuwen, *Multimodal Discourse*, 66.
213. Kress and Leeuwen, *Multimodal Discourse*, 10.
214. Aguiar and Querioz, "Towards a Model."

Music and semiotics

Turino has created a theory of music and dance,[215] and Fitzgerald and Schrag a model of music criticism, both based on semiotics and both useful for the final analysis of the Altai performances.[216] In order to understand these fully, it is necessary to have a basic understanding of Peirce's semiotics and theory of signs.

Peirce's semiotics

According to Peirce, who lived from 1839 to 1914,[217] humans do not directly perceive the outer world or their inner world. Instead, everything is known and said through signs. Examples of signs are a perception, a thought, or a way of communicating. These relate to the object (e.g, a real-world object such as a dog, a television, or a bicycle), which they stand for via other signs.[218] All signs are interpreted by previous signs and may be further interpreted by future signs. Meaning is "the translation of a sign into another system of signs."[219] The semiotic chain of translation is a never-ending line, therefore, that extends both ways.[220] Peirce calls the relating of one system of signs to another system of signs creating interpretants "the process of translation."[221] All meaning is constructed by linking interpretants to interpretants, though this process takes place under sociocultural restraints. This link between translation and semiotics in Peirce's work was first brought to light by Roman Jakobson in 1959.[222] Peirce argues that there are three basic categories of experiences of reality: Firstness, Secondness, and Thirdness.[223] Firstness is pure awareness, the idea of a thing or possibility, without the subject knowing what it is aware of. Secondness is becoming aware of what one is aware of, something in distinction from something else. Thirdness is the mediation by which Firstness and Secondness relate to each other.

---

215. Turino, "Signs of Imagination."
216. Fitzgerald and Schrag, "'But Is It,'" 2–3.
217. Peirce, *Collected Papers*.
218. Peirce, *Collected Papers*, 5.213–263. Citations from Peirce's *Collected Papers* (1931–58) follow the standard practice of listing the volume number and section number.
219. Peirce, "Collected Papers," 4.127.
220. Stecconi, "Peirce's Semiotics," 252.
221. Marais, *(Bio)Semiotic Theory*, 4.
222. Jakobson, "On Linguistic Aspects," 138–43.
223. Peirce, *Collected Papers*, 2.356.

Knowledge is possible only through semiotic relationships. All thought is in signs, and knowledge comes by relating sensory input to existing signs or knowledge that already exists.

A sign is a process of relating three elements: the representamen, the object, and the interpretant. The representamen stands for something (its object) to somebody, forming in the mind of that person a more developed sign called the interpretant of the first sign, which mediates between the sign and the object.[224] Chandler emphasizes that "to qualify as a sign, all three functions are essential."[225] It is not the thing (e.g., a word, smoke) that is the sign; rather the sign consists of the relationship between the sign-vehicle, the object, and the interpretant.[226] A column of smoke is a representamen of a fire (the object), and when an organism sees the smoke, it forms the interpretant of a fire by relating logically this smoke (representamen) to the fire (object), even though the organism may have not seen or felt the fire. The process by which the smoke is related to the fire is a sign process.[227] This sign is not static but is a process relating to other signs and being translated into other signs, which can be called a semiotic process. Translation is the process of turning a sign into another sign or making meaning, and interlingual translation is a type of translation involving two different languages.

Peirce's approach starts with non-linguistic signs.[228] Based on the relationship between representamen and object are three categories of signs: icon, index, and symbol.[229] An icon is a sign that bears a resemblance or likeness to the object it denotes.[230] *Iconic* can be used to describe a translation that has a relation of similarity or resemblance between the ST and the RT (a photo, painting, or sculpture).[231] An index is a sign process that describes a relationship of physical proximity, causality, or logical necessity, such as the example of smoke and fire, or a footprint, or a pointing finger, guiding the observer to the interpretant.[232] The index is affected by the object and has some common features with it. Finally, a symbol describes a more traditional relationship between representamen and object, such as

---

224. Peirce, *Collected Papers*, 2.228.
225. Chandler, *Semiotics*, 30.
226. Marais, *(Bio)Semiotic Theory*, 90.
227. Marais, *(Bio)Semiotic Theory*, 96.
228. Hatim and Mason, *Discourse and the Translator*, 108.
229. Marais, *(Bio)Semiotic Theory*, 95.
230. Peirce, *Collected Papers*, 2.247.
231. Marais, *(Bio)Semiotic Theory*, 96.
232. Peirce, *Collected Papers*, 2.248.

in language.²³³ A symbol is a sign that is related to the object by convention or a law-like relationship. Symbols are arbitrary and must be culturally learned, such as the letters of an alphabet or flags.

Peirce's theory of signs and semiosis is complex and abstract, giving rise to many varying interpretations and theories.²³⁴ However, it does have applications in translation theory and practice, as shown below.

Fitzgerald and Schrag

Fitzgerald and Schrag, who propose viewing songs as signs, provide a model for analyzing the signs in a song to identify how they work and to understand effects they have.²³⁵ The signs in a song include textual signs (the song lyrics), musical signs (rhythm, melody, tempo, etc.), and associate signs, which link to a particular contextual feature: a person, place, or another thing. Fitzgerald and Schrag suggest that these signs relate to objects using Peirce's three meaning-linking mechanisms: lexical symbols relate a sign and an object through language, icons relate a sign and object through resemblance, and an index describes a sign, which calls up emotion when one hears the music.²³⁶ The effects of these signs are then measured according to how they cause things to happen in the real world. Fitzgerald and Schrag give several examples, where either the well-chosen song lyrics function in a symbolic way to influence the listeners, or the poetic and musical syntax functions in an iconic way to achieve effective oral communication for the audience, or the genre type functions in an indexical way to influence the listeners by association. In the Altai performances, the lyrics, the musical syntax, and associate signs all function together so that the performance communicates the meaning of Scripture to the Altai audiences in the most effective way.

Turino

Turino has also developed a theory of music and dance based on Peircean semiotics.²³⁷ Turino maintains that music has power to create emotional responses, based on signs of feeling and experience, and this helps to create

---

233. Peirce, *Collected Papers*, 2.249.
234. Stecconi, "Foundation," 92.
235. Fitzgerald and Schrag, "But Is It," 2–3.
236. Fitzgerald and Schrag, "But Is It," 5.
237. Turino, "Signs of Imagination," 222.

personal and social identities.[238] Turino also uses Peirce's three basic classes of effects created by sign-object relations: an emotional or feeling interpretant, which is a direct feeling caused by a sign; an energetic interpretant, which is a physical reaction caused by a sign such as a foot tapping to music; and a sign-interpretant, which is a linguistic-based concept.[239] Mostly, music sounds functioning as signs will operate as an icon or index. An example of an icon (a sign related to its object by resemblance) in music could be if a song brings another piece of music to mind. Common musical devices such as a rising melody, accelerando, or crescendo will create excitement or tension in a listener because it sounds like human voices becoming excited and rising in pitch, speed, and volume. An index (relating to its object through actual experience) could be, for example, a theme song of a television show acting as index for the program, or a song that indexes a romantic relationship as "our song." Indexical signs relate to emotion and experience and help produce social identification. Members of social groups will share indexical signs relating to common experiences. Music has great semiotic potential, creating social unity and purpose, which is one of the goals for the Altai performances.

Semiotics for oral Bible translation

Naudé also uses Peircean semiotics in application to oral Bible translation, discussing the three sign possibilities outlined by Peirce: icon, index, and symbol.[240] Traditionally the symbolic has been studied by those in translation studies. Naudé provides evidence from the Sesotho Bible translation that in an oral Bible translation, the oral features in the RT may only point to some aspect of the ST, without representing it directly, meaning that the relationship between the two texts is indexical and contiguous rather than iconic.[241] As has been pointed out, it is impossible for the RT to fully resemble the ST, with the result that the relationship in translation can only be weakly iconic.

---

238. Turino, "Signs of Imagination," 222.
239. Turino, "Signs of Imagination," 224.
240. Naudé, "Iconicity and Developments," 388.
241. Naudé, "Iconicity and Developments," 409.

Example from the Altai OBT project

I was involved from June 2019 to June 2024 as a TA in an OBT project in the Southern Altai language in the Republic of Altai (Russian Federation). As part of this project, the translation team has used various modalities which have contributed to the communication of the meaning of the text. After the team had orally translated the book of Jonah, the translation was adapted to the poetic form of an Altai epic story and sung by a well-known throat singer. The recorded performance was accompanied by contextualized pictures drawn by a local artist illustrating the book of Jonah, along with photographs taken by the team's drone showing beautiful Altai nature scenes.[242] This combination of the text of the translation accompanied by music and visual stimuli contributed to the production of meaningful Scripture in the Altai language.

Conclusions for OBT and performance

The multimodal nature of modern communication, including multiple sign systems, is vitally important in oral Bible translation and performance.[243] A simple binary, oral-versus-written model cannot account for the complex semiotic landscape that includes many varied and mixed modes of communication: sign, speech, print, emojis, icons, dance, and other artistic expressions. Harmelink suggests that instead of referring to oral translation, sign language translation, or written translation, the term "multimodal translation" is more appropriate. Methodologies, principles, procedures, and pedagogies will then flow between the different kinds of translation. Maxey suggests renaming OBT "performance translation," which accommodates a more diversely multimedia approach to translation.[244] This involves recognizing that performance is a more complex media interface and that more than the oral medium needs to be considered in translation.[245] Language is only one mode in which meaning is conveyed, and every semiotic process is a meaning-making process. All of this is applied in the final performances of this research, in which the translation team uses local music, costumes, dance, and visual aids such as contextualized drawings, nature photos, and Altai artefacts to create a multimodal experience for the audience.

---

242. This performance can be seen at the following link: http://www.altai-obt.ru.
243. Harmelink, "Narrative Approach," 1.
244. Maxey, "Beyond Print/Oral Translation," 1.
245. Maxey, "Beyond Print/Oral Translation," 6.

The process of translating and performing biblical texts can be described using Peirce's semiotics. The process can be symbolic, whereby the RT bears an arbitrary conventional lexical relationship to the ST. It can be iconic, whereby the RT and performance bear a relation of similarity or physical resemblance to the ST. The visuality of the performance and its movements can provide such an iconic link to the biblical text, providing additional information, which is part of the metatext of the translation, to guide the hearers and the performers. For example, in the case of the Altai performances, this iconic translation is reflected in gestures and dance, physically demonstrating the theme of unity in Ps 133. Musically, if the *jangar* melody (discussed in more detail in chapter 7) is associated with unity in Ps 133, this may also be an indexical resemblance, like smoke indicating the presence of fire. It is indexical in as much as the RT and performance point to the ST showing a relationship of contiguity. This semiotic complexity theory has practical implications for oral Bible translation and the performances of the Altai translation team, with the goal of providing memorable and powerful Scripture.

TRANSLATION AS HOSPITALITY

Maxey partners orality and embodied performance with the hospitality theory of translation.[246] Therefore, I briefly examine this theory and extract some relevant principles that are beneficial for the Altai project. Maxey defines hospitality as "the friendly and generous reception and entertainment of guests, visitors, or strangers" where the host has the power to offer hospitality to the guest.[247] He notes that hospitality is both a biblical theme and a value that Christianity holds in high esteem. Quakenbush comments that "as a major theme in the Bible, hospitality provides a framework for interpreting its grand narrative."[248] Quakenbush gives the example from Gen 18:1–10 where God visits Abraham in the form of three guests as one of the best-known examples of hospitality in the Bible.[249] Pohl describes the distinctive nature of Christian hospitality as offering "a generous welcome to the 'least' without concern for advantage or benefit to the host."[250] Missiologically, God's hospitality is seen in his love for and in his redemption of

---

246. Maxey, "Alternative Evaluative Concepts."
247. Maxey, "Bible Translation as Hospitality," 2.
248. Quakenbush, "Linguistic Hospitality," 286.
249. Quakenbush, "Linguistic Hospitality," 287.
250. Pohl, *Making Room*, 16.

Theoretical Framework

his creation through Christ's death on the cross.[251] Boersma writes, "Christ's death and resurrection constitute the ultimate expression of God's hospitality and form the matrix for an understanding of all God's actions."[252]

As discussed above, semiotics has been used as a theoretical framework for intersemiotic translation (the interpretation of verbal signs by means of non-verbal signs or translation other than print), and in this context fidelity has been interpreted as being faithful to a genre. Maxey proposes another approach to translation: the metaphor of hospitality for translation.[253] Maxey employs this theory to help understand Bible translation as more than just linguistics, also including power relations, issues of identity, and cultural mediation.[254] Maxey prefers the terms "host community" or "host language," as opposed to receptor or recipient community or language.

Maxey argues that equivalence and its associated quality-assessment criteria of accuracy, naturalness, and clarity are insufficient for translation beyond print. Instead, his metaphor of hospitality emphasizes the concepts of carefulness, authenticity, and transparency for biblical performance translation.[255] Maxey makes the point that the Bible is often associated with the printed book, with the consequence that translation theories were developed for the print medium.[256] Non-print translations including song and film were called "adaptations" rather than faithful translations.

In the same vein as Maxey, Derrida describes hospitality simply as inviting a visitor.[257] However, he observes, in a case of "obliged hospitality," the master or the host can effectively become a hostage, a situation which is not atypical of many BT programs. He writes, "So it is indeed the master, the one who invites, the inviting host, who becomes the hostage—and who really always has been. And the guest, the invited hostage, becomes the one who invites the one who invites, the master of the host. The guest becomes the host's host."[258] It was Ricoeur who suggested talking about translation as "linguistic hospitality," which he describes as a state "where the pleasure of dwelling in the other's language is balanced by the pleasure of receiving the

---

251. Quakenbush, "Linguistic Hospitality," 288.

252. Boersma, *Violence, Hospitality*, 26.

253. Maxey, "Bible Translation as Hospitality," and "Bible Translation in the 21st Century."

254. Quakenbush, "Linguistic Hospitality," 290.

255. Maxey, "Alternative Evaluative Concepts."

256. Maxey, "Alternative Evaluative Concepts," 62.

257. Derrida, *Of Hospitality*, 123–25.

258. Derrida, *Of Hospitality*, 125.

foreign word at home, in one's welcoming house."[259] It is a mutual dialogue between the self and the Other, that affirms differences rather than negating the Other. It is a middle road "where one honors the host and guest languages equitably."[260]

Maxey says that the shift from equivalence to hospitality entails a shift from source to host and from text to audience.[261] Translation, and especially performance translation, is always a negotiation which includes conflicts, choices, compromises, and collaboration.[262] Hospitality is relational in nature and allows for difference, whereas equivalence measures what is the same.[263]

Maxey suggests that the category of acceptability by the host community fits well within this concept of hospitality, and he proposes the additional criteria of carefulness, authenticity, and transparency.[264] According to Maxey, for oral materials, carefulness, or manipulating a text with care, is a more appropriate category than accuracy.[265] Authenticity addresses the questions of power relations and colonization, protecting the identity and authenticity of the host community. It also relates to the question of language in translation, the host respecting the foreign but not losing self-respect. In addition, it suggests that each medium remains true to itself, having its own set of internal guidelines for communication.[266] Authenticity also protects the agency of the translator, whose translation choices are evident rather than invisible in the translation. Finally, transparency emphasizes that the host will recognize the alterity or otherness of the guest, rather than wishing the guest to be identical. Towner writes, "For Ricoeur, human diversity is the core reality, alterity is a value, and translation is a means by which those who are 'other to each other' (as well as to themselves) might effectively embrace difference in the creation of something new and enriching for human community—as opposed to understanding translation as a means of reducing or neutralizing alterity."[267]

Maxey proposes that performance translation brings with it a conception of translation not as an act of recuperation but rather as a creative act

---

259. Ricoeur, *On Translation*, 10.
260. Kearney, "Linguistic Hospitality," 17.
261. Maxey, "Beyond Print/Oral Translation," 8.
262. Maxey, "Beyond Print/Oral Translation," 10.
263. Maxey, "Beyond Print/Oral Translation," 11.
264. Maxey, "Alternative Evaluative Concepts," 65.
265. Maxey, "Alternative Evaluative Concepts," 66.
266. Maxey, "Alternative Evaluative Concepts," 67.
267. Towner, "Translation," 154.

of rewriting—not looking back but looking forward to new audiences.[268] Performance itself is translation and is experience-based, "taking place in the performance, through sound, silence, gestures, and interactions with the audience."[269] When biblical material is performed, it is an "intersemiotic translation of previous experiences."[270] With regard to biblical performance translation, carefulness to the tradition entails understanding that, although now in written form, much of the biblical text was originally stories or songs told and received by audiences and then written down. The host culture can also add its own cultural authenticity to the translation. Otherness or alterity can be indicated by adding oral footnotes or descriptions that explain certain foreign customs and concepts. Such a performance translation can be described as hospitable.

Others have also used the term "linguistic hospitality," which is perhaps a clearer metaphor than Maxey's. Quakenbush defines linguistic hospitality as follows: "One practices linguistic hospitality by receiving others in ways that attend to their linguistic repertoire with respect to their identity and communicative needs."[271] Kenmogne used the term in a speech to participants preparing for a SIL International meeting, saying that "we need, in this world, to be exercising a bit more of what I have called a 'linguistic hospitality,' where we learn to create room for all the languages that people actually use."[272] Pasquale and Bierma explain that practicing linguistic hospitality is "making room for the languages of others, welcoming those languages, and acknowledging that language is a vital aspect of a speaker's identity."[273]

Maxey's hospitality theory is particularly suitable for biblical performance, as it emphasizes interpersonal relationships and negotiation. It acknowledges the orality of the biblical texts, designed originally as performances, as well as the authenticity of the host culture, while still recognizing the alterity of certain concepts. It promotes the role of the audience and reduces the dichotomy between translation and performance, asserting that the experience of the performance itself is translation. These are useful concepts for the Altai translation team in their preparation of their performances.

268. Maxey, "Alternative Evaluative Concepts," 70.
269. Maxey, "Biblical Performance Criticism," 14.
270. Maxey, "Alternative Evaluative Concepts," 73.
271. Quakenbush, "Linguistic Hospitality," 292.
272. Kenmogne, "Multilingualism, Urbanisation."
273. Pasquale and Bierma, *Every Tribe and Tongue*, 21.

CONCLUSIONS

In oral Bible translation, features of the ST are represented as oral features in the RT. This has been described as translation from "orality to orality."[274] In the discussion of orality, it became clear that the oral and the written are not mutually exclusive domains but are two intertwined and interdependent modalities of language. In addition, the written ST, the Bible, is actually a complex interface of both oral and written features. Oral Bible translation must begin with an understanding of the oral-written interface of the incipient texts of ancient Israel and the early church. Then, attention must be given to the oral-written interface of the subsequent recipient culture. Because universality cannot be assumed, the oral features of language need to be specifically identified in any given culture. In chapters 5 and 6 of this book, I analyze the oral features in the incipient text (Judg 4–5; Pss 1, 100, and 133), and in chapter 7, I investigate oral features in similar genres in the subsequent recipient culture of the Republic of Altai. I then discuss how to represent oral features of the ST as oral features of the RT.

Functionalism emphasizes the role of the recipient audience in the translation process. As form cannot be separated from meaning, paralinguistic features (volume, speed, intonation of a voice, and quality of the voice) and extralinguistic features (body language, gestures, and facial expressions) should also be considered part of the communication process. Together with the Altai translation team, I have prepared paralinguistic and extralinguistic notes on the passages which are translated and performed.

The process of translation is as important as the finished product, as it is a creative, relational, and interpretive process. The translators themselves have a narrative role of mediation, as they choose which features of the ST should be given prominence and select different strategies. It is important to recognize translators as agents for change in their community. An emphasis is placed on the process of translation and on the importance and role of the translators themselves in the Altai project.

Complexity theory holds that translation is not binary and linear but is instead a recursive process. Also, meaning emerges historically and relationally. The ST and RT can be understood, respectively, as an incipient text and a subsequent text. Performance of the subsequent text can therefore influence the meaning of the incipient text, and so in this research observations and constructive criticism from the audience is fed back into the translation process.

---

274. Maxey, *From Orality to Orality*, loc. 98.

Metatext is used to help make the translation understandable and accessible for the reader/audience by respecting the alterity of the source culture while still ensuring the translation is intelligible to recipient readers. This is reflected in the Altai visual performance in the form of an oral introduction. By explaining key cultural terms and concepts, this helps guide the reader's interpretation of the text.

OBT and performance involve a complex intersemiotic landscape, including multiple sign systems such as gestures, music, and dance, each of which contribute to the meaning-making process. The visual, such as the costumes and contextualized drawings in the Altai performances, are important in providing a contextual addition to words because of the role of intersemiotics and multimodality in the current digital-media culture. Gravelle recommends "using a multimodal approach where visual, oral and written modes all contribute to the complete communication."[275] The translation and performance of the biblical texts will thus be simultaneously symbolic, iconic, and indexical.

Hospitality theory, which construes translation as a mediation between host and guest languages, has particular implications for performance translation. It is a theory that takes into account the oral medium and emphasizes the relational aspect of translation and the role of the audience. It views the performance itself as translation, providing us with the additional criteria of carefulness, authenticity, and transparency for the oral Bible translation and performance.

---

275. Gravelle, "Meaning Making," 7.

3

Oral Bible Translation

INTRODUCTION

This chapter begins with a discussion on how internalization, as the key feature of OBT, affects the oral translation process. This section is developed from interviews with nine OBT teams in different parts of the world, as well as one OBT trainer, and includes conclusions drawn from those interviews about the process of OBT and internalization. In the discussion which follows, I will refer to these interview subjects anonymously as OBT teams 1 to 9. This is followed by a study of how the method of OBT can be used to translate different genres, including poetry. I conclude the chapter with a discussion of when and how emotional exegesis should take place during OBT and how OBT teams in the future can be assisted with this process.

INTERNALIZATION

Younghans, Madden, and Ross emphasize the close similarity between OBT and written translation.[1] The main difference between the two methods is the long process of internalization in OBT that takes place during the preparation of the first draft. They observe that internalization, which includes quality exegesis early in the process, is the signature step of developing the most natural translation. Internalization occurs at the book level, the unit

---

1. Younghans et al., "Time to Reflect," 34.

level (often a chapter), and the block level (often three to five verses), and involves discussion and memory-building activities, as well as relevant exegesis and the development of key terms and concepts. Toler, in his paper on internalization, concludes that it is this process of internalization which is the key ingredient in achieving naturalness in the oral translation.[2] It takes into consideration the needs of oral-preference learners to learn within a community, to process the narrative in an individual and interactive manner, and to comprehend the information in their own language.

The following is a description of the process of internalization as developed by the Seed Company:

> Within an OBT context, internalization is a form of exegesis designed to equip the translation teams with a good understanding of what a particular passage meant to the original audience and how to communicate that meaning in their current context. Internalization is not rote word-for-word memorization. Instead, the process is intended to help the translators understand a passage so well they can repeat its meaning (1) clearly in their language, (2) in an order that respects the uniqueness of the language but retains all the material content, and (3) as naturally as if they themselves had experienced the biblical text first hand.[3]

The need for internalization

One of the turning points for the BT movement was the expansion of the role of mother-tongue translators (MTTs) and a diminishing reliance on missionary translators. Nida writes, "When the United Bible Societies began, fully 90% of BT in the Third World were being made by missionaries with the help of informants or translation helpers. Now in 90% of the projects the translators are nationals, and missionaries have become the resource persons."[4] This shift from non-native translators assisted by native-speaker language-helpers to translators who are themselves native speakers has necessitated a beneficial adjustment in how translation is carried out. In proposing a translation methodology aimed specifically at national translators, Culy underscored the need for internalization to be incorporated into the translation process.[5]

- 2. Toler, "Key Ingredient," 115.
- 3. Seed Company, "OBT Projects," 2.
- 4. Nida, "Trends in Bible Translating," 5.
- 5. Culy, "Top-Down," 33.

Culy drew upon the accepted truth that the native speakers of the RL should be the ones translating because of their native-speaker intuition about the RL.[6] He suggested that the exegete (often an expatriate) should prepare an exegetical explanation of the source passage, presenting the passage's message clearly and simply. Culy points out that this assumes knowledge of English or another Language of Wider Communication (LWC). This means that the exegete's oral explanation effectively becomes the intermediate ST. This is an excellent example of the utility of Marais's views of incipient text and subsequent text. The "intermediate ST" is actually both a subsequent text and an incipient text.

This exegetical explanation of the source passage is then to be internalized by the translator and drafted into the RL. The MTT works from this oral exegesis or explanation of the ST to create a natural rough draft rather than working directly from the ST itself. In this way interference or "shining through" from the SL into the translation is minimized. This kind of top-down approach, born out of a need to train native-speaker translators, focuses on first understanding the ST and then translating as naturally as possible.[7] Understanding the ST has always been a crucial factor in BT. However, this shift from missionary translators to national translators has brought into focus the necessity for internalization in the translation process.

Definition of internalization

Toler adopts the following definition for internalization: "Internalization is mentally processing a piece of information to the point that a translator owns it, as if it were his or her own experience."[8] The emphasis is on the ability to retell the passage in one's own words and even to be able to adapt it to different audiences. Internalization allows improvisation with each instance of telling and retelling. It requires more than just intellectual comprehension of the words; rather, it depends on complete comprehension of and immersion into the passage so that it becomes as if it were part of the translator's own experience. The TA, through the process of internalization, attempts to engage the translator on all levels of experience (actions, emotions, sights, and sounds) to make the passage vivid and more natural when translated. The passage or story needs to become real for the translators personally. Sunil, a translator from the Koch language group OBT project

6. Culy, "Top-Down," 33.
7. Toler and Toler, "Shift in Understanding."
8. Toler, "Key Ingredient," 63.

says, "When we internalize the stories, we feel that we enter into the story, and we become a part of the story. This is a very enjoyable experience."[9]

Harmelink writes, "The internalization process involves, indeed requires, making more holistic, emotional, and visceral connections with intersecting life stories."[10] Stahl offers different descriptions of internalization, as collected from communities involved in oral Bible storying.[11] One community compared internalization to "chewing" on the story like chewing on strong meat before swallowing it down. Another community compared internalizing a story to digging deep and wide around a six-foot yam to harvest it. They do not want to break or cut the yam but need to discover in which direction all the lobes of the yam have grown. These comparisons, drawn from the communities' own life experiences, show that the very process of internalization has itself been internalized.

Dictionary definitions of "internalization" include "incorporating" something within oneself,[12] or "accepting" or "absorbing" attitudes or values.[13] These definitions all involve the idea of obtaining and keeping something inside a person or a system. The word "internalization" is used in a variety of disciplines such as psychology, economics, and sport.[14] When applied to the process of engaging with Scripture, internalization, metaphorically, involves placing God's word "inside" of a person so that it becomes part of the person's personal experience or consciousness. This does not necessarily mean that the translator has to be a Christian believer but that the translator must engage personally in some way with the material. Internalization is a vital part of OBT, although it can also be beneficial for written translation, as it allows the material to be experienced in such a way that translators can truly grasp the passage's core concepts and re-express them both accurately and naturally in the new context of their own language and culture. Internalization is the beginning of a rigorous process of oral translation. Ideally, internalization during the initial exegesis carried out by the TA with the translation team puts the material inside the minds and hearts of translators so thoroughly that, throughout the process, the translators continue working with and refining the material. There are many opportunities along the way for the internalization process to deepen and for the translator's language and expressivity to become more authentic and

9. Alexander, "Joys and Challenges," 5.
10. Harmelink, "Narrative Approach," 4.
11. Stahl, "Internalizing in Storytelling," 4.
12. Merriam-Webster, "Internalize."
13. Cambridge Dictionary, "Internalize."
14. Frost, "Workshop Elements."

convincing. Typically, naturalness improves over time. However, the depth and quality of the whole process depends on the thoroughness of internalization at the beginning.

Internalization versus memorization

Perry contrasts internalization with memorization.[15] The latter implies rote and word-for-word recall, where understanding is not essential. Internalization happens when a person or group has repeated experiences of a passage or story to the point that they embody this in their speech, thought patterns, and bodily responses. A single word may be the trigger for the entire passage or story, in the way that a person who has internalized a song can afterward hear only a few notes and recall the entire song, along with situations in which the song has been performed. It is not only the words that are recalled but also associated emotions, relationships, and experiences. Internalization means that the person who has internalized the passage is able to improvise and retell the passage in different ways to varying audiences.

The role of memory

Although internalization is distinct from memorization, memory is still extremely important in the internalization process. Mnemonics, memory devices which help people remember larger pieces of information, may include music (making songs out of information, especially long lists), name mnemonics (the first letter of each word in a list is used to make a name), expression mnemonics (the first letter of each item in a list is arranged to form a word or a phrase), model mnemonics (some type of representation is constructed to help recall), an ode or rhyme mnemonic, note organization mnemonics, image mnemonics (a picture that promotes the recall of information), connections mnemonics (information is connected to something already known), and spelling mnemonics.[16] In OBT internalization, the most commonly used mnemonics are model, image, or connection mnemonics.

Stahl points out that internalization makes use of a group learning style and collective memory, both of which are features of many oral cultures.[17] Memories are largely constructed of stories, and when people tell

---

15. Perry, "Biblical Performance Criticism," 8.
16. Congos, "9 Types of Mnemonics."
17. Stahl, "We Tell to Remember," 1–4.

stories it enables them to shape their present world, their past, and their future. These stories help people make sense of current events. When people internalize, translate, and retell stories about cultures and events that they are not familiar with, such as the biblical stories, the translators first need to make sense of them in their own minds.

Gravelle, director of research and innovation with the Seed Company, discusses the change from a purely linguistic understanding of meaning-making to a multimodal or intersemiotic visual understanding of how meaning is made. Gravelle points out how languages are not neutral coding systems relaying an objective reality, but rather meaning in language is derived from people's experiences in the world.[18] Meaning is actually created in the mind by imagining, internally visualizing, or performing something in the mind. This embodied meaning is drawn from people's experiences in the real world. Finding meaning is not about looking for the right symbol or sign but about dynamically reconstructing a scene. Instead of understanding translation as a simple process of decoding a message conveyed by the SL and then re-coding it in the RL, oral processing of the ST in the RL gives a clearer understanding to the translator of how to express the text in the RL. Oral processing encouraging the meaning-making process, such as that which goes on during internalization, can help produce similar experiences in the mind of the translators, so that what they simulate matches to a greater extent what was simulated in the mind of the author of the ST.[19]

Farber, writing about memory, agrees that future memory relies not only on having a representation of the original coding but also on simulating a visual representation of the future. He gives an example where, in order to remember to buy milk, rather than just picturing himself with the bottle of milk at home, he envisages driving to the store, parking his car, and walking into the shop.[20] This is effectively the process which takes place in the internalization of Bible passages and stories.

Dinh et al. performed a study to investigate the effects of tactile, olfactory, audio, and visual sensory cues on participants' sense of presence in a virtual environment and on their memory of the environment and the objects in that environment.[21] Results indicated that increasing sensory input in a virtual environment can help increase memory for the objects in that environment, especially with the addition of tactile and auditory cues—and even olfactory cues. Quak, London, and Talsma point out that in everyday

---

18. Gravelle, "More Than Words," 48.
19. Gravelle, "More Than Words," 52.
20. Farber, "Science of Memory."
21. Dinh et al., "Evaluating the Importance," 1.

life, people experience and process information they receive from multiple senses simultaneously (sight, sounds, smell, taste, and touch).[22] They conclude that working memory is also multisensory. Farber notes that a combination of contextual cues serves best to facilitate memory. This would indicate that increasing and combining sensory input during the process of internalization helps the translators in remembering the story or passage.[23]

Pre-internalization

Internalization is made up of several stages, the first of which is getting to know the translators' personal and cultural learning styles and preferences, previous educational experiences, and how they process information.[24] Harmelink emphasizes that open communication and trust are essential elements of the internalization process, saying, "Relationships are critical for the community-based conversational discovery process to work well."[25]

Before the process of internalization begins, some of the teams tell stories from their own culture or personal experience on a similar theme as the story about to be internalized and translated. When the team then come to work on a Bible story, this initial process helps the team apply a Bible story to their own lives and communities, with the result that internalization is more effective. Stahl and Stahl start the internalization process by asking each of the participants to learn to tell their own stories or stories from their community and history that intersect with the biblical text they will be working on.[26] In this process storytellers collect many personal and community stories to help discover what they value as a group. They also work to identify other Bible stories that are linked with the passage they are working on. They look for intersections of their own stories with the Bible stories or for dissonance between the two. They ask each other what other stories the Bible stories remind them of, and they note what stories the original audience may have been thinking of when they heard the Bible story and how that would have shaped the impact of hearing those stories. To help the translation team to immerse themselves in the communication genre of the passage, one can also ask the team to study examples of this genre in their own culture. For example, if the team members are going to translate Jesus' farewell speech at the Passover, the TA, who functions as an

22. Quak et al., "Multisensory Perspective," para. 2.
23. Farber, "Science of Memory."
24. Frost, "Tips for Internalizing Scripture."
25. Harmelink, "Oral Bible Translation," 4.
26. Stahl and Stahl, "Oral Bible Storytelling."

exegete and facilitator in the internalization process, could ask the team to look at farewell speeches in their own cultures.

Exegetical study by the TA

The second stage is a thorough exegetical study of the passage by the TA in order to prepare for the internalization session. Exegesis is the process of analyzing the biblical text to discover its intended meaning. However, oral exegesis is not just carrying out the standard steps of the exegesis orally but is instead the process of "drawing out the meaning consistent with oral communication."[27] Alexander outlines the purpose of oral exegesis: to connect the passage with the daily lives of the translators, to engage with the content, and to make use of the tacit linguistic knowledge of the MTTs. This leads to a translation consistent with oral communication. This exegetical study may include providing an introduction to the book (best provided in narrative form in the LWC); identifying key terms and unknown or difficult concepts; identifying the genre of the passage and the purpose of the genre; understanding the content of the passage; situating the passage in the larger story framework; thinking through setting, sequence, and characters; and looking at the original context and linguistic aspects. Although it is possible to process certain key terms during the study of the passage, Culy says, "By dealing with them before the passage is ever studied, the unknown concepts and how they can be rendered in the target language become 'familiar' and so do not affect the MTT's flow of thought as he records the oral draft."[28]

The oral exegesis can start by conversing about something familiar or relevant to the target people group that the translators can easily identify with. The TA may start culturally appropriate conversations with the translation team using the genre of the passage in the conversation. Alexander gives an example from 1 Tim 3:1–7 about church leaders, in which introductory conversations might include the team's ideas about a good man and how to find a wife for him and what kind of person should be the village leader.[29]

If the content is not very familiar to the translators in their cultural context, it may help to find a Bible story that has the same theme as the teaching in the selected passage. Alexander gives an example of using the scene from the story of Joseph recounted in Gen 39:1–12 (how Joseph fled from sin when he was tempted by Potiphar's wife) to illustrate the passage

27. Alexander, "Oral Exegesis," 4.
28. Culy, "Top-Down," 39.
29. Alexander, "Joys and Challenges."

in 1 Tim 4:12 on Paul's theme of a "model young man."[30] Paul's journeys in Acts (Acts 13–14; 15:36–18:23; 18:24–21:14; 26:30–28:30) could be compared to the translators' travel stories or to different modes of travel on long journeys in the culture. Alexander shares that she even took her translation team on a trip to the beach so they could understand what the sea looks like before translating some of Paul's journey stories in Acts 13–14. There are audio and visual aids to assist with the process of engaging with the content, such as the Lumo Project films[31] and images or drawings of objects from the internet. As a result, the translators learn the passage so well that it becomes a part of them, they are able to use rhetorical devices suitable for the genre without consciously thinking about it, and they become aware of the linguistic differences between the LWC and their mother tongue, even though they may not have the metalanguage needed to describe them. Exegesis and internalization are closely linked and they overlap, as the two often occur simultaneously, intertwining with each other. In fact, internalization could even be considered a form of exegesis.

Internalization techniques

Frost divides internalization into three stages: exposure, experience, and salience.[32] Frost also offers a useful overview of internalization techniques in her document "Introduction to Internalization Techniques," in which she suggests the following, organized by category: visual (sketches, storyboarding); physical/kinesthetic (motions, postures, facial expressions, drama, freeze-frame gestures); random objects (pre-selected or what is available, arrange in an order, move objects around); spatial (associate with rooms, or places, or landscapes); sound cues (one word per thought unit with a tone of voice or emotions for each thought unit); discourse cues (parallel sections, chiastic structures); and meditation or reflection (discuss personal application, thoughts, and feelings of people in the passage).[33]

Exposure

This stage may start out quite passively but leads to more active processing. The initial exposure stage introduces the translators to the passage by having

---

30. Alexander, "Joys and Challenges."
31. https://lumoproject.com.
32. Frost, "Internalization Session."
33. Frost, "Basic Internalization Plan."

them listen multiple times to either an oral telling from memory or to an audio version of the passage in the LWC, preferably in different versions if they are available. The translators should have the opportunity to listen in different ways for different aspects of the message.[34] The team may also listen to the larger context of the passage and may process wider questions, such as when, where, who, what is the sequence of events, and how and why.[35] If the passage is non-narrative, other questions might be asked, such as finding out the reason for the communication, what the main themes are and how they are related, and where the topic shifts occur. At this stage, the emphasis is on basic familiarization and exposure to new concepts in the passage. The goals are to situate the passage in a larger context so the team can relate to it and to introduce new names and vocabulary to the team. While these goals may not be expressed explicitly to the participants, they are important to keep in mind while planning and carrying out the exposure stage. Boomershine, in his book *Story Journey: An Invitation to the Gospel as Storytelling*, suggests identifying the framework or structure of the story by listening to it being read many times.[36] In this way the listener can mentally divide the passage into episodes or scenes, providing a structure on which details can be attached. Structural clues can also be identified by repeated sounds, words, phrases or themes; contrasts; figures of speech; and other rhetorical devices that attract the listener's attention. This process is guided throughout by the translation advisor (TA).

It is also possible at this stage to hold a group devotional on the passage, which can serve to help the translators become more familiar with the passage and its themes and also encourage them to make application to their own lives and personal situations. The following are possible questions which could be used during such a devotional time:

- What did you like about the passage/story?
- What did you not like about the passage/story?
- What did you learn about God?
- What did you learn about humankind?
- What have you taken away that could be applied in your life?

Stahl and Stahl discovered that translators prefer to enter into or engage first with a passage/story through hearing the story and discussing the

---

34. Stahl, "Internalizing in Storytelling," 2.
35. Frost, "Basic Internalization Plan."
36. Boomershine, *Story Journey*.

personal impact.[37] Their crafting process starts with a devotion, hearing the story, and reflecting on the impact of the story. The participants respond intuitively to the storytelling experience based on the images that the storytelling provokes in their mind, along with the impact they experience and how it may relate to their own life stories and experiences. They often discuss the emotions that the story provokes, or they might see themselves in the story in a particular character. They listen for rhetorical devices like repeated sounds, themes, or phrases throughout the story, or they notice stark contrasts, sudden changes, patterns of movements, or figures of speech. The group then uses these discoveries and insights as they explore and discover what the author intended when telling this story.

Experience

The second stage is to assist the translators to engage with the passage, actively involving their senses and analytic abilities.[38] The point is to make mind-body connections between the text and personal experience. It is important to select the internalization techniques that will best help the translation team to make the passage their own. Some activities may work better in different cultures, or with different personalities, and even with different genres. This can be done initially by the TA, but in time one of the local translators could do this in the local context. The second stage may include visuals, kinesthetics, random objects, familiar spaces, sound cues, and discourse analysis. Multimedia combinations are also useful, such as adding sound effects to visuals or using objects and moving them around dynamically. The more senses which are involved, the more effective the associations the translation team can make. The number and nature of activities need to be chosen according to cultural conventions and learning preferences of the team members. Some teams internalize with one or two activities, while some teams require more. Some passages also lend themselves better to certain techniques than to others. A passage with a lot of dialogue is ideal for sound cues, for example, but this may not be effective for remembering a list.

One example of such an activity is a guided imagination exercise in which the translators are encouraged to create vivid mental pictures of what is happening in the passage. Other examples are visual activities, including storyboarding (a series of sketches), or sketching a scene, or using cards with drawn symbols (the latter can be helpful with lists). Dramatization

37. Stahl and Stahl, "Oral Bible Storytelling."
38. Frost, "Preparing for and Facilitating."

using multiple characters can also help the team to get actively involved and internalize the passage effectively. Sometimes groups use freeze-frame moments to capture scenes, which involves making single gestures or posing as "statues" to express certain points in the narrative, "freezing" the action. In another technique, participants can choose objects in the room to represent different moments or characters in the story. People involved in memory competitions often use "memory palaces" to help them remember large sequences of numbers or pictures. A memory palace is based on a familiar layout of a building, and each item to be remembered is connected to a particular item in this building. The items are then remembered in order by mentally walking back through the building. Other ideas include retelling the story from the viewpoint of one of the characters. Dialogues or monologues may require special practice.

Stahl suggests another exercise at this stage, which is to discuss the *Most Important Thing* (MIT) in the passage or section, in order to help the translators focus on what is prominent in the text and prevent them from going off on a tangent.[39] Of course, there may be more than one MIT, and individuals will likely suggest different options. It is important then to assess after the first draft whether the intended audience can identify the MIT from the retelling.

Engagement

This third step, which Frost also calls *salience*, involves deliberately focusing the attention of the translators and helping them to concentrate on prominent points.[40] Here the team has the opportunity to connect more deeply with the passage. In this third stage, the translators discuss the passage in the RL and start preparing to draft the passage. The team searches for points of significance, such as things that may have surprised or challenged the team. The team examines the emotions of the characters involved and perhaps considers the potential reactions of an intended audience. It can be helpful to ask the team what they consider to be the strongest emotion in the passage and then use this as a starting point for beginning to draft the passage. The team may think about what intonation would be most suitable to convey the emotional content of the passage. A discussion of postures, facial expressions, hand movements, and the use of the body can also be helpful. Frost suggests using kinesthetic cues such as body posturing or positioning to reinforce content, including hand gestures, facial expressions, and full

---

39. Stahl, "Internalizing in Storytelling," 4.
40. Frost, "Internalization Session."

body stances.⁴¹ Postures and gestures need to be contextualized to the local culture. Positioning may include showing movement from one location to another, showing where people are standing or how they are interacting with each other, and moving one's body/head in another direction to show a change in speaker.

Frost describes this third stage as time spent emotionally and intellectually processing the passage, talking through difficult concepts and keywords.⁴² Frost also recommends that the team, with the TA, could create aural sound cues to help set the tone, to introduce the tone of a dialogue, or to indicate changes of mood or setting.⁴³ For example, these could include clapping hands, stomping feet, slapping skin, knocking on doors, clearing throat, producing sounds of satisfaction, etc., though of course they need to be contextualized to the local culture. Frost recommends using the devotional questions at this later stage and discussing the impact of the passage on each team member's own life.⁴⁴

Factors influencing internalization

It is important to consider some of the factors that might influence choices about which internalization techniques to use, such as different learning and processing preferences.⁴⁵ Cultural resources also influence choices; for example, drawing would not be used in a culture that does not normally relate to two-dimensional symbols. Other factors to be considered are the following: how big the team is, how much time is allotted for internalization, who does the exegesis, accessibility of exegetical resources, who leads the internalization activities, how exegesis intersects with internalization, and what language is used for internalization.

Tacit knowledge

Earlier on in this chapter, there was a reference to the tacit linguistic knowledge of the MTTs and the importance of leveraging this knowledge in translation. The concept of tacit knowledge was first introduced by Polanyi.⁴⁶

41. Frost, "Basic Internalization Plan," 1.
42. Frost, "Tips for Internalizing Scripture," 3.
43. Frost, "Tips for Internalizing Scripture," 3.
44. Frost, "Preparing for and Facilitating."
45. Frost, "Preparing for and Facilitating."
46. Polanyi, *Tacit Dimension*.

Tacit knowledge is part of many activities in life, such as driving a car or playing music, but it is hard to define and verbalize exactly how this happens. Such knowledge can be shared and transmitted. Tacit knowledge is practical knowledge, expressed in skills or abilities which are developed in time through exercises and practice. Jakubowska has done a sociological study on the transmission of skills through tacit knowledge in sport, and this can be applied to translation.[47] There are many skills in sport which are embodied in the tacit knowledge acquired from practice, repetition, and experience.[48] Jakubowska asserts that since the 1980s, the Cartesian dichotomy between the mind and the body, along with the notion that individuals and their knowledge exist independently of their physical being, has been increasingly criticized and has been replaced by the concept of embodied knowledge.[49] The body is a source of knowledge and a tool for its acquisition. Jakubowska's study of tacit knowledge focuses on the limits of the verbal transfer of knowledge and discusses tacit knowledge transmission in sport based on the repetition and perpetuation of embodied habits.[50] I have observed in working with my OBT team in the Republic of Altai that not only do the translators have tacit linguistic knowledge, but also the skill or activity of internalization in time becomes an embodied habit developed through exercises and practice. This was also confirmed in the interviews with the OBT teams, discussed below.

Frequency and other factors

Frost discusses frequency in internalization, suggesting that a memory needs to be reinforced often enough to result in adequate retention and noting that time between the exercises helps the material to sink in and reappear in natural, local forms of communication.[51] She suggests that new material should be practiced and therefore reinforced twenty minutes (after doing a different short task), two hours (after doing a different longer task), twenty-four hours (next day, same time), and two days after the initial encounter. Stangor and Walinga propose that the loss of information from short-term memory can be prevented by using working memory to rehearse it, by repeating the information mentally or out loud with the goal

---

47. Jakubowska, *Skill Transmission*.
48. Jakubowska, *Skill Transmission*, i.
49. Jakubowska, *Skill Transmission*, 1.
50. Jakubowska, *Skill Transmission*, 9.
51. Frost, "Tips for Internalizing Scripture," 7.

of remembering it. Information can then enter long-term memory, which can be kept for days, months, or years.[52]

Kelley and Whatson describe a learning method called *spaced learning*, in which highly condensed learning content is repeated three times, with two ten-minute breaks during which physical activities can be done by the students (with no stimulation).[53] Their research suggests that spaced learning is more efficient than standard teaching. Lau, as part of her eleven proven techniques to aid memory, includes spaced repetition, chunking, engaging the senses by using visual connections, sharing what one is learning, and creating a memory palace.[54] All of these techniques can be included in the internalization process for translation. The Ebbinghaus Curve of Forgetting graph demonstrates how quickly information is forgotten that is not repeated frequently: immediate recall is 100 percent, 40 percent of the information is forgotten over the first twenty-four hours, and another 60 percent is forgotten within the following twenty-four hours.[55] If the mind is regularly exposed to information, it is much more likely to become embedded in longer lasting memory. If a person occasionally but continually reviews the material in small review sessions with time in between, then gradually the information comes to be remembered more permanently.

Practical considerations

From a practical point of view, it is important during the internalization processes to make sure the translators feel comfortable and rested and have sufficient refreshments and breaks. It is important to eliminate stress for the participants during the internalization process, as stress may create a block that prevents the participants from making the necessary links between the stories or passages and their personal experience. It is these links that help the participants internalize successfully. Farber's article on Brewer's research on memory shows the role that attention plays with regard to future memory.[56] Distractions and divided attention can interfere with memory.

---

52. Stangor and Walinga, *Introduction to Psychology*.
53. Kelley and Whatson, "Making Long-Term Memories."
54. Lau, "How to Memorize Things Fast."
55. Ebbinghaus, *Über das Gedächtnis*.
56. Farber, "Science of Memory."

Collective learning

Toler and Toler suggest that internalization works because it meets the needs of oral cultures and oral-preference learners and involves community orientation (groupwork, collective knowledge, a safe environment) and learning through doing (hands-on learning, apprenticeship, problem-solving).[57] It is evident that these principles are interwoven throughout the internalization process. This process satisfies the education needs of the oral learner in a way that values traditional forms of passing on information. Internalization is learner-centered: all the activities involve the learner as active participant. Seeking out the learning activities that work best for the translators encourages the internalization process to be learner-centered. This type of learning explicitly builds on what the translators already know and gives structures for them to build upon, rather than reintroducing things already known as if they were completely new information.

Internalization also meets the need for community orientation, a hallmark of oral cultures. Oral cultures are by nature communal. During internalization there is a strong sense of community built into the project, as the process is facilitated through group work and participation. This intentional focus on community allows oral learners to make use of their collective knowledge rather than just their individual knowledge. This also creates an effective learning environment by promoting a sense of safety in the group.

Learning by doing occurs through participatory learning. Internalization is designed to have translators participate in the activities from the very beginning. The experience stage in internalization, in particular, includes many hands-on activities, such as drama, storyboarding, and the use of objects to retell the story or passage. Oral cultures' preference for learning by doing can be easily seen in their practice of apprenticeship and their approach to problem-solving. Many oral cultures utilize apprenticeship for the passing on information when learning a new skill or job. In like fashion, this type of learning allows the translator to engage in the learning process, resulting in a more practical learning experience which is more likely to be remembered. Self-discovery is an important part of this learning process. Internalization also makes use of discovery questions to allow the translator to interact with the passage.

Stahl and Stahl, based on their experience with oral Bible storytelling, also discuss how group work is productive in both translation and storytelling.[58] Storytelling naturally needs an audience for feedback, review, and

---

57. Toler and Toler, "Shift in Understanding."
58. Stahl and Stahl, "Oral Bible Storytelling."

encouragement. Group work creates synergy, cooperation, motivation, and collaboration and also encourages team members to build on each other's knowledge and talents. It allows team members with a variety of talents and experiences to participate. Stahl and Stahl have designed on-the-job group-based training for participants in Oral Bible Storying (OBS), based on Kolb and Fry's experiential learning cycle.[59] Kolb and Fry outline four broad stages for learning and mastery: concrete experience (telling stories in small groups); reflection and observation (giving each other feedback); abstract conceptualization (learning a story-telling principle); and active experimentation (revising the story). In their training, members of an OBS team enter the learning cycle at the concrete experience stage as they hear the stories in the group and reflect on the impact of the stories. By repeatedly going through this experiential learning cycle, the participants hear the story multiple times, refine their understanding of the story, improve their ability to visualize the story, and then tell it in their own language. With each pass through the cycle, they address more questions or points of confusion, and they test their impressions of the emotions, motivations, and intentions of the characters in the story. They also learn to recognize clues such as rhetorical devices which the original author included in the story to help focus the attention of the audience and draw conclusions about what is important in the story. In the experiential learning cycle, there is a lot of repetition and practice, meaning that the participants benefit from managed learning on the job and also learn how to give feedback to each other, gaining confidence gradually and continually.

The conversational discovery of meaning

In a personal discussion with Swapna Alexander, she talked about the conversational discovery of meaning.[60] She was involved in oral drafting in translation teams doing written Bible translation (BT) who used the process of internalization during an oral drafting stage. However, instead of using group internalization techniques such as those described above, which were unfamiliar to her team's culture, the team discovered the meaning of passages during oral drafting through extended conversation and discussion. She commented that many internalization devices are in fact techniques for literate people, when in actual fact internalization is more cognitive. It is important to find out first how the oral target culture processes information; often this is brought out through conversation, rather than by acting or

59. Kolb and Fry, "Toward an Applied Theory," 34.
60. Alexander, personal discussion, Feb. 9, 2021.

storyboarding. The most effective strategy for internalization may in fact be conversation blended with the different techniques of internalization that are most familiar to that culture.

Conclusions

Internalization is most effective when carried out in a team whose members already know and trust each other and when done in a stress-free environment. It is learner-centered and community-oriented and so appeals to oral-preference communities. An effective entry point into the passage can involve sharing stories on a similar theme or discussing devotional questions. The TA then leads the team through the oral exegesis of the passage and through the three parts of internalization—experience, exposure, and engagement (salience)—using perhaps also conversational discovery. Through this process, the TA is helping to leverage the tacit linguistic knowledge of the translators. Research into memory has shown that it relies heavily on mental visualization. Increasing and combining different types of sensory input and helping the translators to mentally reconstruct the scene during the process of internalization helps the translators to recall the story or passage. Frequent but timed repetition enables the translators to remember the material more permanently.

SURVEY ABOUT INTERNALIZATION

I decided to do a survey among active OBT teams and trainers around the world in order to carry out further research on several questions about internalization. I contacted a number of different OBT teams by email to ask for help with my research, and nine teams and one trainer responded voluntarily to my request. I asked these nine functioning OBT teams and one OBT trainer, whose identities will remain anonymous, to answer questions on the oral translation process and internalization, and I have summarized the results of this research. I prepared this questionnaire on internalization in English, which was then also translated into French for the one team whose members do not speak English. This questionnaire consists of general questions about internalization and its timing, a question for the TA, and questions about emotional exegesis and performance.

General questions on internalization

Describe the internalization process that you use.

According to their accounts submitted in response to my questionnaire, the OBT teams all listen to the passage several times in the LWC, and they all use a variety of internalization techniques combined with discussion and exegesis of the passage. A variety of different activities seem to help the process. One team provided the excellent idea of having the two translation peer teams do the internalization of a passage together. In this way, the team knows the passage when they give feedback to their peer team. The OBT trainer who responded reported that he encourages teams to invent their own methods of internalization and combine them. He recommends using one method to get to an initial stage of retelling and then using another method to consolidate and reinforce.

Which of these activities helped you internalize the passage best and why?

Table 1 summarizes the most commonly used techniques reported by the OBT teams and the OBT trainer.

Table 1: Summary of the internalization process used

		OBT Teams									OBT team trainer
		1	2	3	4	5	6	7	8	9	
Internalization activities	Drama		x	x	x	x	x		x		
	Storyboarding/drawing	x	x	x	x	x	x	x	x	x	
	Watching a film						x		x		x
	Random objects		x	x	x	x	x	x	x	x	
	Popcorn		x	x			x				
	Retelling	x			x	x	x	x			
	Felt board									x	
	Conversation and discussion	x									x
	Gestures/actions		x	x					x	x	
	Imagination				x		x	x	x		

Almost all the internalization techniques were mentioned, including storyboarding, random objects, acting, retelling, gestures, and emotional and sensory visualization. In one case, there were as many answers as people on the team! It can be concluded that there is not a single most effective technique for internalization. Rather, effectiveness depends on the number of people on the team, the culture, the personalities of the team members, and the genre of the passage.

Do you prefer one (or more) method of internalization over others? If so, which do you prefer and why?

Table 2 summarizes the preferred methods of internalization of the OBT teams and trainer.

Table 2: Summary of preferences for different methods of internalization

		OBT Teams									OBT team trainer
		1	2	3	4	5	6	7	8	9	
Internalization activities	Drama		x						x		
	Storyboarding/drawing	x	x	x	x	x	x	x	x	x	x
	Watching a film										
	Random objects						x		x		
	Popcorn										
	Retelling					x					
	Felt board										
	Conversation and discussion	x									
	Gestures/actions										x
	Imagination										

There are different factors which influence which method is preferred and why, one of which is certainly the activity which was introduced first to the team. Overall, storyboarding/drawing pictures seems to be the preferred technique of internalization, as it combines drawing, retelling, and using the imagination. Several teams commented that a combination of the activities is the most helpful strategy, combining storyboarding with acting or gestures. Different techniques are appropriate for different genres, and it was noted that storyboarding is particularly useful for remembering the structure of a longer narrative passage.

Are there internalization activities that you have decided are ineffective? How did you decide that?

All the activities are helpful to a certain extent depending on the genre of the passage, the personalities in the team, and the culture. However, it can be concluded that gestures and drama are the least helpful. Drama can be difficult on smaller teams and embarrassing in many cultures. Gestures are very individual, and it can be hard to remember other people's gestures.

Does the size of the group doing the internalization affect your experience, and if so, how?

The general conclusion was that a larger group finds it easier to internalize, due to the convenience of having more people involved, and leads to improved creativity, discovery, and discussion.

How would you describe your learning styles and previous educational experiences?

For some teams, these methods of OBT remind them of storytelling methods of their ancestors. Some of the more oral-preference teams commented that they are used to learning by group interaction. In general, in today's modern culture, most people enjoy a multimodal approach to learning. Internalization takes advantage of these preferences.

Do you enjoy internalization? What do you enjoy and not enjoy?

The teams were not all overwhelmingly positive about internalization; some reported that they initially found it to be uninteresting or more of a routine activity like driving. However, the majority of the teams used words like fun, joyful, and entertaining in describing the process.

Does internalization play a role in your everyday life? If so, give some examples.

For some teams the process of internalization was completely new. For others, they had encountered similar techniques in other aspects of life such as school, church, or work.

Do you help others outside the team to internalize the stories? If so, how do you do this?

Some teams do encourage passing on the story to others and helping others internalize the stories. This happens most often in an informal fashion during community checking. The story fellowship group is also an effective way of passing on the story to others. The teams that were interviewed are not deliberately attempting to pass on this method of internalization to others.

How does internalization assist a more natural and effective translation?

All the teams were in agreement that internalization helps the teams understand the meaning of the passage, particularly the structure of the passage, and to imagine it more clearly. Therefore, it contributes to a more natural translation.

Does the team discuss extralinguistic features within the biblical text?

All the teams, apart from one, said they do extralinguistic exegesis during the internalization process and that it is very beneficial because it helps inform translation choices which need to be made during the drafting process.

How does internalizing a non-narrative biblical passage differ from narrative?

About half the teams have had some limited experience in translating non-narrative genres. Those who had experience said that, with non-narrative genres, the process of internalization differs and is harder, and some had to rely more on rote memorization.

Timing

How many times do you listen to the passage initially normally, and do you have breaks?

Most teams listen to the passage between three to five times, often taking breaks between the listening sessions to retell or discuss.

Do you normally have other breaks during the whole internalization process?

The general opinion of the teams was that the process of internalization is more effective if the teams have breaks during the process.

How long does internalization take normally? (e.g., for one story or one chapter)

The process of internalization is quite long, and often it takes teams several hours or more to internalize a passage. Although the process of internalization is very effective, it is time-consuming and requires a lot of energy and effort from the team. There are various internal and external factors that influence the process.

Is it easier to internalize with more practice?

All the teams concluded that internalization does become easier with practice.

Retention rate

How long can a team member remember one passage?

The teams differed greatly in their conclusions on this question. Clearly it depends on the genre and the size of the passage, as well as the people and cultures involved. Many teams cannot remember passages from week to week, but some can retain the information for several months. The teams agreed that using the internalization techniques and discussing the emotions in this passage, combined with frequent review, enables them to remember the passages for longer.

Have you considered internalizing more material for long-term memory?

Again, here conclusions varied vastly. Some thought that they could internalize and retell whole books such as Jonah and Ruth and, with practice, retain them for a lifetime. This was especially the case if the internalization techniques used enable people to mentally visualize the passage and the sequence of events, such as drama, storyboarding, or objects. It appears that internalization using the techniques discussed, rather than just rote memorization, may enable a person to understand the passage deeply, mentally visualize it, and remember it for a long period of time.

Questions for the TA

How do you prepare the internalization session?

The preparation by the TA differs widely, but all include using commentaries and translation helps, which are then adapted and discussed orally with the translation team during the process of internalization.

Questions for the team concerning the performance of a biblical passage

When you perform the passages, are there changes to the stories after the performance?

Other than as part of community checking, most teams have done retelling only within their own translation team. They all agree that retelling the stories to each other helps them adapt the stories and correct them. The teams adapt the translation according to any feedback they get from within or from outside the group.

Are there advantages of performing the stories?

The teams agree that retelling or performing the stories to each other, using the collective memory of the group, is very beneficial. It allows group participation, aids memory, and allows the team to experiment and to adapt the retelling.

Has the team performed passages outside of the group?

Not all the teams have done performances outside the group. However, the ones that have done this received positive affirmation from their audiences and had feedback, which was encouraging and which helped them make changes in their translations.

Conclusions from the survey

Internalization is considered by the teams mostly as an enjoyable and useful method of learning, reflecting both modern and traditional preferences for group and multisensory learning. In some cases, similar techniques have been used by people previously in their schools, churches, and work environments. Most teams begin internalization by listening to the passage between three to five times, often taking breaks between the listening sessions to retell or discuss. Following this initial stage, internalization techniques differed among the teams. It seems that all the techniques of internalization can be helpful to the translation teams, and it is popular to combine these techniques, using one to retell and another to consolidate. There is no single preferred technique for internalization, and this depends on the number of people on the team, the culture, the team itself, and the genre of the passage. However, overall, storyboarding seems to be one of the most popular and effective techniques of internalization, as it combines drawing, retelling, and using the imagination. Different techniques are appropriate for different genres. Storyboarding is particularly useful for remembering the structure of a longer narrative passage. Overall, it can also be concluded that gestures and drama are perceived to be the least helpful techniques.

In general, it is more convenient to do internalization in a larger group. All the teams agreed that internalization helps the teams understand the meaning of the passage and contributes to a more natural translation. The TAs from all the teams prepare extensive exegetical notes in advance and then discuss these orally with the translation team during the process of internalization.

Although the process of internalization is very effective, it is time-consuming, requiring several hours or more for a team to internalize a passage and requiring a lot of energy and effort from the team. There are various internal and external factors that influence the process. All the teams agree that internalization becomes easier with practice.

The team's ability to retain passages in their memory for long periods of time clearly depends on the genre and the size of the passage, and on the people and the cultures involved. Many teams cannot remember passages from week to week, but some can retain the information for several months. However, the use of the internalization techniques and discussing the emotions in this passage, combined with frequent review, enables team members to remember the passages for longer.

All the teams, apart from one, said that doing extralinguistic exegesis during the internalization process is useful because it informs choices which need to be made during the drafting process. Teams which had experience in translating non-narrative genres reported that, with these genres, the process of internalization differs and is harder. Some had to fall back on rote memorization.

The teams interviewed are not deliberately attempting to pass on this method of internalization to others, although in some cases it happens informally. Most teams have done retelling only within their own translation team, apart from during community checking. They all agree that retelling the stories to each other helps them adapt the stories and correct them. Those teams who have done performances have received positive affirmation from their audiences and had encouraging feedback, which helped them make changes in their translations.

These conclusions will be utilized in the process of internalization for the Altai translation team.

INTERNALIZATION FOR NON-NARRATIVE GENRES

Introduction

There are many different types of non-prose narrative genres in the Bible (e.g., epistles, non-narrative poetry, sermons, prophecy, laments, histories, law, genealogies, descriptive procedures such as building the tabernacle or temple, and apocalyptic literature). The diversity of non-prose narrative genres means that internalization methods for this material, as could be expected, often take different forms. In fact, perhaps the most pressing questions about internalization currently are whether it is even possible to translate non-prose narrative genres and poetry using OBT and whether the process of internalization works for these genres. These are relevant questions for my research because the chosen passages (three psalms and Judg 5) contain poetry (Judg 5 is in fact narrative in poetic form).

This section discusses the importance of *understanding* as a key aspect in internalization. A key question is whether internalization techniques can be transferred from narrative to non-prose narrative genres and poetry, passing on this essential element of understanding of the passage to the translators. This section discusses approaches which have been used to internalize the NT epistles and biblical poetry and attempts to assess them.

Results from the interviews

There was one question on the questionnaire for OBT teams asking about internalizing non-narrative material. The interviews with various teams indicated that in almost all cases, the teams find it easier and quicker to internalize narratives.

Understanding as a key aspect of internalization

Internalization involves focusing long enough on each significant aspect of the text to connect or associate it with things that are familiar in the translators' lives.[61] In the process of making these mind-body connections and adapting the material through discussion, applications, or other activities, the story or concept becomes part of the person's experiences or part of a new set of associations. Ultimately, it could be said to "become part" of the person and is thus internalized. Associations are a temporary tool for internalizing the concepts. This process of handling or shaping the material is extremely important to the process of internalization. Each exercise allows the team to adapt the material in a slightly different way, enabling the person to process the material and make new connections.

In order to make accurate associations, people first need to understand the text, including the concepts, the setting, and the relationships depicted in the text.[62] If there is a concept that people do not understand, it is difficult to make an association for that concept. Therefore, understanding is the foundation for internalization. As the concepts are being internalized, the goal is to be able express the concepts in a different language. A process of "handling" the material through internalization activities tends to bring to light the most significant questions that the translators need to answer to achieve deeper understanding. This process also allows the translators to identify gaps in their understanding.

For non-narrative internalization, this emphasis on understanding may unlock people's ability to internalize such material.[63] In internalizing narrative, the TA and the team usually study and discuss the following: setting and context, including the "when" and the "where" of the narrative; cultural information; new vocabulary and key terms; key players or characters, including who they are, how they are related, and how they develop; information flow, structure, and the story arc (conflict, building tension, climax, resolution, implications); and relatability, which refers to how the characters' experiences may resonate with the life experiences of the team members. The above process often happens intuitively.

Preparing for non-narrative translation involves looking at similar kinds of information: setting and context, including the purpose or goal of communication and genre conventions; key players and concepts, i.e., who or what they are and how they are related; information flow, including

---

61. Frost, "Non-Narrative Internalization."
62. Frost, "Non-Narrative Internalization."
63. Frost, "Non-Narrative Internalization."

sections, points of emphasis, and order in lists; and relatability, or how the concepts can apply to personal lives. In other words, the basic techniques that are used for narrative internalization can be transferred effectively to non-narrative.[64]

Transferring internalization techniques to non-narrative passages

Visually, the team can use symbols or sketches to represent abstract concepts, creating one symbol per thought unit, e.g., fruit of the spirit. This could also be done, for example, by imagining for each concept on the list a space that one associates with this concept—a favorite room in the house, a place at work, a space in the city, etc. The association needs to permit the person to hold the memory long enough for the brain to make the correct connection. The facilitator reads the list slowly while people are silently making associations of concepts with spaces. The facilitator then reads the list again while the team imagines moving from space to space and from concept to concept. In this way the list "solidifies" in a person's brain, and connections are created that make the order easier to recall.[65]

In addition to a storyboard, the team could create a web to show how concepts are related in the way that a tree diagram can be used to represent a genealogy. Kinesthetically, the team could associate one posture or facial expression with each line in a poem, each item in a list, or each thought unit, depending on the genre. The team could make a series of motions to help outline the concentric structures of certain psalms, giving one motion per line. Random objects, spaces, and sounds can also be associated with non-narrative thought units.

Stahl and Stahl shared about their experience working with OBS teams in South Asia as they internalized the non-narrative sections of the Sermon on the Mount.[66] From this experience they analyzed how to craft and tell non-narrative Bible portions and how to adapt the internalization process to non-narrative genres. Their internalization process was divided into two sections: first, the elicitation of the participants' intuitive impressions from hearing the story (recognizing images; discussing any impact on senses; and identifying, from their own culture, stories which are used to reinforce an understanding of what constitutes good deeds); then following up on their intuition by digging deeper through group discovery (literary

64. Frost, "Non-Narrative Internalization."
65. Frost, "Non-Narrative Internalization."
66. Stahl and Stahl, "Sermon on the Mount OBS."

analysis including a particular focus on rhetorical devices, image-building and memory activities, practice through peer review, practice with a fresh audience, checking with a consultant). Rhetorical devices in the Sermon on the Mount include the use of polar opposites, the images that Jesus uses in his metaphors, repetition of themes, the use of synonyms, and the framing of the story (repetition at the beginning and the end of the section). In conclusion, the following components were important for the non-narrative internalization of the Sermon on the Mount: knowing the context around the passage; tapping into the intuitive knowledge of the translators by researching different persuasive speeches in their own cultures; identifying rhetorical devices (not dissimilar from those used in narratives but more densely packed); discussing which rhetorical devices to use in their local language; telling personal stories as part of the internalization; lengthy discussion to explore the meaning of Jesus' words; and targeting the stories more for discipleship than for evangelism. Stahl and Stahl observed that the process took longer than for narrative biblical passages.[67]

Oral drafting of epistles

In a personal email, Swapna Alexander, an OBT consultant, shared her previous experience of oral drafting in India.[68] This was not a complete OBT project but was instead oral drafting for a written translation of biblical epistles. She notes that, because the drafting process was entirely oral, the resulting translation was both very natural and well received by the receptor audience. Alexander used oral drafting because very few of the team were literate and many did not understand the LWC sufficiently. She writes,

> The MTTs and I would discuss the passage we were to translate, and they would translate it orally. We did not use any of the internalization techniques we use now. I did not see them do many group activities. So, it really did not make any sense to act things out or draw pictures. As you can imagine, the narrative genre was far easier than the epistles. But what I enjoyed the most was drafting the epistles. I made my own exegetical notes ahead of time and we would go on to talk, talk and talk and finally do the drafting.

She calls this process "the conversational discovery of meaning." Using this conversational discovery of meaning, rather than any other deliberate

---

67. Stahl and Stahl, "Sermon on the Mount OBS."
68. Alexander, personal email, Sep. 9, 2021.

internalization group activities, the team was able to produce an oral draft for the epistles. However, Alexander comments that using this technique to translate biblical epistles was more difficult than drafting the narrative genre.

In an interview that I heard with an OBT team in India, the discussion touched on how the team translated the epistle of James using OBT methods.[69] Initially they tried internalization using storyboarding but found that unsuccessful. After a month of trying oral approaches, they decided to commit to writing a draft of the epistle, so as not to leave anything out of the first draft. To avoid relying on a written draft in future sessions, it was suggested that the team, during the internalization phase, develop sequences of pictorial symbols to reflect the logical connectors in the epistles.

In an interview with another OBT team in India, the consultant discussed their team's internalization and oral Bible translation of 1 and 2 Thessalonians and 1 and 2 Peter.[70] He shared that the team of translators used basically the same process as they did for narratives but that it took longer with the epistles. It was suggested that internalization techniques other than storyboarding might be more beneficial with epistles, in which argument structure is important. Further research was recommended on how persuasive argument structures used in the biblical epistles are also employed in receptor cultures.

This OBT team in India started working in 2019 with three teams from oral-preference communities. After an initial survey, the decision was made to do OBT, and a training seminar was held. The teams translated three gospels and the book of Acts and then continued with 1 and 2 Peter and 1 and 2 Thessalonians. When the teams were working on the narrative books, they were very fluent at storytelling and used storyboarding consistently. They used the same approach with the epistles but struggled with the process. It took longer for the teams to do the exegesis and the storyboarding for the epistles. It was also more challenging to record. The team was often unable to progress on their own and had to go back to ask the TA for help discussing the difficult sections and to clarify the meaning of key words and concepts. Because the information load is higher in the epistles, the team had to spend a lot of time in discussion with the TA and the consultant in order to get the meaning clear. Accidental omission in the recordings was greater when working on the epistles than when doing the narrative books, and there was a greater tendency to copy the LWC discourse structures as a shortcut. The team had to translate shorter sections and often needed to shorten passages

69. Interview with OBT team 11 in India on Nov. 12, 2019.
70. Interview with OBT team 10 in India in Apr. 2021.

(using the knife-cutting tool in the Render software). It took the team about five months to complete 1 and 2 Peter, and 1 and 2 Thessalonians, working full-time. When asked, the team said that additional guidelines and training from the consultants to translate the epistles would have been helpful.

Ballarin Ducasse, in her paper "Developing an Oral Interpretation Translation Method," discusses how her translation team translated Galatians in written format using an oral drafting method.[71] In the first phase of the process, labelled "basic knowledge acquisition," the translators received all the information they needed to construct a coherent picture of the text (background information; information on the author, genre, and main theme; and the logical structure of the text).[72] The second phase was the listening session, during which the text is read three times in different versions followed by a time for silent thinking. Finally, there was the reformulation phase, when the translators translate the passage orally and work on the rewording of the text. In this final phase, each of the team members initially records him or herself expressing the entire context of the passage in one go. Then the group listens to all these interpretations, evaluates the oral translation, and decides if there needs to be another attempt. The group then selects the best, most accurate, and natural translation. Finally, the group makes their written draft.

To summarize, from the research done on the oral translation of epistles, one team was unable to produce an oral draft. Another team produced an oral draft through the conversational discovery of meaning, but it took significantly longer than drafting for narrative. Another team used the same internalization techniques that they had used in narrative, but the process took longer, and it was more challenging. The team translating Galatians used an approach involving individual oral translation and voting on the best option, a technique that is suggested again below for translating poetry. The idea of doing supplemental OBT training for teams attempting the translation of epistles has been proposed, especially in the area of using pictorial symbols to represent the logical connectors in the epistles.

Translating poetry using OBT

The method Ballarin Ducasse describes is somewhat similar to the method Rees (director of the South Asia Division of Pioneer Bible Translators) uses to translate biblical poetry orally with his translation team in Pnar, India.[73]

71. Ballarin Ducasse, "Developing an Oral Interpretation."
72. Ballarin Ducasse, "Developing an Oral Interpretation," 5.
73. Rees, *"Pnar Audio Translation."*

Rees has developed his own translation strategy by which each person records his or her own version of the poetry, and then the team either chooses the best version, or they even mix and match the parts they appreciate from each version. Rees writes that the poetry section (Gen 49) of the translation project took much longer to complete than the rest of the book and that the team spent more time on internalization, using the technique of storyboarding. The community response to the end product was extremely positive.

Rees's approach to translating poetry also has some similarities to Balarin Ducasse's method for preparing an oral translation of Galatians. Each translator prepares an individual rendering of the verse, initially according to poetic effect rather than accuracy, and then the team either chooses the best, or the team mixes and matches the best versions. Finally, the question of accuracy and any remaining exegetical problems are addressed in the best poetic version.

Conclusion

It is possible to transfer the internalization techniques from narrative to non-narrative genres; however, the process of internalization for non-narrative is more difficult. It may be that narratives are easier to internalize because they have a defined, understandable story structure, with easily recognized elements such as conflict and resolution. Also, narratives seem to be more universal across languages and cultures, while many other biblical genres are not universal. The main emphasis in the internalization process should be on complete understanding of the passage. Non-narrative internalization requires increased creativity and effort on the part of the TA, who should choose internalization techniques that fit the genre of the non-narrative passage in question. If internalization techniques do not work, the conversational discovery of meaning is another option. One method of translating poetry orally is to allow all the translators to attempt a translation, the best of which is then chosen by the team according to poetic effect, and then to mix and match the best version. Exegetical issues are then examined at a later stage to ensure accuracy. Also, it is recommended that poets be involved in the translating of poetry. During the translation of the poetic passages in the Altai project discussed in this book, there were Altai poets and musicians present, who assisted the translation team in retelling the passage and shaping the content poetically. The method of mixing and matching the best versions was used.

EXTRA-LINGUISTIC EXEGESIS

Introduction

Another distinctive feature of the OBT process is extralinguistic or emotional exegesis. This is a critically important aspect of OBT because it is inherently connected to the voice quality of the speaking voice of an oral translation. Voice quality is, in effect, a "metatext" of OBT which cannot be ignored. During the internalization stage, there is usually a discussion on what kinds of feelings the characters in Bible passages may have been experiencing and expressing. Especially as OBT and sign language translation work have become more prevalent, translators are seeking guidance from their TAs and consultants on matters concerning emotional exegesis.

Reconstructing emotion

Emotions are often not directly mentioned in the biblical text, requiring translators to plausibly reconstruct them based on inferences from the written text. Determining which emotions are suitable for each story or passage can be difficult; when there is no explicit comment by the biblical author, it may be necessary to use other indicators from the biblical language in order to understand the emotional character of the text or to identify emotions associated with a given character. This can be a challenging task, as Voinov acknowledges in his research on the linguistic expression of politeness in Tuvan. In this language of the Tuvan Republic in Siberia, politeness is expressed through morphological, syntactic, pragmatic, and sociolinguistic means.[74] When conducting emotional exegesis, it is important to remember that the vocal prosody of the original biblical text cannot be accurately determined. Furthermore, all recordings of the passage, whether in translation or in the original language, represent simply one interpretation of the biblical text. The team should identify a range of appropriate emotions as well as those that are not appropriate, based on both the words and the context of the passage. It also must be remembered that certain audiences may prefer an emotionless rendering, even in audio versions.

Frost and Beal suggest that the main requirement for doing emotional exegesis on biblical passages is empathy, which enables the reader to understand life from another's perspective. They provide guidelines for reconstructing the biblical context (by looking at the frame of mind of the participants, their relationships, their event expectations, their locations,

---

74. Voinov, "Politeness Devices."

their default responses, and the foundational values of the culture).[75] This reconstruction is intended to enable the translation team to create what they call "an emotionally compelling backstory" for the passage.[76]

Notes for OBT teams on emotive force and performance

Maxey presents an example of a script corresponding to Mark 1:40–45, which he developed for his oral translation team.[77] This script consists of three columns: the middle column holds the translated text; the left contains paralinguistic instructions like volume, speed, and intonation; and the right column is for extralinguistic instructions, such as gestures or body movements, applicable to the performers or translation team. Maxey suggests that comments in the margin instead of footnotes are more convenient for the performer. Annotated scripts of this sort highlight the reality that translation is fundamentally an interpretive action and that the performance of the script will be impacted by both the audience and the setting. In a nonliterate or oral-preference environment, the written medium can be entirely bypassed through employing mentors who initially perform the script and apprentices who learn from their mentors' performances.

In response to this request from OBT teams for more guidance on emotional exegesis, I have prepared my own notes for OBT teams on the books of Jonah and Ruth.[78] Designed to supplement existing Translator's Notes, these OBT notes contain an analysis of the structure and climax of the passage, in addition to reflections on its intended effect such as imagery, emotions and feelings, performance features and supporting evidence for them, plus potential performance ideas that could be tailored to the receptor culture. These include some suggestions for culturally appropriate gestures which could be made part of the performance. With regards to gestures, Dickie notes that the value of performance was highlighted in her workshop on Ruth in Africa, when distress, frustration, disappointment, and even love were expressed in gestures more effectively than in words during their

---

75. Frost and Beal, "Leveraging Biblical Artistry," 20–21.
76. Frost and Beal, "Leveraging Biblical Artistry," 24.
77. Maxey, *From Orality to Orality*, loc. 3670.
78. These are not yet available but will be accessible through Translator's Notes in Paratext, the software internationally used by Bible translators. Translator's Notes (TN) is a verse-by verse commentary geared specifically for local Bible translators, produced by the SIL International Translation Department, and authored by experienced translation consultants.

performance of Ruth.[79] I am collecting feedback from OBT teams on how useful these notes are and how they may be adapted for future use.

Voice and performance

Van Aswegen and Koroma emphasize that in oral translations the role of the voice is crucial throughout the entire process, from the beginning to the end.[80] Communication is not only about the words that are said but also about the way they are said.[81] In OBT the voice actually gives meaning to the text and is viewed as an integral part of the communication process.

Several key voice prosody features can be effectively utilized by teams as they verbally retell passages.[82] Utilizing silence or pauses to create emphasis or mark boundaries in speech is the first. Secondly, altering the speed and duration of one's speech is important. Varying volume—speaking louder or softer—is an effective approach. The fourth element is accent or dynamics, which denotes speaking with greater or lesser force, or emphasizing a particular aspect of a speech by stressing it. The fifth is articulation or enunciation, wherein the words are articulated with precision. Sixth is voice quality, also known as timbre; this involves utilizing the oral cavity in varying ways to achieve different tones such as lightness, flat tone, smoothness, smokiness, breathy sound, and roughness. Lastly, there are pitch, intonation, tone, and rhythm. Pitch refers to the highness or lowness of the voice, and intonation denotes the way that pitch fluctuates (the highs and lows of speaking). Additionally, some languages make semantic or grammatical use of tone, in which the meaning of a word or its grammatical function is encoded tonally. Rhythm is concerned with how the vocal sound is distributed throughout a clause or sentence and is responsible for creating an overall melody while speaking. Kress and Van Leeuwen note that several material qualities of the voice can have meaning potential, a phenomenon which can be expressed in speech by vocal tension, roughness, breathiness, loudness range, pitch range, and vibrato.[83]

Given that native speakers naturally vary their voices, the translation team can generally incorporate important prosodic features of speech fluently.[84] Nevertheless, training is necessary to assist the team to be mindful of

79. Dickie, "Interacting With," 26.
80. Van Aswegen and Koroma, *Understanding Oral Bible Translation*, 12.
81. Frost, "Workshop Elements."
82. Schrag, *Creating Local Arts*, 114.
83. Kress and Van Leeuwen, *Multimodal Discourse*, 82.
84. Frost, "Non-Narrative Internalization."

both their own and others' speaking patterns. The team can promote better verbal communication by making minor modifications, allowing them to reach a point of fluency and natural expressiveness. It is then essential to conduct community testing with target listeners to confirm the outcomes. The team can explore various possibilities and analyze them with peers for a more informed result.

In relation to OBT, voice synchrony is harmony between the text and the voice prosody used. Fotso defines synchrony as "a situation where the elements of a set are operating together, simultaneously and harmoniously without internal contradictions."[85] During the combined exegesis and internalization stage, the team must take into account the age and gender of the characters in the text.[86] The inflections of the speaker often indicate their age, gender, and status (often conveyed through dialect). Children's voices are easily identifiable through their prosody, as are those of adults and seniors. When people of different social ranks are interacting, Fotso notes that those of a lower rank may use particular prosodic voice characteristics to show respect or deference—a phenomenon referred to as "character synchrony."[87] An example of voice synchrony could be seen in Jesus' command to his disciples after the stilling of the storm, "Why are you so afraid? Do you still have no faith?" (Mark 4:40 NIV84). His voice would likely come across as authoritative yet assuring.

The team must also consider the characters' emotions; Fotso speaks of this as "pragmatic synchrony."[88] Furthermore, vocal qualities will influence listeners and their reactions. It is also important to pay heed to emphasis, figures of speech, and genre, which Fotso labels as "literary synchrony." As an example, consider how a rhetorical question like "if that is how God clothes the grass of the field, which is here today and tomorrow is thrown into the fire, will he not much more clothe you—you of little faith?" (Matt 6:30 NIV84) can be spoken in varied ways to express rebuke, concern, or ridicule.

Often, translation teams tend to leave voice and performance considerations until the end of the process, but this is not an optimal approach. Rather, voice elements should be taken into account from the outset. Van Aswegen and Koroma propose that qualified personnel should be recruited and trained in voice prosody right from the start.[89] The most effective ap-

---

85. Fotso, "Voice Synchrony," 7.
86. Van Aswegen and Koroma, *Understanding Oral Bible Translation*, 12.
87. Fotso, "Voice Synchrony," 19.
88. Fotso, "Voice Synchrony," 7.
89. Van Aswegen and Koroma, *Understanding Oral Bible Translation*, 12.

proach is for the person responsible for the final recording to be present during all preceding exegesis and internalization sessions, to ensure they comprehend the story as fully as possible. Should the team wish to invite voice actors who will not have been present at preceding stages, they must be careful to convey which sections require emphasis and which components demand special emotion.

In his paper "Song of Songs 5:2–9," Fotso outlines the key points that are crucial when transforming the original written poetic features from Song of Songs 5:2–9 into oral and performance features.[90] These are voice changes, emotion dynamics, pause and silence, and background sound effects. Pause and silence can represent structural breaks in the passage in an oral translation. Additional background sound effects may help evoke the atmosphere of the passage.

OBT consultant checking

An OBT consultant should have had experience with orality, OBT, and performance principles to effectively perform a checking process that is distinctly different from written BT consultancy. The consultant should listen carefully to the oral recording as well as consult a transcribed back-translation. Asking the following key questions is also beneficial:[91]

- Do the voices of the recording distract in any way from the contents of the message? Are those whose voices are recorded in good standing with the community?
- Is the voice prosody of the recording in harmony with the discourse and the context?
- Is the rate of information flow appropriate?
- Are there any expressions which are inappropriate or offensive?
- Is the dialect acceptable to the greatest number of listeners?
- Does the type of language used correspond to that of the original text?
- Is the type of language used appropriate to the receptor audience in terms of politeness, degree of formality, register, etc.?
- Is the quality of the recording acceptable from a technical standpoint?

---

90. Fotso, "Voice Synchrony," 19–20.
91. Cleaver, "Oral Bible Translation," 19.

- Does anything in the translation or recording hinder the audience from reacting to the message in the same way that the original audience are assumed to have reacted to it?

Conclusion

Emotional exegesis is an important part of OBT, and the team needs to attempt to reconstruct a range of possible emotions for the characters depicted in the passage being translated. Notes prepared for OBT teams giving guidance on emotional exegesis and hints for performance are helpful for these teams. The role of the voice is crucial in OBT. The OBT facilitator should be aware of voice prosody issues and be able to organize training for the translators in this area. TAs should include the issues of voice synchrony in their exegetical discussions, and voice synchrony should be considered during the testing and review stages of OBT. Consultant checking should be carried out with all the above points in mind.

SUMMARY

This has been intended as a thorough investigation of the internalization process, including an overview of my interviews with a selection of OBT teams from various parts of the world. The research's findings, which are summarized above, will aid OBT teams, trainers, exegetes, and consultants to better comprehend internalization and to successfully implement and adapt these techniques.

Second, in this chapter I have presented my research into the use of OBT to translate genres other than narrative. I conducted a comparative analysis of the experiences of OBT teams worldwide that have endeavored to translate poetry orally. Based on my findings, I have provided suggestions for OBT teams which want to translate biblical poetry orally in their own contexts.

Additionally, there is a growing necessity for guidance in the area of extralinguistic exegesis within the fields of OBT and sign language translation. It is hoped that my comprehensive notes on extralinguistic and paralinguistic elements of performances or retellings can serve as a valuable resource for teams working in these fields now or in the future.

4

Biblical Performance Criticism

INTRODUCTION AND DEFINITION

This chapter discusses the discipline of Biblical Performance Criticism (BPC), first by considering why this discipline is foundational to my research. BPC represents a fundamental shift from "a text-orientation to a performance-orientation."[1] This discipline began to become more widespread after Rhoads's publication in 2006, "Performance Criticism: An Emerging Methodology in New Testament Studies." Rhoads defines BPC as follows:

> It seeks to re-imagine ancient Israel and the early church as predominantly oral and memory cultures, to construct scenarios of ancient performances as means to interpret anew the traditions of the Bible, to reconsider the disciplines we use to study the Bible so as to take account of orality, and to develop steps in a process of performance analysis of biblical texts.[2]

Schechner lists nine diverse kinds of performance: in everyday life (e.g., cooking, socializing), in the arts, in sports and entertainment, in medicine, in business, in technology, in sex, in ritual both sacred and secular, and in play.[3] He also finds seven functions of performance: to entertain, to create

---

1. West, "Art of Biblical," 50.
2. Rhoads, "From Narrative in Print," 1.
3. Schechner, *Performance Studies*, 7–8.

beauty, to mark or change identity, to make or foster community, to heal, to teach or persuade, and to deal with the sacred and the demonic.[4] Rhoads's definition of performance, as related to biblical studies, is "any oral telling/retelling of a brief or lengthy tradition—from saying to gospel—in a formal or informal context of a gathered community by trained or untrained performers—on the assumption that every telling was a lively recounting of that tradition."[5] Similarly, West says that biblical dramas "do not reach their fullest expression until they are embodied and voiced by a performer, or a group of performers, who present the drama to a gathered audience."[6]

BPC is a bridge between the origins of the biblical text and the contemporary audience for whom the performer performs. A performance entails memorizing and internalizing a section of Scripture, then delivering it with gestures and emotion to an audience of any size. Following the performance, the performer and audience can engage in a dialogue about various aspects of the performance, including understanding of the text, potential improvements, and any insights gained. The performer and each member of the audience may experience the impact in unique ways and to different degrees. Each person constructs meaning based on the performance event, their specific local and cultural situation, their triggered individual memories, and their combined cognitive processing of all these factors.

Proponents of BPC claim that, because ancient Israel was mainly an oral culture, the exegesis of passages must therefore shift from the perspective of a modern print culture to that of an oral/scribal culture to understand the biblical texts in the context of oral cultures.[7] In a print translation, the focus is on faithfulness to the ST, to the author's intention, to a single meaning, and, typically, to the process of acquiring information by the individual reader. In contrast, in performance translation, the focus is more on the audience and their collective experience, creativity in the RL, the impact on the audience, the potential for diverse interpretations, and the ability to evoke emotion in the listeners. However, a print translation may be used by individual readers as well as the community, such as in liturgical settings.

ORIGINS AND A BRIEF HISTORY OF BPC

BPC grew out of a new approach to biblical criticism called narrative methodology, well demonstrated in the book *Mark as Story*, widely considered

4. Schechner, *Performance Studies*, 19.
5. Rhoads, "Performance Criticism," 119.
6. West, "Art of Biblical," 72.
7. Makutoane et al., "Similarity and Alterity," 4.

as one of the foundational books pertaining to BPC.[8] In this book Rhoads places his study of Mark against the background of orality, aiming to view Mark as a unified narrative designed to be performed.[9] Shiner, similarly to Rhoads, also views the text of the Gospel of Mark as a script for a performance, searching for clues in the text to discover the original performance features and setting.[10] Shiner describes the context of the oral media culture in which Mark was composed and performed, identifying five key features of its oratorical style: texts were memorized for performance; performance was not word-for-word but with a stable structure; oral performances were dramatic, including emotions and gestures; the performer was expected to feel those emotions and convey them; and the audience participated actively.[11] Rhoads presents the performance dynamics which assist in understanding the meaning and rhetoric of NT writings: acting, presenting the world of the text, using personification, onstage/offstage focus, nonverbal communication, emotions, states of consciousness, humor, temporal experience, and rhetoric.[12] Boomershine's performance commentary on the passion-resurrection narrative in Mark was the next major milestone in BPC, using a method based on sound mapping, emphasizing the impact of performance on the original audience.[13]

Doan and Giles applied BPC to the Hebrew Bible, looking for remnants of orality in the written text, claiming that "performance resides just beneath the surface of much of the Hebrew Bible text."[14] They call performance criticism a conceptual framework for analyzing the remnants of oral performances contained in the Hebrew Bible text.[15] This conceptual framework uses the imagination as well as cognition. In their work, the audience dynamic has become more important, and they emphasize that the performer must acknowledge the presence of the audience.[16] For them, the genres of Song of Songs and of the prophet books make them obvious choices for BPC.[17] Doan and Giles also conclude that Miriam's song in Exodus

---

8. Agnew, *Embodied Performance*, 47.
9. Rhoads, *Mark as Story*.
10. Shiner, *Proclaiming the Gospel*.
11. Shiner, *Proclaiming the Gospel*, 3.
12. Rhoads, "Performance Criticism," 126.
13. Boomershine, *Messiah of Peace*.
14. Doan and Giles, "Performance Criticism," 278.
15. Doan and Giles, *Prophets, Performance*, 157.
16. Doan and Giles, "Performance Criticism," 21–22.
17. Doan and Giles, *Story of Naomi*.

chapter 15 is suitable for the application of performance criticism.[18] Work on the prophetic books in BPC was continued by Jeanette Mathews, who is interested in reconstructing the performed history of the text and looking for performance features and themes in the script of Habakkuk.[19] She also discusses the potential for reenacting the script for modern audiences today.

Maxey argues that BPC is not primarily about reconstructing ancient performances but also extends to translating for modern biblical performances.[20] According to Maxey, BPC challenges the idea that written text is the primary and most important medium of communication. It asserts that there was not a fixed biblical written text but rather that the text was fluid. BPC places great value on memory but not in the sense of rote learning and retelling by heart. It is also not only storytelling but is instead story creation through the performance event, so audiences do not hear just a story but experience a communicative event. BPC also presupposes a community, an active audience, who can even sometimes provide missing pieces to the performance. All translation involves interpretation, and in BPC meaning is not only interpreted but is revealed and negotiated in the performance itself. Maxey compares BPC to reader-response criticism, or, rather, "audience-response" criticism, as authority lies also in the community, rather than being solely in the biblical text. BPC understands that performance itself is translation, and the performance event is central. Translation takes place in the performance through the sound, silence, gestures, and interaction with the audience. Maxey asserts that there is a difference between a recorded performance and a live performance, but the difference is of degree rather than of type.[21] A recorded performance anticipates an audience, but BPC normally presupposes a live audience.

There have also been several scholars who have applied BPC to the Pauline Epistles, an example of which is Rhoads's performance of Philemon.[22] Here, Rhoads uses his method of story-based BPC, based on narrative methodology, with the goal of recreating historically a first-century performance. Oestreich also analyzes Pauline letters using BPC, focusing on how the letters were received in their first-century context, although he does not engage in performance himself.[23] Other scholars are using performance to teach the gospels and other books of the NT, working with students to

18. Doan and Giles, *Twice Used Songs*, 163.
19. Mathews, *Performing Habakkuk*, 200.
20. Maxey, "Biblical Performance Criticism," 16.
21. Maxey, "Biblical Performance Criticism," 22.
22. Rhoads, "New Testament."
23. Oestreich, *Performance Criticism*.

prepare performances for modern audiences, such as Ruge-Jones, who aims to help communicate the composition for an audience in a culturally appropriate way.[24] Swanson also uses performance for education, in a series of workshops in which the actors try different ways to perform his text of "St. Mark's Passion," aiming to create the same impact in a contemporary audience that would have been evoked for a first-century audience.[25] His book on methods to embody biblical storytelling through drama presents biblical interpretation as an embodied public physical act that "provokes" the stories and enables the stories to provoke the audience.[26]

Perry composed a method of BPC using the three stages of preparation, internalization, and performance.[27] Hearon analyzes characters in John, focusing less on discovering the first-century context and more on the interpretive decisions of the performer before a live audience.[28] Cousins, in her recent PhD dissertation using a performance-critical methodology to inform a theological interpretation of the Psalms of Ascent, assesses multiple performances of the psalms for different audiences in Australia.[29] She describes a hermeneutic circle in which her rehearsals and psalms performances then result in changes in translation.[30] Following performances, Cousins also asked audiences to participate in discussions and to complete a questionnaire.[31]

BENEFITS OF BPC FOR THE TRANSLATION PROCESS AS SCRIPTURE ENGAGEMENT

Eight conditions

Germain discusses the benefits of BPC for the translation process, using seven out of Dye's eight conditions of Scripture engagement to summarize the benefits.[32] Dye's first condition, Appropriate Language, states that people can interact with the Scripture in the language that speaks most strongly to

---

24. Ruge-Jones, "Those Sitting Around Jesus," 27.
25. Swanson, *Provoking the Gospel*.
26. Swanson, *Provoking the Gospel of Mark*.
27. Perry, *Insights from Performance*, 40.
28. Hearon, "Characters in Text," 76.
29. Cousins, "Pilgrim Theology."
30. Cousins, "Pilgrim Theology," 185.
31. Cousins, "Pilgrim Theology," 204.
32. Germain, "Benefits of Performance," 1–3.

them.[33] Performances have a great impact among minority language speakers if done in their local language, and a text could even be performed in related dialects to discuss translation options.

Dye's second condition is Acceptable Translation.[34] BPC methods can help achieve an acceptable translation through experimenting with different key terms during performances and then discussing these with the audiences after performances. In this way the performance can serve as a basis for community testing. The participants will also have a greater sense of ownership of the translation if they are actively engaged in post-performance dialogue. Dye's third condition, Accessible Forms, is met by BPC when oral learners can interact with Scriptures in an oral performance, meaning they can access Scriptures without literacy or technology.[35] Even literate audiences can find new ways of engaging with the text through oral performance. Dickie comments that performance has the potential to reach many more people, including the nonliterate and those who are attracted to the arts.[36]

Dye's fourth condition, Background Knowledge, is a key way in which BPC can be used as a teaching tool.[37] The performer can talk about the biblical world during a performance, and discussion after the performance can help add further background knowledge. Dickie points out that performance can help show which supplemental biblical information is needed for an audience to understand a passage correctly.[38] The fifth condition, Availability, could be met if the audience is taught the story after the performance in such a way that they can then become performers of the story.[39] Perry notes that the biblical writers were participants rather than objective observers and were themselves storytellers who internalized these stories and were shaped by them.[40] This means that people who experience BPC can become performers of the text rather than merely being objective observers. BPC can therefore be used as an instrument for evangelism, meeting condition six, Spiritual Hunger.[41] If the community is open to trying BPC, this helps satisfy condition eight, which is Partnership.

33. Dye, "Eight Conditions," 92.
34. Dye, "Eight Conditions," 92.
35. Dye, "Eight Conditions," 92.
36. Dickie, "Community Translation," 40.
37. Germain, "Benefits of Performance," 1–3.
38. Dickie, "Community Translation," 41.
39. Germain, "Benefits of Performance," 1–3.
40. Perry, *Insights from Performance*, loc. 2464.
41. Germain, "Benefits of Performance," 1–3.

Community benefit

Germain points out that BPC can also have a great benefit in the host community.[42] The performance event is communal, and, as the community gathers to hear the Scripture and then discuss it, the community fully understands the stories, and the group is transformed as they hear the stories and identify with these stories of faith. Through this performance and discussion, the people will learn more about the text, offer their own community exegesis, and will have a sense of local ownership of the text. BPC can also lead to other forms of art in the community, such as composing songs or dance. Dickie notes that if the audience interprets the meaning of the text together, there will be less chance of errors of understanding, and the text will become owned by the community and become part of their collective memory.[43] Performance can give the community deeper insights into the text than would likely be possible with a print version. Performance can also strengthen the unity of the group through joint participation in the communication event. It also gives preference to the community, using the media they prefer and asking them to help define the meaning of the text. Perry adds that meaning is made in community, so that performance is a participatory way of knowing rather than an individual one.[44]

Emotional engagement

BPC engages the whole body and all the senses.[45] Oral performance will help the translation team add the emotive dimensions to the text, such as repetition, word associations, rhyme and rhythm, word order, alliteration, and moments of contrast. Nonverbal communication can be used to communicate emotions that are not found in the text, including tone and attitude. Ruge-Jones discusses how hearing a text differs from reading a text.[46] In the oral performance the audience gets visual clues to help guide them through the story, including the tone, gestures, intonation, and pace. It shows the thoughts, feelings, and dynamic interactions between the characters and elicits the same emotions in the audience. Dickie agrees that using media such as song, dance, or performance of a text activates the senses of the audience, which gives them an emotional connection to the text and helps them

42. Germain, "Benefits of Performance," 7.
43. Dickie, "Using Psalms," 39.
44. Perry, *Insights from Performance*, loc. 2464.
45. Germain, "Benefits of Performance," 1–3.
46. Ruge-Jones, "Word Heard," 107.

remember it better.⁴⁷ Performance and the human voice help to influence the emotions of the audience, which was in many cases the original purpose of the biblical text. Perry's experience showed that audiences remembered more emotions than ideas from the performance.⁴⁸ He also comments that biblical texts are a whole-body experience, or an embodied experience. BPC helps people to connect the body, including emotions, with the mind when engaging with the text.

Multiple interpretations

Ward agrees with Germain that the performance may present several different interpretations, as it facilitates experimentation with many varied possibilities of meaning before the audience.⁴⁹ Maxwell emphasizes that in today's hypertext culture, internalizing and performing Scripture can bring with it freedom to impact the hearer in new ways, embodying the story and inviting the audience to engage and participate.⁵⁰ It is a way to communicate multiple layers of interpretation, including emotive force. Noting that one of the goals of the ancient authors was to engage the audience, Maxwell claims that narrative fails without audience participation.⁵¹ Perry also adds that performance opens some interpretations and closes others.⁵² Therefore, it offers a new way to explore and compare interpretations of a text. Performance can also help a difficult text convey a stronger message.

EMBODIED PERFORMANCE ANALYSIS

Embodied Performance Analysis (EPA) is a new method of BPC developed by Agnew and used by her for a performance of Romans. EPA begins with embodiment.⁵³ It employs the tools of the body, the emotion, and the audience, integrated with a range of other interpretive approaches to discern meaning in a biblical composition. Through preparation, performance, and reflection, the performer-interpreter employs these tools, together with several relevant exegetical approaches, to discern meaning in a biblical

---

47. Dickie, "Using Psalms," 39.
48. Perry, *Insights from Performance*, loc. 2464.
49. Ward and Trobisch, *Bringing the Word*, 57.
50. Maxwell, "Embodying Scripture," 75.
51. Maxwell, *Hearing Between the Lines*, xiii.
52. Perry, *Insights from Performance*, loc. 2464.
53. Agnew, *Embodied Performance*, 16.

composition, presented in an analysis comprised of performance interpretation and critical reflection. The critical reflection takes the performer-interpreter behind the scenes of the preparation and discusses the impact of the composition on the performer and the decisions made for performance. It may be necessary to follow the process several times before arriving at a definitive performative interpretation and critical reflection. Telling stories, inhabiting them, and internalizing them is not just communication but is in itself interpretation, making meaning out of the Bible. Interpretation is not just carried out by the cognitive mind, detached from physical, emotional, and relational aspects of our being; instead, a wholistic meaning-making process is needed. EPA embraces the personal (shaped by the story and experience of the interpreter) and the particular nature of engagement with the Bible (shaped by the time, culture, and the context of the interpreter and their audience). It is also intentionally immersive and intuitive, taking seriously the fact that humans are physical, emotional, and relational in their whole being. Agnew calls it "an approach to exegesis by and through performance."[54]

Step 1 is preparation, which will involve a translation or adapting a translation of the composition, making a layout of the script, and some preliminary performances.[55] Step 2 is the main performance or a series of performances for an audience. Step 3 is reflection, which is going behind the scenes, integrating insights from the preparation and the performance, exploring questions arising using scholarship or other interpretive methods, and having a coherent discussion of the composition in performance. It might be necessary to proceed through these steps several times, implementing insights from reflection in the adaptation or changing the translation and rehearsing again, before arriving at a more definite performance and analysis.

The first tool to be used is the body, employed with an awareness of how the body moves in response to the composition (instinctive movements, gestures, posture, and voice).[56] The body is used as a tool for interpretation because cognitive knowledge is interpreted through the medium of the body. The second tool is emotion, which means paying attention to how the performer feels in response to the composition, assessing the composition's impact on the emotions, and discerning what it is telling the performer-interpreter about either himself/herself or about the composition. Emotions are a vital tool in our interpretation of the world. The final tool

---

54. Agnew, *Embodied Performance*, 25.
55. Agnew, *Embodied Performance*, 38.
56. Agnew, *Embodied Performance*, 114.

is the audience, which includes envisaging the audience during preparation and anticipating how the audience today might receive the composition. A live audience can be understood not only as recipients of the performance but also as participants.

Agnew's EPA method begins with embodiment and uses performance to interpret biblical compositions, integrating other tools when necessary.[57] BPC uses performance today to reconstruct the historical performance situations of the biblical compositions in their origins. The goal in BPC is to seek an understanding of the passage and its impact and then find ways to perform the composition which agree with that interpretation.[58] Performance is used to tell the story rather than to interpret the story. The earliest BPC method was also limited to narrative analysis and texts and looked at the text in its origins, rather than reception through performance today to a modern audience. However, later, practitioners such as Perry and Hearon have developed BPC further to a stage where the interpreter-performer is learning through the process of performance. Agnew further develops BPC to the method of EPA, which begins with performance and uses it to interpret biblical compositions.

CONCLUSIONS AND APPLICATION

Perry suggests three modes of BPC: analytical, heuristic, and practical.[59] The analytical mode of BPC examines the remains of ancient performance events, rather like an archaeologist who examines an ancient site looking for clues to help reconstruct the performance event. The heuristic mode of BPC creates contemporary performance events to find out what meanings can be produced, an approach which has been developed further by Sarah Agnew. The practical mode is the daily performance of biblical materials that happens in Bible studies, churches, YouTube videos, and conversations when someone performs a biblical tradition.

The idea of BPC to produce performances of a text as part of the translation process is both innovative and inspiring. My research is interested in the heuristic mode of BPC—creating contemporary performance events in the Altai context to find out what meanings can be produced and using performance as an interpretive tool in translation. Performance can help the process of exegesis, by using the performance and subsequent feedback from the audience to interpret the biblical passage and discover meaning.

57. Agnew, *Embodied Performance*, 16.
58. Agnew, *Embodied Performance*, 51.
59. Perry, "Biblical Performance Criticism," 10.

Agnew's "Embodied Performance Analysis" begins with embodiment and uses performance to interpret biblical compositions. Such performance involves an epistemological shift in how the Bible is regarded. Conquergood has written about how performance requires an epistemological shift away from the dominance of textualism in communication.[60] He suggests that performance and text should be kept in tension, in a "text-performance hybridity."[61] He comments that performed experience will become a way of knowing and understanding.[62] Knowledge gained through performance is a different type of knowledge from that provided by analytical study.

I initially conducted my own preparation, internalization, and performance process of Judg 4–5 and the three psalms in English. This was done together with a team from the United States, working by teleconference. The starting point for this performance process was doing a translation into English from Hebrew. I then used Embodied Performance Analysis to reflect on my own performances to reinterpret the biblical passages. The Altai team and I prepared an initial performance in two places in the Republic of Altai, before the final performances, and we used the responses to the initial performances to further reflect exegetically on the chosen passages.

By using performance, I am challenging the tendency to separate translation from engagement. Translation instead should be viewed as a form of engagement, and engagement can include translation. Performance translation helps draw both translation and engagement together as part of a larger process, because it is collaborative and iterative, construing translation as a process rather than as an end product. Viewed this way, performance itself is an act of translation, which takes place in the performance through the interaction with the audience. Translation, performance, and engagement can come together to address the felt needs of the community. The use of performance also expands the scope of translation beyond orality, pointing to the complexity of media in all communication.

With regards to Scripture engagement, performance is an ideal way to engage with the audience. It leads to increased partnership with the local community and the church—and to the community more fully understanding Scripture, having ownership of the text, and being transformed. It can lead to other forms of art and can give oral-preference learners increased access to Scripture. Performance can address the felt needs of the community and can strengthen the unity of the group. It can be used as a teaching tool and as an instrument for evangelism, all the more since the audience can

---

60. Conquergood, "Performance Studies," 148.
61. Conquergood, "Performance Studies," 152.
62. Conquergood, "Rethinking Ethnography," 190.

themselves become performers of the story. In the case of the Altai project, the performed psalms include refrains in which the audience members can participate and sing. Several times during the concerts the audience got up and began to sing and dance themselves, spontaneously taking part in the performance.

Performance can also be used as a type of community testing, so that feedback from the audiences following the performances can be fed back into the translation process. Initial practice performances, as well as the final performances, were used in the Altai project to facilitate discussion of translation options and key terms.

In the next chapters I will describe how I explored the oral performance traditions of the target culture together with the translation team, including music and poetic genres, in order to discover what is available and what is suitable for use in BT and in performance. I, as an orality-oriented exegete, then identified the oral characteristics of the original text, and, together with the translation team, searched for the functionally equivalent correspondents in the RL. Then after the Altai team and I had completed the preparation, internalization, and translation of the chosen passages, we prepared an initial and final performance of Judg 4–5 and the three psalms, according to the suitable local genres. In this way the team went through Perry's three steps which form a repetitive circle: preparation, internalization, and performance.[63] The performance was presented in ten different venues in the Altai Republic. Following performances, audiences were asked to participate in focus group discussions and to complete a survey, which will be discussed in chapter 9.

---

63. Perry, *Insights from Performance*, loc. 39.

5

The Poetic Features of Judges 4 and 5 for Oral Translation and Performance

INTRODUCTION

My research focuses on designing a performance-based oral Bible translation of Judg 4–5 and Pss 1, 100, and 133 in Altai, in the style of their traditional epics. This chapter discusses the features of orality in these passages in preparation for oral translation and performance.

The chapter begins with Judg 4, with exegetical notes I have prepared for the oral translation team in Altai and with broader applicability for other OBT teams. In the appendices is a story chart of this passage (see Appendix 1), and a table showing the oral and performance features of this passage (see Appendix 2). The story chart is based on the five major elements of stories: plot, conflict (the tension that drives the story forward to a conclusion), setting (the details of time and place in which a story occurs), characters (the people of the story), and theme (the main idea of the story).[1]

The poetic dimension of the ancient text of Judg 5, as well as many textual difficulties, can cause a serious challenge for interpretation and translation. The large variety of poetic features needs careful attention as oral translation and performance of the passage is considered. In the appendices is a story chart of this passage (see Appendix 3), as well as a table showing the oral and performance features of this passage (see Appendix 4).

---

1. Andrews and Andrews, "Teaching the Classics," 5.

DIFFERENCES BETWEEN THE PROSE AND POETRY ACCOUNTS OF JUDGES 4 AND 5

General differences between Hebrew prose and poetry

Block describes the differences between Hebrew prose and poetry as follows: common language with everyday words and spellings, as opposed to elevated literary language with rare words and archaic expressions; grammar with commonplace elements, as opposed to creative grammatical forms; a logical and chronological style with many coordinating and subordinating clauses and plot development, as opposed to expressive and abstract description with parallelism; a controlled and realistic tone, as opposed to an emotional tone with frequent hyperbole and figures of speech; and, finally, the aim to inform, educate, and indoctrinate, as opposed to an aim to celebrate and inspire.[2]

Features such as wordplay, figures of speech, images, rhetorical questions, and irony can be present in both Hebrew poetry and prose.[3] However, in Hebrew poetry these features are used more frequently, as if piled up one on top of the other. In Hebrew poetry there is usually no background information given to the audience, and there is no strict chronological presentation of events. The expression is usually more condensed than in the poetic narrative account, though there are exceptions such as in the account of the death of Sisera in Judg 5 as compared with Judg 4. The poet assumes that the listener knows the story, and events may occur out of order and be repeated. The goal of the poet is not to retell a story but to recast the narrative so as to appeal to the emotions of the audience, and, in the case of Judg 5, to call the listeners to praise God for his victory.

Differences Between Judges 4 and 5

The poem in Judg 5 is distinguished from the narrative in Judg 4 by the introduction (5:1), where it is described as being sung. The Hebrew word describing the victory song in Judg 5 is שִׁיר *shir*—song or poem. This term is used to describe the Song of Songs (1:1) and various psalms.[4] The poem has the marks of typical Hebrew poetry: parallelism, chiasmus, formulaic

---

2. Block, *Judges/Ruth*, 175.
3. Zogbo and Wendland, *Hebrew Poetry*, 3.
4. Zogbo and Wendland, *Hebrew Poetry*, 13.

constructions, alliteration, and paronomasia.[5] It is also divided into a series of stanzas.

There is strong characterization in the poem, compared to the narrative, with more actors who are colorfully described.[6] It is more intense and more personal than the prose account in Judg 4. The language is emotive, and irony is present at the end. The battle description is short and filled with metaphorical language, and even natural phenomena are depicted as divine opposition to Canaan. The audience is also invited to participate by the use of several imperatives aimed at the listeners. In addition, the use of the first person in the song helps the performance become more immediate for the audience. Levy notes that although chapter 4 does contain some elements of drama, the poetry of chapter 5 is "a story-poem, a grand public oratory, part of a victory celebration."[7]

The two versions of the same event highlight different aspects.[8] Schneider notes that the poem is more focused on the battle and praising God and therefore does not deal with many of the themes of the book which are stressed in the prose narrative, such as the role of leadership, foreigners helping Israelites, and the role of women.[9] The prose version consists of a logical and chronological plotline leading up to the final climax in 4:23–24, but the poetic version consists of independent scenes put together with no logical thread.[10] The prose version highlights the role of the Lord overtly and then focuses on Barak, who first of all pursues the enemy, scattered by the Lord, and secondly pursues Sisera, who is then killed by Jael. The poet does call people to praise the Lord for the victory (5:2, 9), but the Lord's role is mentioned less specifically than in the prose. In the prose account, the narrator also highlights the role of the women and deliberately humiliates the men. However, the poem shows Deborah and Barak in a partnership, and gender is not as significant an issue in chapter 5.

JUDGES 4 AS A STORY

Beck states that stories are art forms crafted by the storyteller, intended to make meaning, maintain the focus of the audience and elicit their response.[11]

5. Block, *Judges/Ruth*, 212.
6. Mathews, *Prophets as Performers*, 84.
7. Levy, *Bible as Theatre*, 52.
8. Block, *Judges/Ruth*, 181.
9. Schneider, *Judges*, 2388.
10. Block, *Judges/Ruth*, 183.
11. Beck, *God as Storyteller*, 4.

Beck notes the importance of context in reading a story, including the whole biblical story line, allusions to other stories, and the historical, temporal, sociocultural, and geographical context of the story.[12] Stories also have an organizing plot which gives the story movement and flow and arouses the emotions and interest of the audience.[13] A typical plot includes exposition, crisis, complication, climax, resolution, and conclusion. According to West, the dramatic structure, plot, or story arc is the clearest evidence that the biblical narratives are designed as drama or scripts of ancient performances.[14] West identifies the setting, the central conflict, resolution, and denouement as the key stages in such a plot. He emphasizes again that these written biblical texts originated with and were developed from oral performances. Although the genre, drama, has a textual element, it is an event or experience which takes place between actors and performers on stage.

Characterization also plays a crucial role in the art form of the story, including varieties of characters, methods of characterization, and their names.[15] The narrator controls the point of view of the audience, benefitting from awareness of events and conversations that happened when no one was present. In addition, the narrator can provide not only the details of the event but also controls the viewpoint from which those details are presented, sometimes deliberately leaving gaps as a way to influence the reader.[16] The storyteller's use of time, space, and setting (geographical, architectural, and social) also help with the development of the story and impact the listener.[17] Beck especially highlights the importance of geography when an event is placed in story form.[18] It is important in Judg 4 for the translation team to understand the context of the narrative, the organizing plot, the characters, the narrator's role, the use of time and setting, conflicts, and the geographical setting of the story. Geography has an important part to play in the story of Judg 4–5.

INTRODUCTION TO JUDGES 4

Judges 4:1–3 and 4:23–24 provide a clear introduction and conclusion, respectively, to the prose account. The conclusion of the poem (5:31b), with

12. Beck, *God as Storyteller*, 23–24.
13. Beck, *God as Storyteller*, 28.
14. West, "Art of Biblical," 57.
15. Beck, *God as Storyteller*, 36.
16. Beck, *God as Storyteller*, 60–64.
17. Beck, *God as Storyteller*, 68.
18. Beck, *God as Storyteller*, 99.

the final familiar Deuteronomic formula, *And the land had rest for forty years*, shows the narrator's intention that Judg 4–5, the prose and the poem, should be read together.[19] Chapter 4 initially introduces Deborah as prophetess and judge in 4:4 and then introduces Heber the Kenite in 4:11. There are two overlapping plotlines in chapter 4, which both include rising and falling tension. The first describes the battle between the two tribes of Israel and the Canaanite enemy, consisting of the lead up to the battle, the turning point where the Lord throws the enemies into a panic, and Israel's victory. The second plotline is about Sisera, who escapes, thinks he has found protection, and then is killed by Jael, the wife of Heber the Kenite. The account is highly ironic, as Jael, seeming to offer hospitality to Sisera, murders him instead, showing her determined character and her loyalty to Israel. Davidson comments that the Deborah/Jael story is constructed playfully, with over thirty details that emphasize a parallel and contrast with the Samson story later in the book (Judg 13–16).[20]

KEY ORALITY FEATURES OF JUDGES 4

The narrator of Judg 4 uses several oral rhetorical features throughout the chapter: surprise, irony and ambiguity, repetition of key terms, wordplays, dramatic effect, an *inclusio*, dialogue, and characterization.[21]

Surprise, irony, and ambiguity

By virtue of the broader context of the book of Judges, the defeat of the enemy can be predicted by the reader even before Deborah appears on the scene.[22] Judges 2 outlines the cyclical plot of disobedience, punishment, cry for help, and deliverance, and chapter 3 gives examples of various deliverers (Othniel, Ehud, Shamgar) and Israel's enemies (Mesopotamia, Moab, the Philistines). However, the audience does not yet know exactly how this is going to happen in chapter 4, and there is still a considerable amount of suspense in the account. The first surprise for the audience is that in this episode the deliverer is a woman. However, this is a variation on the theme, already introduced by the narrator, that God is working through unexpected and unusual heroes, such as the left-handed Ehud and Shamgar,

---

19. Mathews, *Prophets as Performers*, 83.
20. Davidson, *Intricacy, Design*, 110.
21. Block, *Judges/Ruth*, 186.
22. Sternberg, *Poetics of Biblical Narrative*, 271.

whose weapon is an ox-goad.²³ Although the audience already guesses the final outcome, the ways and the means by which this will take place are still unknown at this point in the narrative.

However, as soon as the audience begins to think that it is a woman, Deborah, who will lead Israel into battle, Barak appears on the scene as the would-be hero, only to then reveal his timidity and lack of self-confidence. When Deborah announces that the glory will go to a woman, again the audience expects that to be Deborah. This is confirmed when the battle is won *before Barak*, with Barak playing a very diminished role in the victory. However, just as the audience is beginning to wonder how these expectations have gone wrong, because Deborah has disappeared from the stage, they suddenly come true, as the narrative introduces a third character. The prediction did not mean what the audience initially understood it to mean. There was a clue left for the audience in 4:11 where Heber the Kenite was introduced, and the last act (4:17–22) finally puts an end to the suspense.²⁴

The tension is heightened with the narrator following each action of Jael as she invites Sisera warmly into her tent, reassures him, offers milk, and covers him again (4:18–19). Sisera never suspects that the real threat lies in a woman, warning her in verse 20 about a man who may pass by. Finally, Jael murders Sisera with her female camping equipment (tent peg and mallet), as opposed to the weapons of a warrior in battle.²⁵ Barak arrives too late to kill the enemy but in time to see the army general lying dead, killed by a woman. The narrator attributes the victory to God.

Repetition and lexical features

It is important to note the narrator's use of key terms in Judg 4, including:

– יָד *yad* [hand] (4:2, 7, 9, 14, 21, 24). This expression is primarily used in the context of *being sold into the hands of*, or *give the enemy into your hands*, but in verse 21 it emphasizes the fact that Jael took the hammer and tent peg into her hands to murder Sisera.

– אִישׁ *ish* [man] (4:6, 10, 14, 20, 22). The word *man or men* is mentioned several times, but it is the women who are the heroes in these chapters. Traditional roles are overturned and subverted; women are manly, and

---

23. Sternberg, *Poetics of Biblical Narrative*, 272.
24. Sternberg, *Poetics of Biblical Narrative*, 272.
25. Sternberg, *Poetics of Biblical Narrative*, 272.

men are womanly.²⁶ In this story, it is women who are honored and come to the rescue of their families and their people.²⁷

– the verbs *go up* עָלָה *alah* (4:5, 10, 12), *go* הָלַךְ *halach* (4:6, 8, 9, 24), and *go down* יָרַד *yarad* (4:14,15).²⁸ Movement and geography are significant in this story, including the location of the Israelites on top of the mountain before the battle, and the presence of the enemy in the valley.

There are also wordplays in the Hebrew text, e.g., with the words חֶרֶב *cherev* [sword] and חֶבֶר *chever* [Heber] in 4:16–17, and with the words כְּנֵעַ *chena* [subdue] כְּנַעַן *Kena'an* [Canaan] in 4:23.

Dramatic effect and *inclusio*

Dramatic effect is created by an aside, giving the audience background information in verse 11, with the introduction of Heber the Kenite and an anticipation of future action in verse 17 with a second reference to him.

The Hebrew word הִנֵּה *hinneh* behold occurs twice in verse 22 to draw attention to the shocking discovery that Barak is about to make. These markers are followed by the participles רֹדֵף *rodef* [to pursue] and נֹפֵל *nofel* [to fall], used by the storyteller for dramatic effect to describe the death of the enemy Sisera.²⁹

There is an *inclusio* structure which frames the story with the two strong women: Deborah at the beginning and Jael at the end.

Dialogue

The first dialogue in Judg 4 takes place between Deborah and Barak in verses 6–9. Barak's words show his lack of self-confidence. His timidity highlights by contrast Deborah's role as she gives the prophecy that the glory will go to a woman.³⁰ Robbins emphasizes how Deborah is honored and Barak is shamed by the challenge-response communication between them.³¹ Sternberg notes that Deborah's announcement, "Hasn't the Lord, the God of Israel, commanded you" legitimizes her role as judge, further reinforced

---

26. Zucker and Reiss, "Subverting Sexuality," 32.
27. Le Roux, "Battle Against Hazor," 21.
28. Ogden and Zogbo, *Handbook on Judges*.
29. Ogden and Zogbo, *Handbook on Judges*.
30. Sternberg, *Poetics of Biblical Narrative*, 274.
31. Robbins, *Exploring the Texture*, 80.

by the assignment she gives to Barak.³² Deborah then has another line of exhortation to Barak, imparting courage to him, in verse 14, beginning with "Go!"

The concluding dialogue of chapter 4 occurs between Jael and Sisera in verses 18–20. It begins with Jael making an alluring offer, followed by Sisera's attempt to regain his authority over the situation. However, Sisera's words are full of irony, though he does not realize it himself, because he tells Jael to say that there is "no man" or "no one" there. Eventually a man comes to the door of the tent, and he sees only Sisera's dead body there.³³

Characterization

Deborah's story demonstrates how the downward spiral of spiritual degeneration in Israel is continuing.³⁴ There are four main characters depicted in Judg 4: Deborah, Barak, Sisera, and Jael. These characters are juxtaposed, Deborah with Barak and Jael with Sisera.³⁵ Barak should have been the judge and main hero in the story, but instead the two women are the heroines, one an Israelite prophetess and the other a non-Israelite, although the victory and honor are attributed to the Lord. Deborah was a talented woman, both a judge and a prophetess, who can be compared to Moses. Levy calls Deborah "a decisive, strong-willed and God-fearing woman."³⁶ Jael, a Kenite who took the opportunity to kill the military leader Sisera in an unconventional way, is described as a heroine in chapter 5:24.³⁷ Barak is also an unusual character. Traditionally men were expected to fight and be brave, but Barak is reluctant to fight without Deborah, and even Sisera runs cowardly away from the battle.³⁸

Imagery

The theme of trees occurs repeatedly in Judg 4. Deborah sits and judges underneath a palm tree (4:5). Heber the Kenite moved his tent away from the Kenite tribe and lives near the terebinth tree at Zaanannim (4:11). As

---

32. Sternberg, *Poetics of Biblical Narrative*, 274.
33. Butler, "Judges," 106.
34. Schneider, *Judges*, 1432.
35. Le Roux, "Battle against Hazor," 9.
36. Levy, *Bible as Theatre*, 53.
37. Levy, *Bible as Theatre*, 2.
38. Levy, *Bible as Theatre*, 4.

discussed below in more detail, if חֲרֹשֶׁת *Charoshet* (Harosheth) can be translated as *forested*, then this theme of trees is further repeated. When the army chased the enemy back to the forested area (*Harosheth Haggoyim*), the trees would have slowed the progress of their chariots and made them vulnerable to the attack of the foot soldiers. Their judgment day came under the trees, just as Deborah judged from under her tree.

Mountains are also significant in this story, as the Lord summons Barak to the top of Mount Tabor with his army (Judg 4:6), and it is from there that the attack is mounted on Sisera's troops below in the Kishon valley. In the OT, mountains were often places where God's presence was felt and where God gave a victory (Gen 22:2; Exod 19–20; Deut 34:1; 1 Kgs 8:1; 1 Kgs 18:14–65; 2 Chron 3:1).

THE ORALITY OF THE SONG OF DEBORAH IN JUDGES 5

As already discussed previously, recent research shows that both oral tradition and scribal activity were important in the formation of the Bible.[39] It is highly probable that the Song of Deborah was initially created and passed down orally. Koller compares the Song of Deborah to a genre of oral Arabic poetry called *qaṣīdā* poems (often translated *ode*), which were an ancient and respected genre, many of which have a military theme.[40] The narrator would recite such a poem, composed after a military victory, and others would memorize it and circulate it orally more broadly. Koller suggests using this Arabic oral poetry as a model for considering the Song of Deborah as a poem composed immediately after the event (within days or weeks), which was then circulated orally by reciters with certain additions or deletions occurring over time. Davidson detects Canaanite influence on the Song of Deborah, comparing it to the myth of Baal's battle against the powers of El and Yam.[41]

THE EDITOR, DATE, AND THEME OF JUDGES 5

Block defends the traditional view that Deborah was responsible for the composition of the poem.[42] However, this is impossible to know for certain. The composer often speaks in the first person, particularly during the first

---

39. Naudé and Miller-Naudé, "Translation of Biblion," 1.
40. Koller, "Composing the Song."
41. Davidson, *Intricacy, Design*, 306.
42. Block, *Judges/Ruth*, 215.

half of the chapter. In verse 7, the first-person speaker is named Deborah and described as the mother of Israel. This identification matches the order of the names in the title and the use of the feminine singular verb *she sang*. The leadership of a woman in such victory songs and celebrations corresponds with the role of women in other biblical and extra-biblical texts and agrees with Deborah's prophetic status described in chapter 4. Alter, who suggests a date of around 1100 BC, claims that this is one of the most ancient poems in the Old Testament.[43] This passage is often noted for its archaic language and is considered one of the oldest texts in the Hebrew Bible.

GENRE OF THE POEM

The Hebrew Bible contains two narrative poems which tell the stories of battles: the Song of the Sea (Exod 15) and Song of Deborah (Judg 5). Classifying the genre of Judg 5 is not an easy task, yet its biblical context demonstrates that it is a triumphant hymn in honor of the Lord, similar to the Song of the Sea in Exod 15 and with analogies to Egyptian victory poems.[44] In contrast to other extra-biblical poems which celebrate human victories, the two biblical victory poems contain praise to the Lord. In Judg 5 there is some focus on individual human activity, especially towards the end, with Jael's murder and Sisera's waiting mother. This has led some to identify the poem as a ballad, but the poem is more than a ballad. The poet does admire the female characters, but Jael is a participant in the divine victory, and the hymn can be identified primarily as a hymn of praise to the Lord.

The editorial note in verse 1 says that the song was sung by both Deborah and Barak, a thanksgiving hymn for a military victory.[45] Globe notes that singing such songs after a victory was common in ancient Israel, such as after the Exodus or during the reign of David, and that the composer most likely drew upon an established tradition of Middle Eastern victory hymns. Butler writes that Israel's victory songs may commonly have been sung by women.[46]

Judges 5 as a poem is a carefully constructed unity.[47] The metrical structure and the use of chiasm, parallelism, paronomasia, and repetition all point to this. The passage is also centered around one unique theme.

43. Alter, *Hebrew Bible*, 5126.
44. Block, *Judges/Ruth*, 212.
45. Globe, "Literary Structure," 495.
46. Butler, "Judges," 122.
47. Coogan, "Structural and Literary," 144.

STRUCTURAL ANALYSIS OF JUDGES 5

Following this introductory survey of issues related to the passage, this section will now discuss its structure.

The structure of the poem

The poem is divided into stanzas, as is typical in Hebrew poetry. Block finds nine stanzas:[48]

Judges 5:2–3, Stanza 1: Introduction

Judges 5:4–5, Stanza 2: The introduction of the Lord

Judges 5:6–8, Stanza 3: The emergence of Deborah

Judges 5:9–11c, Stanza 4: A call for praise for the Lord's righteous acts

Judges 5:11d-18, Stanza 5: A recitation of Israel's righteous actions

Judges 5:19–23, Stanza 6: A description of the battle

Judges 5:24–27, Stanza 7: The death of Sisera

Judges 5:28–30, Stanza 8: Sisera's mother waiting for his return

Judges 5:31a, Stanza 9: Conclusion of the poem

The last stanzas focus more on individual human activity, highlighting Jael's participation in the divine work of victory of the Lord over his enemies. However, although the reader is inspired by the heroism of the two women, in the end the poem is a celebration of the Lord's triumph.[49]

Scholars do not completely agree on the number of stanzas. An extensive study has been done by Coogan, who has divided Judg 5 into five stanzas, with the first and final subdivided into two strophes each:[50]

Judges 5:2–8 (divided into 2–5, and 6–8), Stanza 1: Preliminaries of the battle with a focus on the Lord

Judges 5:9–13, Stanza 2: Preliminaries of the battle with a focus on Deborah

Judges 5:14–18, Stanza 3: The response of the tribes

Judges 5:19–23, Stanza 4: The actual battle focusing on cosmic events

---

48. Block, *Judges/Ruth*, 212.
49. Block, *Judges/Ruth*, 217.
50. Coogan, "Structural and Literary," 151.

Judges 5:24–30 (divided into 24–27 and 28–30), Stanza 5: The sequel to the battle, focusing on Jael and Sisera's mother

Coogan bases his analysis on the conclusion that verses 14–18, the description of the tribes, is at the center of the poem. Verse 19 has a clear change of subject matter, so this marks the beginning of the fourth stanza, as is the case again in verse 24 marking the beginning of the fifth stanza. Coogan acknowledges that the first part of the poem is more difficult to divide, but he suggests the first stanza from verses 2–8, and the second from 9–13, both beginning in a similar way with a brief description of the situation and the imperative *bless the Lord*.[51] The first and last stanzas are divided into sub-stanzas which are parallel to each other.[52] This is a thematic parallel describing the actions of the two women in relation to Sisera.

A POETIC ANALYSIS OF JUDGES 5

Parallelism

Judges 5:3 is an example of parallelism:

שִׁמְעוּ מְלָכִים
הַאֲזִינוּ רֹזְנִים

Shim'u melachim
ha'azinu rozenim

Hear, O kings;
Listen, O rulers.

These two lines have a similar meaning as well as a similar grammatical pattern.[53] שִׁמְעוּ *shim'u* [hear] and הַאֲזִינוּ *ha'azinu* [listen] are parallel verbs, while מְלָכִים *melachim* [kings] and רֹזְנִים *rozenim* [rulers] are parallel nouns, providing syntactic parallelism. In both lines imperative verbs are followed by vocative nouns. Parallelism is also evident in the first two lines of verse 4:

יְהוָה בְּצֵאתְךָ מִשֵּׂעִיר
בְּצַעְדְּךָ מִשְּׂדֵה אֱדוֹם

Adonai betzetcha misse'ir
betza'decha missedeh edom

O Lord, when you came down from Seir,

---

51. Coogan, "Structural and Literary," 152.
52. Coogan, "Structural and Literary," 153.
53. Ogden and Zogbo, *Handbook on Judges*.

when you marched from the land of Edom

Staircase (or incremental) parallelism refers to parallel lines that build on each other. For example, in Judg 5:7 there is a progression from one line to the next as follows:

חָדְל֥וּ פְרָז֖וֹן
בְּיִשְׂרָאֵ֖ל חָדֵ֑לּוּ

*Chadelu ferazon
beyisra'el chadellu*

Village life ceased,
ceased in Israel,

The word חָדְל֥וּ *chadelu* [ceased] occurs in the first line and is built upon in the second line.

Verse 21 is another example of staircase parallelism, where the second line is built on the first (ABC/ADAB):

נַ֤חַל קִישׁוֹן֙ גְּרָפָ֔ם
נַ֥חַל קְדוּמִ֖ים נַ֥חַל קִישׁ֑וֹן

*Nachal kishon gerafam
nachal kedumim nachal kishon.*

The torrent of Kishon, it swept them away
The ancient torrent, the torrent of Kishon.

Verse 23 gives another example of this type of parallelism:

א֣וֹרוּ מֵר֗וֹז אָמַר֙ מַלְאַ֣ךְ יְהוָ֔ה
אֹ֥רוּ אָר֖וֹר יֹשְׁבֶ֑יהָ

*Oru meroz amar mal'ach adonai
oru aror yosheveiha*

'Curse Meroz,' said the Lord's messenger,
'Curse, O curse its inhabitants,

Verse 27 is one of the best examples of staircase parallelism in the Hebrew Bible:[54]

בֵּ֤ין רַגְלֶ֙יהָ֙ כָּרַ֣ע נָפַ֣ל שָׁכָ֑ב
בֵּ֥ין רַגְלֶ֖יהָ כָּרַ֣ע נָפָ֑ל
בַּאֲשֶׁ֣ר כָּרַ֔ע שָׁ֖ם נָפַ֥ל שָׁדֽוּד

*Bein ragleiha kara nafal shachav
bein ragleiha kara nafal*

---

54. Block, *Judges/Ruth*, 241.

ba'asher kara sham nafal shadud

Between her feet he sank, he fell, he lay.
Between her feet he sank, he fell.
Where he sank, there he fell, dead!

Chiasm

Chiastic structures are similar to parallelism except that the order of certain phrases is reversed, forming an X pattern, which often emphasize a point or signal the beginning or ending of the poem. Full verbal chiasm is used, for example, in 19ab (ABC/DCB):

בָּאוּ מְלָכִים נִלְחָמוּ
אָז נִלְחֲמוּ מַלְכֵי כְנַעַן

Ba'u melachim nilchamu
az nilchamu malchei chena'an

The kings came, they fought,
Then fought the kings of Canaan,

It is also used in 24ac (ABC/BDA), which emphasizes the blessing on Jael:

תְּבֹרַךְ מִנָּשִׁים יָעֵל
מִנָּשִׁים בָּאֹהֶל תְּבֹרָךְ

Tevorach minnashim ya'el
minnashim ba'ohel tevorach

Most blessed of women is Jael,
Of tent dwelling women most blessed.

Partial verbal chiasm, where just one element is repeated, is present in 7ab (AB/CA):

חָדְלוּ פְרָזוֹן
בְּיִשְׂרָאֵל חָדֵלּוּ

Chadelu ferazon
beyisra'el chadellu

Village life ceased,
ceased in Israel,

Inclusio

There is an *inclusio* (a bracketing or envelope structure) בָּרֲכוּ יְהוָה *barachu adonai* [bless the Lord] around the section from verses 2–9.

Key words

Israel and *the Lord* are repeated many times throughout the poem. *Israel* occurs eight times in Judg 5, in the first section of the poem from verses 2–13. Coogan points to its usage in 8b and 9a to link what he has identified as the first two stanzas.[55] *The Lord* occurs ten times in stanzas 1 and 2 but only three times in the rest of the poem.

Multiple verb phrases

Multiple verb phrases are another common feature in Hebrew poetry. They occur in Judg 5, such as in Judg 5:4, where there is a movement from one line to the next:

אֶרֶץ רָעָשָׁה
גַּם־שָׁמַיִם נָטָפוּ
גַּם־עָבִים נָטְפוּ מָיִם

eretz ra'ashah
gam-shamayim natafu
gam-avim natefu mayim

the earth shook,
the heavens poured,
the clouds poured down water.

In 5:10 there are three verb phrases describing actions of people:

רֹכְבֵי
יֹשְׁבֵי
וְהֹלְכֵי

Rochevei…yoshevei….veholechei
You who ride…you who sit…you who walk…

In 5:26 describing Sisera's death there are four verbs in quick succession:

וְהָלְמָה *vehalemah* struck
מָחֲקָה *machakah* crushed

---

55. Coogan, "Structural and Literary," 156.

וּמָחֲצָה *umachatzah* shattered
וְחָלְפָה *vechalefah* pierced

Word pairs

Craigie finds eighty-two word pairs in Judg 5, twenty-two of which he notes also occur in Ugaritic poetry.[56] Some examples are שִׁמְעוּ *shim'u* [hear] and הַאֲזִינוּ *ha'azinu* [pay attention], and מְלָכִים *melachim* [kings] and רֹזְנִים *rozenim* [rulers] in verse 3. Another is כָּרַע נָפַל שָׁכָב *kara nafal shachav* [he sank; he fell; he lay], which are found together in other parts of the Hebrew Bible. In verse 3 שִׁיר *shir* [sing] and זַמֵּר *zamar* [make music] is a common word pair in Hebrew.

Paronomasia

Paronomasia, or punning, is used in verse 12 דְּבוֹרָה and דַּבְּרִי *Devorah* and *dabberi* [Deborah; speak].[57]

Meter

This poem does have a noticeable meter, but Block argues that it is too inconsistent to suggest definitive conclusions.[58] Coogan, analyzing the poem metrically based on the syllable count, concludes that this reveals a chiastic structure to the whole poem.[59] Freedman also bases his analysis of meter of Hebrew poetry on syllable count.[60] Others base their metrical analyses on stress beats.[61] Fokkelman argues that the 864 syllables and 352 words of the song in Judg 5 occur in 108 cola and 50 verses, which he combines into 20 strophes and 7 stanzas, and three sections or parts (verses 2–8, verses 9–23, and verses 24–31ab).[62]

---

56. Craigie, "Parallel Word Pairs," 16.
57. Coogan, "Structural and Literary," 156.
58. Block, *Judges/Ruth*, 212.
59. Coogan, "Structural and Literary," 158.
60. Freedman, "Pottery, Poetry," 7.
61. Lindars, *Judges 1–5*, 219.
62. Fokkelman, "Song of Deborah," 313.

Alliteration

In the poem, alliteration is used to highlight parallel elements.[63] Examples of this are in verse 4 מִשֵּׂעִיר בְּצַעְדְּךָ מִשְּׂדֵה אֱדוֹם *misse'ir betza'decha missedeh edom* [when you came down from Seir and from the land of Edom], and in verse 26 מָחֲקָה *machakah* [crush] and וּמָחֲצָה *umachatzah* [shatter]. Alliteration is also used for aesthetic reasons in the poem, such as the use of words with the initial *mem* in verse 14:

מִנִּי אֶפְרַיִם שָׁרְשָׁם בַּעֲמָלֵק
אַחֲרֶיךָ בִנְיָמִין בַּעֲמָמֶיךָ
מִנִּי מָכִיר יָרְדוּ מְחֹקְקִים
וּמִזְּבוּלֻן מֹשְׁכִים

Minni efrayim shorsham ba'amalek
achareicha vinyamin ba'amameicha
minni machir yaredu mechokekim
umizzevulun moshechim

The emphasis on *I* in verse 3 is *emphasized* by the repetition of אָנֹכִי *anochi*, the use of the first-person singular verbs, and the alliteration of the vowel *a* with the consonant א, which starts every word except one in the first line.[64]

אָנֹכִי לַיהוָה אָנֹכִי אָשִׁירָה
אֲזַמֵּר לַיהוָה אֱלֹהֵי יִשְׂרָאֵל

Anochi ladonai anochi ashirah
azammer ladonai elohei yisra'el

Repetition

It is important to know that repetition always has a function in Hebrew poetry. For example, repetition may be used to emphasize a point, to create irony, to anticipate an event, or to mark the beginning and end of the poetic units.[65] Repeating words or sounds is a major feature of Judg 5 and helps give emphasis in the text. For example, in 5:12 עוּרִי *uri* [awake] is repeated four times. Repetition often occurs at the climax of the story, for example, in 5:27 the verbs כָּרַע נָפַל *kara nafal* [he sank, he fell] are repeated, as is the expression בֵּין רַגְלֶיהָ *bein ragleiha* [at her feet]. This creates rhythm and

---

63. Coogan, "Structural and Literary," 159.
64. Hauser, "Judges 5," 28.
65. Ogden and Zogbo, *Handbook on Judges*.

emphasizes the expressions שָׁכַב shachav [he lay] and שָׁדוּד shadud [dead]. In verse 19 מְלָכִים malachim [kings] and נִלְחֲמוּ nilchamu [fought] are repeated, and the word שָׁלָל shalal [spoil] occurs four times in verse 30. Hebrew roots are also repeated as both the verb and the object providing emphasis, such as in 5:23 אָרוּ אָרוֹר oru aror [curse a curse]. In 5:22 the hooves of Sisera's horses הָלְמוּ halemu [hammer (strike)] the ground, and in 5:26 Jael takes a הַלְמוּת halmut [hammer] to kill Sisera.

Formulaic passages

The theophany is a highly significant part of the poem, as it dramatically shows the role of the Lord in the battle. The theophany in Judg 5:4–5 has formulaic features very similar to the theophany in Ps 68:8–9.[66] It may be that the composer of Ps 68 was alluding to the poem of Deborah, but it is not directly quoted.

The second passage containing formulaic features in the poem of Deborah is the tribal list in verses 14–18, which can be compared to Gen 49 and Deut 33.[67] The general form is similar, but the lists vary and are not dependent on each other.

Parataxis

Parataxis is the placing side-by-side of words, images, or scenes without connectors that are dissimilar or juxtaposing. The lack of links between the concepts causes the listeners to reflect, use their imagination to fill the gaps, and see a unity that exists behind the whole.[68] Syntaxis (writing using complex syntax) tends to be used to express logical and orderly relationships, whereas parataxis is dramatic. An example of paratactic style can be seen in verse 3:

שִׁמְעוּ מְלָכִים
הַאֲזִינוּ רֹזְנִים

Shim'u melachim
ha'azinu rozenim

Hear, O kings;
Listen, O rulers.

---

66. Coogan, "Structural and Literary," 161.
67. Coogan, "Structural and Literary," 162.
68. Hauser, "Judges 5," 26.

Here, the kings suddenly appear on the scene of the poem and are told to listen as praise is sung to the Lord. The kings are the defeated Canaanites, defeated in the battle by the Lord. The songwriter hints already at the final defeat of the enemy in verse 3 but does so implicitly. The center of attention then moves rapidly to the I who sings to the Lord.

אָנֹכִי לַיהוָה אָנֹכִי אָשִׁירָה
אֲזַמֵּר לַיהוָה אֱלֹהֵי יִשְׂרָאֵל

Anochi ladonai anochi ashirah
azammer ladonai elohei yisra'el

The repeated emphasis on the I who sings in victory, who is in close relationship to the Lord, is at the expense of and in contrast to the kings who have to listen to this victory song.[69] This verse leads into a dramatic change of scene in verses 4–6, which introduces the Lord in a cosmic theophany, with a description of the Lord's great might. The verse is highly repetitive, only using five words, and the paratactic style uses these few words to convey many images.

With an abrupt change from verse 23, Jael and her blessing are introduced. Verses 24–27 also contain many examples of parataxis. The reason for the introduction of Jael is not immediately apparent to the reader, and Sisera's name is not yet mentioned. Jael even appears hospitable to the enemy, until she reaches for the tent peg and hammer. The beginning of verse 25 also is staccato and terse, as Sisera blurts out a few words, desperate for water:

מַיִם שָׁאַל חָלָב נָתָנָה

Mayim sha'al chalav natanah
Water he asked, milk she gave

Finally, again there is a quick transition from the murder of Sisera to the final scene, where Sisera's mother is waiting for him to return.[70] This final section allows the audience to reflect on the brutal murder of Sisera, using dramatic irony to describe the Canaanite ladies waiting for war booty, while the audience knows that the enemy is already defeated and that the Lord is the victor. In his paratactic style the narrator leaves gaps for the audience to fill in. In verse 28, the narrator does not immediately identify Sisera's mother, but then the audience realizes who the worried and fearful mother is.

---

69. Hauser, "Judges 5," 30.
70. Hauser, "Judges 5," 38.

CONCLUSION

Although there is no clearly chronological structure in the Song of Deborah, there is unity.[71] The poem is constructed from snapshots of scenes of the battle, the killing of Sisera, and the waiting in vain of Sisera's mother, which are presented in intensified detail. The death scene is vivid and emotional. The poem ends with a dramatic contrast of the two women, and the contrast of a curse for the Lord's enemies and a blessing for those who love him. There are no metaphors or similes, but instead there is dynamic repetition, where one emphatic word or descriptive phrase is repeated, either unchanged or slightly altered, to lend emphasis and passion.

Such a dramatic and passionate victory poem provided the ideal text for the Altai translation team to design a performance-based oral Bible translation in Southern Altai in the light of their traditional epics. The contrast between the portrayal of the same story in prose narrative form in chapter 4 and in poetic narrative form in chapter 5 provides an interesting case study for oral translation and performance.

Rushing considers the Song of Deborah as an example of the genre of heroic poetry, a song designed for marginalized peoples, highlighting the heroic role of women and tent-dwelling peasants in the history of ancient Israel.[72] There is one Altai epic poem that features a female warrior heroine, called Ochy-Bala, who possesses unusual beauty and skill and who defeats the enemy Ak-D'alaa. Following the above analysis of the main features of the original oral rhetorical-literary features of this poem in Hebrew, the next step is to consider how different features of the Altai language can serve some of these same functions. This will be done in chapter 7, where I will describe the process of employing the genre of Altai epic poetry to adapt this biblical poem to the Altai culture and language.

---

71. Gerleman, "Song of Deborah," 171–75.
72. Rushing, "God's Women," 12–13.

6

The Poetic Features of Psalms 1, 100, and 133 for Oral Translation and Performance

INTRODUCTION

In this chapter I identify and discuss the features of orality in Pss 1, 100, and 133. The chapter begins with comments on the orality of the psalms and then for each psalm discusses its date of composition and the major themes and message of the text. This is followed by a reflection on the biblical genre of the passage and the unity of the passage. In Appendices 5–10 are the story charts for these passages, accompanied by tables showing the oral and performance features of these passages that I have prepared for the oral translation team and for the use of other oral Bible translation teams.

ORALITY OF THE PSALMS

Gunkel was one of the first scholars to develop methods of "Form Criticism," basing his approach in part on the oral use of the psalms and their function within society as laments, expressions of thanksgiving, psalms of praise, etc.[1] Brueggemann states that all psalms were poetry, often joined

---

1. Gunkel, "Einleitung."

with music, and designed to be performed.² They were sung first and written later.

PSALM 1

Theme of the psalm

Schaefer calls this psalm "Choice between two ways."³ The one who is following the Lord's commandments is the ideal and most respected member of the community. Those who disobey these directives are destroyed and lose their connection to the source of life.

The psalm can be summarized as follows:

- The one who rejects the wicked (verse 1)
- And delights in the Lord (verse 2)
- Will succeed (verse 3).
- But the wicked will not last (verse 4):
- They will be rejected by the righteous (verse 5)
- And disregarded by God himself (verse 6).

The purpose of the psalm is to give the audience the desire to study the Torah.⁴ Anderson calls this psalm a "Torah Psalm."⁵ The primary objective is to incite the audience to contemplate the qualities of those worthy of admiration, igniting a desire within them to be admired and establishing a connection between this admiration and the study of the Torah.⁶ Dedication to the Torah leads to boundless prosperity, symbolized by a flourishing and majestic king (represented by a tree), which is highly desirable, healthy, and aesthetically pleasing. This stands in stark contrast to the destiny of the wicked. Those who reject the Torah not only become worthless and futile like discarded chaff but also face condemnation from God and expulsion from the righteous community. Ultimately, there is no court of appeal. God safeguards the righteous, while the wicked are left to their own fate.

The psalm investigates the question of who truly experiences happiness. In the book of Malachi, which canonically immediately precedes the

---

2. Brueggemann, "Psalms," 124.
3. Schaefer, *Psalms*, 1.
4. Robar, "Discourse."
5. Anderson, *Out of the Depths*, 152.
6. Robar, "Discourse."

Psalms in the Hebrew Bible, one of the prominent themes is the seeming futility of serving God, as the wicked appear to thrive and are even referred to as "happy" (Mal 3:14, 15). However, Ps 1 challenges this assumption by asserting that it is not the wicked who are truly fortunate and happy. The psalm aims to convince its audience that the key to success lies in wholeheartedly following the Lord's teachings. The truly happy and admirable individual is one who resembles a royal figure, wholeheartedly devoted to the Lord. True happiness is found in embracing the Lord's instruction rather than rejecting it, for it is the Lord himself who directs each path towards its ultimate destination.

Genre of the psalm

Psalms were a common poetic genre throughout the ancient Near East.[7] Psalm 1, as an introductory psalm, is thought to be characteristic of the psalms in general. The introductory formula אַשְׁרֵי *ashrei* [happy or fortunate] occurs in other psalms (2:12, 32:1, 33:12, 41:2), as does its praise of God's teaching תּוֹרָה *Torah*, and the idea that the wicked will receive punishment, and the righteous, success. It is a wisdom psalm, describing the consequences of the good and evil life.

Psalm 1 as a unit

There is some evidence, in both the early Jewish and Christian traditions, to suggest that Ps 1 was originally joined to Ps 2, and together they were considered to be the first psalm of the book of Psalms.[8] The first verse of Ps 1 אַשְׁרֵי־הָאִישׁ *ashrei-ha'ish* [happy is the one] and the last verse of Ps 2 אַשְׁרֵי כָּל־חוֹסֵי בוֹ *Rei kol-chosei vo* [happy are all who take refuge in him] form an *inclusio*, which lends support to the Jewish tradition that they were originally considered a literary unit. According to Codex Bezae, Paul, speaking in the synagogue at Pisidian Antioch in Acts 13:33, quotes from Ps 2:7 but refers to it as "the first psalm," suggesting that the early Christians also considered Pss 1 and 2 as one unit.[9] Seow concludes that the two psalms were not composed as one piece, but they were probably intentionally combined at some point to serve as an introduction to the psalter. In this research, Ps 1 has been translated and performed as an independent unit.

---

7. Alter, *Art of Biblical Poetry*, 142.
8. Craigie, *Psalms 1–15*, 59.
9. Seow, "Exquisitely Poetic," 292.

Structural analysis of Psalm 1

Alter describes the compact antithetical structure of Ps 1, based on the contrast between the righteous and the wicked.[10] There are four logical points of transition introduced by כִּי אִם *ki im* [but] (verse 2), לֹא־כֵן *lo-chen* [not so] (verse 4), כִּי אִם *ki im* [nor] (verse 4b), and עַל־כֵּן *al-chen* [therefore] (verse 5). The psalm itself is like an equation where the righteous man will not do certain things but instead does the opposite, and the fate of the wicked is then contrasted to the fate of the righteous. The final verse is presented as a generalizing summary of retributive justice. An envelope structure encloses the poem, with the end echoing the beginning. The poem begins with the wicked and sinners and concludes with them. Alter notes that this poetic structure presents the message of the psalm as if it is "built into the structure of reality."[11]

Bratcher and Rayburn divide the psalm into two sections.[12] The first section (verses 1–3) describes the truly righteous person, stating what he refuses to do (verse 1), what he does (verse 2), and then describing him as resembling a healthy tree (verse 3). The second section (verses 4–6) compares the evil person to chaff, which is blown away by the wind. Such a person will not share the future happiness of the righteous but will instead be destined to destruction. Craigie finds the following structure: the solid foundation of the righteous (1:1–3), the impermanence of the wicked (1:4–5), and a contrast of the righteous and the wicked (verse 6).[13] He points out a chiasm in the first two sections: A (verses 1–2), B (verse 3), B' (verse 4) and A' (verse 5). Verse 6, using antithetical parallelism to contrast the righteous and the wicked, has its own internal chiastic structure.

Poetic features

Psalm 1 exhibits the following prominent oral-poetic features: parallelism, chiasm, *inclusio*, contrast, assonance, repetition, ambiguity, sound-play, and metaphors or imagery.

Parallelism is used in verses 1, 2, 4, 5, and 6. In verse 1 there are three parallel lines, which is an exception to the normal two. There is a progression in verse 1 from more movement to less, and progression from the generic wicked to the pattern of actions as a sinner and finally to a mocker

---

10. Alter, *Art of Biblical Poetry*, 143.
11. Alter, *Art of Biblical Poetry*, 143.
12. Bratcher and Rayburn, *Handbook*.
13. Craigie, "Parallel Word," 59.

The Poetic Features of Psalms 1, 100, and 133 for Oral Translation and Performance   139

who actively despises others. The second verse has two positive synthetically parallel lines, where the second line develops the thought of the first. Verse 4 is an example of emblematic parallelism, where the second line repeats as a simile the thought of the first line. Verse 5 contains synonymous parallelism. Verse 6 shows antithetical parallelism, in which the second line of the couplet expresses a contrasting idea to the first.

If אַשְׁרֵי־הָאִישׁ אֲשֶׁר *ashrei-ha'ish asher* is taken as the title of Ps 1 or even of the entire Psalter, then the poem begins with a triplet:[14]

לֹא הָלַךְ בַּעֲצַת רְשָׁעִים
וּבְדֶרֶךְ חַטָּאִים לֹא עָמָד
וּבְמוֹשַׁב לֵצִים לֹא יָשָׁב

*Lo halach ba'atzat resha'im
uvederech chatta'im lo amad
uvemoshav letzim lo yashav*

Verse 3 contains a poetic quatrain, which is more unusual in Hebrew poetry, pointing here to the profusion of the growth of the tree:[15]

וְהָיָה כְּעֵץ שָׁתוּל עַל־פַּלְגֵי מָיִם
אֲשֶׁר פִּרְיוֹ ׀ יִתֵּן בְּעִתּוֹ
וְעָלֵהוּ לֹא־יִבּוֹל
וְכֹל אֲשֶׁר־יַעֲשֶׂה יַצְלִיחַ

*Vehayah ke'etz shatul al-palgei mayim
asher piryov yitten be'ittv o
ve'alehu lo-yibbol
vechol asher-ya'aseh yatzliach*

One possible structure of Ps 1 sees verses 1–5 in the form of a chiasm, ABB'A'. A is verses 1–2, B is verse 3, B' is verse 4, and A' is verse 5. This inner chiasm in the first two parts of the psalms is then summarized in verse 6, which also has an internal chiastic structure. An inner chiasm could also be seen in verses 5 and 6, where the outer frame is the wicked, and the righteous appears twice in the middle.[16]

The poem begins and ends with an *inclusio* describing the wicked in verses 1 and 6. Also, the last word of the poem תֹּאבֵד *toved* [perishes] begins with the last letter of the Hebrew alphabet, *tav*, and the first word of the poem אַשְׁרֵי *ashrei* [happy] begin with the first letter of the alphabet, *aleph*.[17]

---

14. Seow, "Exquisitely Poetic," 280.
15. Seow, "Exquisitely Poetic," 284.
16. Craigie, *Psalms 1–15*, 59.
17. Seow, "Exquisitely Poetic", 289.

This forms a basic acrostic or letter-*inclusio* around the psalm. This may suggest totality or comprehensiveness, indicating that the psalms present all that the blessed person needs for living life in God's way.[18]

Psalm 1 is based on contrast. The happy individual is contrasted with the evildoers, the sinners, and the mockers. The sounds are reversed in אַשְׁרֵי *ashrei* and רָשָׁע *rasha*, indicating that the *happy* and the *wicked* are complete opposites and their paths head in the opposite directions.[19] In the first half, the wicked are in the plural but the man of faith is an individual. He is the one solid tree among many unrighteous. These contrasts are sharpened by the use of the grammatical markers at the beginning of verses 2a, 4a, 4b, and 5a.

The first three words of Ps 1 exhibit assonance אַשְׁרֵי־הָאִישׁ אֲשֶׁר *ashrei-ha'ish asher*.

There is repetition of the word תּוֹרָה *Torah* in verse 2, which corresponds with how the person is meditating continually on God's instructions.

There is probably an instance of deliberate poetic ambiguity in verse 3d, where the subject of the verb יַעֲשֶׂה *ya'aseh he does* could be the tree or the man, and likely both.

As is common in Hebrew poetry, there is ellipsis in verse 5, where the verb in the first line acts as the verb in both lines of the couplet.

Sound play is used to create a connection between בַּעֲצַת רְשָׁעִים *ba'atzat resha'im* [the counsel of wicked people] and בַּעֲדַת צַדִּיקִים *ba'adat tzaddikim* [the congregation of righteous people]. The righteous are to reject the counsel of the wicked, and the wicked are to be rejected from the congregation of the righteous. The sound play hints that these are the only two options in life.

Psalm 1 employs various metaphors and imagery, including the journey, the tree, winnowing, and the judgment court. However, the journey stands out as the primary controlling metaphor throughout the poem. Even though the journey is explicitly mentioned only in verses 1 and 6, it permeates the entire psalm as the dominant image.[20] It is demonstrated by the use of the word דֶּרֶךְ *derech* [way] (1a, 6a, 6b) three times, and the reference to walking (1a).[21] אַשְׁרֵי *ashrei* is often associated with walking (Pss 89:16; 119:1; 128:1; Prov 20:7) and with a journey (Pss 84:6; 119:1; 128:1; Prov 8:32). The concept of a path or a journey symbolically signifies an individual's way

---

18. Anderson, *Out of the Depths*, 94.
19. Scriptura, "Psalm 1."
20. Scriptura, "Psalm 1."
21. Seow, "Exquisitely Poetic," 279.

of life, their demeanor, actions, and decisions.[22] Each journey commences and progresses with guidance. Also, in verse 3, the tree or the man succeeds in all it does. This same word צָלַח *tzalach* can refer to the success of journeys (Gen 24) as well as of plants (Eze 17). Another word with multiple significance is תֹּאבֵד *toved*, meaning both *perish* and *become lost*, as in losing one's way on a journey. The way of the wicked either leads nowhere or ends in a dead end. Also, the opening word אַשְׁרֵי *ashrei* [happy] both looks and sounds like the word אֲשׁוּרָי *ashurai* [footsteps]. Finally, the relative particle אֲשֶׁר *asher* is usually absent in poetry, but it is conspicuously repeated throughout this psalm, sounding like the word for footstep.

The metaphor of the tree illustrates that just as a tree always relies on its water source, people always require the guidance of the Lord. Dedication to the Lord is enough to bring about success and respect. The depiction of the judgment court aligns with the winnowing metaphor and creates its own metaphor for God's justice.

Formulaic passages

The Hebrew word אַשְׁרֵי *ashrei* at the start of Ps 1 is a formulaic beginning, introducing the idea of honor, and marking out the one whom society honors or aspires to be like. Psalms 30, 40, and 112 also begin in this same formulaic way. The verb is used in reference to the testimony of one's standing in society, for example in Job 29:11.[23] It does not guarantee blessing or joy but rather suggests that an individual is deserving of commendation and praise.

PSALM 100

Theme of the psalm

Psalm 100 is a joyous call for celebration, inviting all the nations of the world to join in Israel's faith and to enter into God's presence and to share in Israel's witness to God's character. This universal psalm declares that the Lord, and no other, is God.[24] Anderson calls this psalm "A Hymn to the God who Created and Chose Israel."[25]

22. Scriptura, "Psalm 1."
23. Seow, "Exquisitely Poetic," 278.
24. DeClaissé-Walford et al., *Commentary on Psalms*, 734.
25. Anderson, *Out of the Depths*, 102.

Genre of the psalm

Psalm 100 is a praise psalm. These typically have a three-part structure: an opening praise (a call to praise and sometimes a meditation on praise), a reason for praise (the cause for praise often introduced by כִּי *ki* [for or because]), and a concluding call to praise.[26] Psalm 100 is מִזְמוֹר לְתוֹדָה *mizmor letodah* [a song for giving grateful praise]. There are two meanings to the biblical word תּוֹדָה *todah* [praise] or [thanksgiving]. According to Koehler et al., מִזְמוֹר לְתוֹדָה *mizmor letodah* is a title which can either mean a *psalm for a sacrifice of thanksgiving* or a *psalm for the offering of thanks*.[27] The second meaning is probably preferable because of verse 4, where תּוֹדָה *todah* means *song of thanksgiving*. Wendland places Ps 100 in his category of psalms of thanksgiving.[28] These psalms all contain some variation of the word *thank* or a reference to thanksgiving, and, as in the case of Ps 100, they often overlap with psalms of praise.

It may be that such a psalm was accompanied by the thanksgiving offering in Lev 7:12. Tate calls Ps 100 a hymn.[29] Gunkel proposed that this hymn may have been sung on the second day of a pilgrimage festival during the entrance into the sanctuary.[30] Kraus agrees that this was probably an "entrance hymn for a celebration of thanksgiving."[31]

Psalm 100 as a unit

Segal suggests that this psalm was intended to conclude the group of psalms Pss 95–100.[32] The term תּוֹדָה *todah* [thanksgiving] could be a theme for this group of psalms, appearing first in Ps 95:2. Psalm 100 draws on key terms from Ps 95 such as *thanksgiving*, *bless*, and *come*, and indeed from all the psalms in this set. The similarity of 95:7 and 100:3 with the shepherd theme shows the connection with Pss 95 and 100.[33] Psalm 100:1a is identical to 98:4a.

---

26. Salisbury, "Praise Psalms."
27. Koehler et al., *Hebrew*, 1695.
28. Wendland, *Analyzing the Psalms*, 32–60.
29. Tate, *Psalms 51–100*, 534.
30. Gunkel, *Introduction to Psalms*, 42, 45.
31. Kraus, *Psalms 60–150*, 274.
32. Segal, *New Psalm*, loc. 9517.
33. Tate, *Psalms 51–100*, 535.

Zenger and Hossfeld argue that Ps 100 is the climax for the group of psalms from 93–100 around the theme "The Lord is king."[34] Although the term *king* does not appear in Ps 100, the psalm uses royal terminology and theology throughout. Boerger argues that it could be a "partner psalm to the Royal Cycle providing unity across that boundary," referring to Pss 95–100.[35] Also, in Ps 100 there are five statements from Pss 93–100 that are repeated with only slight changes. Zenger and Hossfeld go on to suggest that because these statements are only in Pss 93, 95, 96, and 98, Ps 100 was originally intended to be the concluding psalm of a collection made up of these *The Lord is king* psalms.[36] According to this theory, Pss 94, 97, and 99 were inserted later. Howard says, "The crescendo of praise that has been building since Psalm 93 reaches a climax in Psalm 100."[37] Futato agrees that Ps 100 concludes a celebration of the kingship of the Lord.[38]

Structural analysis of Psalm 100

The structure of the poem

Brueggemann divides the psalm into two parts, each of which he states could stand alone (verses 1–3 and 4–5).[39] Salisbury also suggests a structure in which the psalm has two stanzas, each with two strophes. Stanza 1 (verses 1–3) gives a call to praise (verses 1–2) and reasons to praise (verse 3).[40] According to Brueggemann, this is a summons to reorient life away from confidence in oneself and back to trusting in the Lord.[41] Stanza 2 (verses 4–5) gives a call to praise in verse 4, and verse 5 gives the reasons to praise. Salisbury argues that although verse 3 begins with an imperative, which normally signals a call to praise, here the content is describing the attributes of God, and so it should be interpreted as a reason to praise.[42] There is a clear break before verse 4 and the verse starts with an imperative. Verse 5 gives a final reason to praise indicated by כִּי *ki*.

---

34. Zenger and Hossfeld, *Commentary*, 494.
35. Boerger, "POET Psalms," 23.
36. Zenger and Hossfeld, *Commentary*, 495.
37. Howard, *Structure*, 180.
38. Futato, *Cornerstone Biblical Commentary*, 319.
39. Brueggemann, "Psalm 100," 1.
40. Salisbury, "Praise Psalms."
41. Brueggemann, "Psalm 100," 65.
42. Salisbury, "Praise Psalms."

Segal argues that the middle verse (verse 3—*Know that the Lord is God, He has made us, and we are his, We are his people and the sheep of his pasture*) is the physical and semantic center of the psalm, indicating that the basis of thanksgiving is the righteous person's understanding that he or she is in a living relationship with God.[43] The central imperative of the seven imperatives in the psalm, דְּעוּ *de'u* [know], is set between two uses of the verb בֹּאוּ *bo'u* [come]. In the exact physical center of the psalm is the Hebrew word עַמּוֹ *ammo* [his people], with twenty words in Hebrew before and after.[44] The psalm begins with *all the earth* and moves onto the more specific concentration of God's people. DeClaissé-Walford et al. agree that the psalm is centered on the middle imperative clause דְּעוּ כִּי־יְהוָה הוּא אֱלֹהִים *de'u ki-adonai hu elohim* [Know that the Lord is God], declaring that there is one universal Lord.[45]

Bratcher and Reyburn propose that verses 1–3 may have been sung by pilgrims as they approached the temple, while verses 4–5 were sung by the choir inside the temple.[46] In this view the psalm may have been a processional hymn used in corporate worship.[47] Amzallag suggests that תּוֹדָה *todah* in the title of Ps 100 was a musical indication for an antiphonal performance. He speculates that verse 5 could have been sung as a refrain after each of the verses 1–4 or that the text of the song divides into two parts, with each part sung by a different voice.[48] In the latter case, verse 5 would belong to the second voice.

Oral-Poetic Features

Psalm 100 has the following prominent oral-poetic features: parallelism, *inclusio*, repetition, metonymy, ellipsis, the arrangement of imperatives, and metaphors or imagery.

Verse 5 contains an example of synonymous parallelism:

לְעוֹלָם חַסְדּוֹ
וְעַד־דֹּר וָדֹר אֱמוּנָתוֹ

Le'olam chasdv o
ve'ad-dor vador emunato

43. Segal, *New Psalm*, 9477.
44. Howard, *Structure*, 96.
45. DeClaissé-Walford et al., *Commentary on Psalms*, 735.
46. Bratcher and Reyburn, *Handbook*.
47. Amzallag, "Meaning of Todah," 535.
48. Amzallag, "Meaning of Todah," 538.

His loyal love forever,
His faithfulness until generation to generation.

Segal suggests that the term תּוֹדָה *todah* [thanksgiving] could be as an *inclusio* for this group of psalms (95–100), appearing first in Ps 95:2.[49]

There are two repetitions of key words in the psalm, which are תּוֹדָה *todah* [thanksgiving] and בֹּאוּ *bo'u* [come], though תּוֹדָה *todah* [thanksgiving] occurs the first time in the superscription.

Verse 1 starts with a call to praise:

הָרִיעוּ לַיהוָה כָּל־הָאָרֶץ

ari'u ladonai kol-ha'aretz

Shout to the LORD all the earth!

All the earth here means *all the inhabitants of the earth* and is therefore a metonymy.

As is common in Hebrew poetry, there is ellipsis in verse 4 of the verb בֹּאוּ *bo'u* [come]:

בֹּאוּ שְׁעָרָיו ׀ בְּתוֹדָה
חֲצֵרֹתָיו בִּתְהִלָּה

bo'u she'araiv betodah chatzerotav bithillah

Enter his gates with thanksgiving,
His courts with praise.

There are seven imperatives in total in this poem:[50]

וְעִירָה *hari'u*—shout

וְדִבְעוּ *ivdu*—serve/worship

וּבֹאוּ *bo'u*—come/enter (verse 2 and 4)

וְדְעוּ *de'u*—know

וְהוֹדוּ *hodu*—give thanks

וּבָרְכוּ *barachu*—bless

The fourth imperative is in the very center of the poem. In the last sentence the psalmist gives the reason for the listener to obey all these imperatives: the Lord's loyal love combined with his faithfulness.

The psalm contains the metaphor that God's people are his sheep and therefore he is their shepherd, taking care of his people. צֹאן מַרְעִיתוֹ *tzon*

49. Segal, *New Psalm*, 9518.
50. Segal, *New Psalm*, 9468.

mar'ito [sheep of his pasture] is a Hebrew idiom meaning that the Lord personally pastures his sheep, not delegating this role to anyone else. Israel is shepherded by the Lord.[51]

PSALM 133

Theme of the psalm

This is a psalm about togetherness and unity, depicting the people of God coming together to worship him. Armstrong comments that the theme expressed as *living together in unity* is a blessing that comes from God.[52] This sets God's people apart for him, invigorating them to make them more fruitful and bringing blessing of the most enjoyable and abundant kind.[53] Cousins sees the key point of the psalm as being "communal life is a good thing," as expressed in the opening line.[54] She also comments that the whole poem is addressed to an audience as a third-person commentary, with no change in the discourse direction. Schaefer titles this psalm "Everlasting Life for a Blessed Community."[55] Alter describes this poem as an "idyll" commemorating life in harmony and unity in a fruitful land.[56] Anderson calls this psalm a "Wisdom Psalm."[57] It celebrates both family and community.[58]

Salisbury comments that through this psalm, King David is promoting Zion as the place where God dwells in order to centralize the worship of Israel and to avoid the worship of false gods.[59] David's goal was to unite all twelve tribes centralized around Jerusalem. He is giving a vision for the future for his people, preparing for the building of the temple. This is one of four pilgrimage songs that David wrote for the people of God to sing on their way to Jerusalem.

---

51. DeClaissé-Walford et al., *Commentary on Psalms*, 737.
52. Armstrong, "Psalms Dwelling", 502.
53. Salisbury, "Translating and Performing."
54. Cousins, "Pilgrim Theology," 340.
55. Schaefer, *Psalms*, 315.
56. Alter, *Hebrew Bible*, 5588.
57. Anderson, *Out of the Depths*, 151.
58. Dickie, "Psalm 133," 1.
59. Salisbury, "Translating and Performing."

Genre of the psalm

שִׁיר הַמַּעֲלוֹת לְדָוִד

Shir hamma'alot ledavid
A Song of Ascents. Of David.

Psalm 133 is a wisdom psalm praising fellowship and harmony.[60] Kuntz also identifies Ps 133 as a wisdom psalm.[61] The title is *A Song of Ascents, by David*. מַעֲלָה *ma'alah* probably refers to the ascent up Mount Zion on which the temple was built. The occasion for the prayer is a pilgrimage, sung by pilgrims going to a festival in Jerusalem.[62] In conclusion, it was probably a song of Zion influenced by wisdom poetry.

Structural analysis of Psalm 133

The composer of the psalm uses poetry to persuade his listeners, creating a vision of the future in their minds.[63] The subject matter of the psalm, as well as the Hebrew poetic features in the text, indicate that the poem has three sections.[64] The middle section (verses 2–3a) is framed by verses 1 and 3b. Both of the frames contain strong exclamatory statements which have persuasive force, and the middle section contains figurative, colorful images. The outer frames are linked by the following features: the same final sounds, such as מַה *mah* [how] twice in verse 1 and צִוָּה *tzivvah* [he commands] and הַבְּרָכָה *habberachah* [blessing] in verse 3; the same sounds in the plural morpheme in verse 1 in נְעִים *na'im* [pleasant] and אַחִים *achim* [brothers], and at the end of verse 3 חַיִּים *chayyim* [life]; two positive word pairs both in verse 1 טוֹב *tov* [good] and נְעִים *na'im* [pleasant], and in verse 3 הַבְּרָכָה *habberachah* [blessing] and חַיִּים *chayyim* [life]; an intensifier in both verses, הִנֵּה *hinneh* [behold] in verse 1 and כִּי *ki* [indeed] in verse 3; the repetition of a word טוֹב *tov* [good] in verses 1 and 2a; and alliteration in verse 3 with צִיּוֹן *tziyyon* and צִוָּה *tzivvah*. There is also assonance between גַּם *gam* in verse 1 and עוֹלָם *olam* in verse 3b.

The psalm is short with frequent repetition, which attracts the attention of the listener in such a brief poem. The section in the middle (verses 2–3a) contains repetitions of sounds and of words, both of which bind it

---

60. Bratcher and Reyburn, *Handbook*, 1096.
61. Kuntz, "Reclaiming Biblical," 151.
62. Allen, *Psalms 101–150*, 278.
63. Salisbury, "Translating and Performing."
64. Dickie, "Psalm 133," 3.

together.⁶⁵ זָקָן *zekan* [beard] is repeated in verses 2a and 2b, כְּ *ka* [like] in verses 2a and 3a, and יֹרֵד עַל *yored al* [going down] is in verses 2a, 2b, and 3a. Verses 2b and 3a are linked by the final sounds in אַהֲרֹן *Aharon* [Aaron], חֶרְמוֹן *Chermon* [Hermon] and צִיּוֹן *Tziyyon* [Zion]. There is also a pun between כַּשֶּׁמֶן [like oil] in verse 2a and כִּי שָׁם [indeed there] in verse 3b.

The climax of the poem is in verse 3b, with the truth that where people are living in unity, God gives a blessing of life.⁶⁶ The poem can be described as a staircase leading to this climax. In every colon, apart from verse 3b, a word or phrase is repeated from the previous colon, which Berlin calls a "word-chain";⁶⁷ Doyle, an "extended parallel terrace";⁶⁸ and Tsumura, "sorites."⁶⁹ An example of this is טוֹב *tov* from verse 1, which is repeated in verse 2a; זָקָן *zekan* from verse 2a, repeated in verse 2b; and שֶׁיֹּרֵד עַל *sheyyored al* in verse 2b, repeated in verse 3a. However, there is no repetition from verse 3a to 3b.

Oral-poetic features

Psalm 133 has the following prominent oral-poetic features: ambiguity, *inclusio*, hyperbole, wordplay and phrase repetition, metonymy, puns, word-pairs, alliteration, assonance, and imagery, and metaphors.

There is possibly deliberate ambiguity in verse 2. Is it the beard or the oil that runs down onto Aaron's clothes? It is more likely that it is the continuation of the metaphor of the abundant oil. שָׁם *sham* [there] in verse 3 is also ambiguous in terms of its reference.

There may be an *inclusio* based on phonetic wordplay, giving a concentric structure, with אַחִים *achim* in verse 1 and חַיִּים *chayyim* near the end of verse 3.

This psalm is full of hyperbole, beginning with the twofold use of *how*, followed by *look* or *wow!* The two metaphors in the center of the poem, of the finest oil and bountiful dew, continue the hyperbolic emphasis found in the first verse. In verse 3 the verb צִוָּה *tzivvah commands* is hyperbolic, emphasizing the final statement.

The poem uses frequent wordplay and phrase repetition. The repetition of יֹרֵד *yored* [coming down; descending] three times implies that such

---

65. Dickie, "Psalm 133," 3.
66. Dickie, "Psalm 133," 3.
67. Berlin "On the Interpretation," 141.
68. Doyle, "Metaphora Interrupta," 14.
69. Tsumura, "Sorites," 416.

blessings, unity, and life for evermore come down from God above. There is also repetition of טוֹב tov, זָקֵן zeken, עַל al, and כְּ ka.

Leow argues that both oil and dew, when used individually, are stock metonyms referring to the Lord's blessings in Zion.[70]

There is a pun between כַּשֶּׁמֶן kashemen [like oil] in 2a and כִּי שָׁם ki sham [indeed there] in 3b.

The poem is made up of couplets, apart from a closing triplet in verse 3.[71] All the couplets, and the closing triplet, are enjambed (the meaning of one line runs over into the next).

There are two positive word pairs both in verse 1 טוֹב tov [good] and נָעִים na'im [pleasant], and in verse 3 הַבְּרָכָה habberachah [blessing] and חַיִּים chayyim [life].

There is alliteration in verse 3 צִיּוֹן tziyyon and צִוָּה tzivvah. Alliteration is also used in כַּשֶּׁמֶן kashemen [like oil] in 2a and כִּי שָׁם ki sham [indeed there] in 3b.

There are the same final vowel sounds in מַה mah [how], which occurs twice in verse 1, and צִוָּה tzivvah [he commands] and הַבְּרָכָה habberachah [blessing] in verse 3. There is also assonance between גַּם gam in verse 1 and עוֹלָם olam in 3b. Verses 2b and 3a are also linked by the final vowel sounds in אַהֲרֹן Aharon [Aaron], חֶרְמוֹן Chermon [Hermon], and צִיּוֹן Tziyyon [Zion].

There are the same sounds in the plural morpheme in verse 1 in נָעִים na'im pleasant and אַחִים achim brothers, and at the end of verse 3 חַיִּים chayyim life. There is an intensifier הִנֵּה hinneh behold in verse 1.

Psalm 133 includes geographical images and metaphors, highlighting downward movement.[72] In the opening line, the psalmist declares how good it is to be in community in physical closeness. The text invites the audience to consider their unity as a community, and perhaps even imagine other members of the community joining them. Although the focus is on the relationship of the community members to one another, the Lord's presence is in the background.[73] The geographical images can help the performer and audience imagine themselves within the land of Israel and under the Lord's blessing.[74]

There are two striking metaphors of unity in this psalm. Hebrew poetry typically has intensity, impact, and power but uses very few words.[75]

---

70. Leow, "Form and Experience," 194.
71. Dobbs-Allsopp, "Psalm 133," 8.
72. Cousins, "Pilgrim Theology," 342.
73. Cousins, "Pilgrim Theology," 343.
74. Cousins, "Pilgrim Theology," 344.
75. Salisbury, "Psalm 133."

Living together under the blessing of the Lord is compared to fine oil on the head (verse 2) and abundant dew on the mountain of Zion (verse 3a). Cousins remarks that these are unusual rather than conventional metaphors.[76] However, in context they would have been understood by the original audience.[77] Metaphors are especially useful when describing emotional states, since these may otherwise be unobservable.[78] The first metaphor evokes movement and abundance, as oil is seen pouring down the face and even further down the beard.[79] The second metaphor is also flowing liquid. Both a heavy dew in Jerusalem, such as the dew at Hermon, and the anointing of a high priest were rare occurrences, happening perhaps once in a lifetime.[80] Both the dew and the oil come down on the most fitting place. In the case of the oil this is the head of the high priest, who was the mediator of worship and blessing between people and God, symbolizing blessing coming down from God above. The fitting place for the dew is Zion, the place of pilgrimage, of worship, and of blessing. In both cases, the dew and the oil are the best in both quantity and quality. These images generate feelings of pleasure and abundance for the listener. In translation it may be necessary to turn the metaphor into a simile, but it is more powerful to keep the metaphor if possible.

Previous oral performances of the text

Dickie conducted workshops with three groups in South Africa using Ps 133, to see if the groups would perceive the psalm as relevant to them and to observe how they might choose to communicate the psalm's meaning to their peers.[81] The groups were a women's support group, a youth group, and a collection of performance artists from a local church. Dickie initially held a short session with each group, reading the psalm and discussing its structure, seeing artists' impressions of the poem and hearing songs based on the psalm, and thinking with the group about what living in harmony would look like for them. According to Dickie, it was determined that Ps 133 is adaptable to suit the various contexts of its listeners.[82] Moreover, the community in question had the ability to interpret the psalm's meaning in

---

76. Cousins, "Pilgrim Theology," 340.
77. Dickie, "Psalm 133," 8.
78. Macky, *Centrality*, 224–25.
79. Macky, *Centrality*, 341.
80. Salisbury, "Psalm 133."
81. Dickie, "Psalm 133," 1–2.
82. Dickie, "Psalm 133," 14.

relation to their own situations, thus establishing a sense of ownership over the psalm.

CONCLUSION

Many of the psalms were composed and transmitted orally, and there may not have even been a single original version but, instead, several oral alternatives. This chapter has analyzed the oral features of the chosen psalms, finding that they are ideally suited for oral translation as songs and performance and for enabling the community to determine its own context.

7

Altai Epics and *Ochy-Bala*

INTRODUCTION

After the presentation of the exegesis of the chosen biblical passages in chapters 5 and 6, I will now move to the research of the local genres in the Altai Republic. My focus is especially on Altai oral epics in the history and culture of the Altai people. This includes interviews with Altai throat singers and musicians and research into one particular Altai epic, *Ochy-Bala*. This research and these interviews helped the translation team decide which poetic features of the Altai epic poems can perform the same function as the features of orality in the biblical text.

THE ALTAI EPICS

The Altai Republic

The Republic of Altai in Siberia is an area of approximately 92,600 square kilometers located 500 kilometers south of Novosibirsk.[1] It borders China, Mongolia, and Kazakhstan. Historically, the region has been occupied by various nomadic groups and was colonized by Russians during the eighteenth century. Between 1918 and 1922, a civil war broke out between the Altaians and Bolsheviks; as a result, in June 1922 the Oyrot Autonomous Oblast was established. In June 1991 an additional milestone was achieved

---

1. Yagmur and Kroon, "Objective and Subjective," 244.

when the Gorno-Altai Soviet Socialist Republic was proclaimed, which subsequently led to the adoption of its current name, the "Altai Republic," in May 1992.

The Altai people are estimated to number approximately 76,000 and comprise six distinct groups: Telengit, Altai Kizhi, Tubular, Kumandin, Shor, and Chalkan. Of these, 55,000 (Telengit and Altai Kizhi) fluently speak the Turkic language of Southern Altai.[2] This language continues to be vibrant with great potential for further growth due to increased ethnic identity in the area. The Altai language is prominently used across various mediums such as art forms, media outlets, education settings, and everyday communication. In addition to this, the large majority of the Altai people are conversant in Russian, with the exception of a minority residing in more isolated villages.

Epics

The term *epic* has been long used the West, likely due to influence of the great works of Homer.[3] According to Aristotle, an epic is a long narrative which features the heroic deeds and adventures of legendary figures.[4] Bowra further defined an epic as "a narrative of some length that deals with events of grandeur and importance, coming from a life of action—especially violent action such as war."[5] Furthermore, Niles suggests as an alternative the Persian term *dastan*, which is used in many areas of Central Asia to describe lengthy oral narratives performed by professional singers.[6] Epic songs are found not only in the Altai region but have also been circulated across Asia for centuries, from Eastern Turkey, Mongolia, Siberia, to Northwest China.[7]

Altai folklore

The intense affection that the Altai people have for epic tales is evidence of their orality. These epics are part of their oral tradition and hold a great significance in their culture. Pegg emphasizes the importance of these

2. Yagmur and Kroon, "Objective and Subjective," 244.
3. Niles, "Introduction," 254–255.
4. Reichl, *Oral Epic*, 11.
5. Reichl, *Oral Epic*, 11.
6. Niles, "Introduction," 255.
7. Niles, "Introduction," 255.

stories, claiming that "heroic epics are vital to contemporary Altaian culture and identity."[8] Harvilahti and Kazagacheva refer to the Altai oral epic as "a mythical heroic epic."[9]

Wilhelm Radlov (1837–1918), considered the founder of Turkology and one of the earliest collectors of Altai folklore, published ten epic oral texts in St. Petersburg.[10] S. S. Surazakov (1925–80), another researcher whose work contributed greatly to understanding Altai epics, recorded the renowned *Maadai-Kara*, a song consisting of 7,738 verses which was published in bilingual form (Altai and Russian) by the Institute of World Literature of the Russian Academy of Sciences in 1973.[11] In addition, Surazakov created a twelve-volume series titled *Altai Heroes*, which features over eighty texts associated with these epics.[12]

As well as researching literature about the Altai epics, I conducted interviews with famous singers of the Altai epics and musicians in the Republic of Altai. The selection includes both younger and older performers, including one woman, all experienced in the telling of Altai epic poetry.

Moral values in Altai epics

Plueckahn suggests that performance of epic songs is associated with the mythology, customs, history, and lived experience of Mongolian Altai as well as their social, political, and musical identity.[13] Wood, in her research on Altai epics, demonstrates how Altai heroic epic poetry provides insight into the values held by this people group, including reverence for the heavens, collective unity with the land of Altai and its natural environment, emphasis on family as a valuable asset, peacefulness and tolerance, courage in liberating their homeland from oppression, hospitality to guests and assistance to others, a communal mindset, unique composition of beauty inspired by nature, and proficiency in art and music.[14]

Harvilahti posits that one of the primary objectives of an epic narrative is to bolster the self-esteem of the people and establish admiration for their history and culture.[15] The hero, as a sort of embodiment of his people, is

8. Pegg, "Re-sounding," 128.
9. Harvilahti and Kazagacheva, *Holy Mountain*, 77.
10. Radlov, *Obraztsy Narodnoy*.
11. Harvilahti, "Altai Oral Epic", 216.
12. Surazakov and Shinzhin, *Altai Baatyrlar*.
13. Plueckahn "Musical Sociality," 186.
14. Wood, "Mudrost Naroda", 10.
15. Harvilahti, "Epos," 45–46.

unconquerable. Even if he suffered defeat once, he is ultimately indomitable and will eventually return. Harvilahti believes that using epics in cultural life can have numerous beneficial impacts, particularly in reinforcing cultural and national identity. In a personal interview, Emil Terkishev describes the Altai epic as a heroic tale, the foundation of wisdom for the Altai people left by their ancestors.[16] In Altai he calls the epics *the gold peg* (a peg that holds a tent to the ground) that anchors the Altai people. Emil Terkishev and Daniel Danzheev compare the Altai epics to the Bible, saying that they contain prophecy for the Altai people.[17] Emil Terkishev sees his life's calling as helping revitalize the epic stories in Altai. He said, "One should live life as if one is part of an epic, and once one has understood the epics, one will live differently."[18]

Plots of the Altai epic

Harvilahti and Kazagacheva note that there have been multiple layers of influence on the content and imagery of the Altai epics.[19] The two greatest influences have been shamanist traditions and Altai hunting culture. Van Deusen confirms that there are numerous shamanic images in the epic tales, such as shape-changing and voyages to other worlds.[20] The themes of the Altai epic are timeless, addressing the ongoing battle between good and evil, light and darkness, truth and falsehood. The hero is endowed with magical abilities; his horse has the ability to see and understand everything; the hero's wife has prophetic powers; and young women know who they will marry before the event takes place. This hero often finds himself at war, defending his homeland, people, and love—wars against those who threaten Altai land and possessions, wars to win over prospective brides when there are too many suitors, and wars to reclaim thieved livestock. He consistently triumphs in these battles through miraculous acts. He ascends to the higher realm seeking counsel from deities, while descending into the underworld to combat its demonic forces.

The Altai warrior's faithful steed is his best friend, providing essential help and support. This is reflected in the fact that Ancient Turkic people would always bury a horse alongside their warriors. Gejin observes that no Mongolian epic exists without the presence of the horse; it is quite

16. Personal interview with Emil Terkishev, Jul. 2022.
17. Personal interview with Daniel Danzheev, Jul. 2022.
18. Personal interview with Emil Terkishev, Jul. 2022.
19. Harvilahti and Kazagacheva, *Holy Mountain*, 26.
20. Van Deusen, *Singing Story*, 94.

often a pivotal character possessing wisdom, magical powers, supernatural strength, and speed.[21] Moreover, the steed can transform into various animals to assist its owner in times of danger or even warn him of events yet to come. Thus, the importance of horses in this tradition cannot be overstated. They are indelible components of nomadic epics.

Throat singing

In the Republic of Altai, heroic epic tales are sung using a technique known as throat singing or overtone singing. This type of guttural singing enables singers to produce more than one pitch at a time by taking advantage of the resonance capacity of their vocal organs (lips, tongue, jaw, velum, and larynx). As Sul'gin notes, the Altai people employ such a tone that resembles "the buzzing of a flying beetle."[22] It is believed that this practice originated in southwestern Mongolia.

In the Altai Republic of southern Siberia, the native Altai people created their own type of throat singing called *kai*. The term for a storyteller in this tradition is *kaichy*, meaning "a kai person."[23] There are three different types of throat-singing styles in both the Republic of Tuva and the Republic of Altai: *köömey*, *sygyt*, and *karkyra*.[24] According to Van Deusen *köömey* resembles the sound of boiling porridge; *karkyra*, the wail of a mother camel who has lost her young; and *sygyt*, a whistling sound.[25] Nogon Shumarov describes the phenomenon of *kai* not as throat singing but as laryngeal singing.[26] For sung epics, the Altai singers use *karkyra*, the low sound of which Daniel Danzheev said reflects the Altai landscape setting with mountains and forest.[27] The Tuvans mostly sing *köömey* and *sygyt*, which have a higher frequency because they live in the steppe. Bair Turulanov described *karkyra* as having a very low-bass, rich, spiritual sound.[28] The sustained notes yield the overtone effect of *kai*. Bair Turulanov also commented that *karkyra* is connected to the lower world, *köömey* to the middle world (earth), and *sygyt* to the upper world. Nogon Shumarov also describes the recitative style of *kai* as chanting without the accompaniment of an instrument but also

21. Gejin, "Mongolian Oral," 335.
22. Sul'gin, "Ob Altajskom Krae," 459.
23. Pegg, "Re-sounding," 128.
24. Personal interview with Nogon Shumarov, Jun. 2022.
25. Van Deusen, *Singing Story*, 112.
26. Personal interview with Nogon Shumarov, Jun. 2022.
27. Personal interview with Daniel Danzheev, Jul. 2022.
28. Personal interview with Bair Turulanov, Jul. 2022.

agreed that the Altai epics are sung traditionally with the *topshur* (a small two-stringed lute) in the *karkyra* style.²⁹

Linguistic evidence suggests that the term *kai* was originally linked to shamanism and symbolized the spiritual might of the shaman's words.³⁰ In ritual performances, throat singing is essential, as it allows a *kaichy* to alter his state of consciousness, thereby allowing him to traverse through the three realms (the underworld, earth, and the upper world) and possibly even into parallel worlds. Moreover, it grants them access to "*kai*-time" or "epic space-time."³¹ *Kai* has been described as opening a door into the spiritual world. Bair Turulanov described his feelings when singing *kai* as pleasant, positive, and yielding satisfaction for the *kaichy*.³² In a personal interview, Emil Terkishev said that *kai* was the first sound heard when the world was created, and it is the sound of nature.³³ In a personal interview, Natalya Enchinova remembered that when she was seventeen years old, she went into the forest and heard the sound of *kai* in nature from the mountains and the rivers, and she still has this sound ringing in her ears.³⁴ Daniel Danzheev said that after living several years in the forest environment, he felt that the forest spirits were encouraging him to sing *kai*.³⁵ He also commented that when children are born and cry, they are singing a type of *kai* from a very early age.

The singer

A *kaichy* typically begins his or her training from a young age, submitting to several years of dedicated instruction.³⁶ Singers often have been exposed to epics since childhood, sons imitating their fathers, and some may go on to receive more formal instruction. In a personal interview with Natalya Enchinova, she remembers crying as she listened to her father singing *kai*.³⁷ She herself did not learn *kai* officially but just began singing at the age of forty. Bair Turulanov does not remember deliberately sitting down and

---

29. Personal interview with Nogon Shumarov, Jun. 2022.
30. Reichl, *Oral Epic*, 78.
31. Pegg, "Re-sounding," 129.
32. Personal interview with Bair Turulanov, Jul. 2022.
33. Personal interview with Emil Terkishev, Jul. 2022.
34. Personal interview with Natalya Enchinova, Jul. 2022.
35. Personal interview with Daniel Danzheev, Jul. 2022.
36. Reichl, *Oral Epic*, 28.
37. Personal interview with Natalya Enchinova, Jul. 2022.

learning but listened to his father and then attempted it himself.[38] He commented that *kai* is passed down through the family line through experience and practice. Nogon Shumarov is a professional actor, musician, and theatrical director.[39] He is a teacher of *kai* and initially founded a school of *kai* for children. He now teaches adults online, in his home and in person, and believes that anybody is capable of learning *kai*. Emil Terkishev said, "One does not become a *kaichy*, but one lives as one."[40] It is considered a destiny. A *kaichy* is a person of the people, and it is believed the people will recognize a real *kaichy*. Kidrash Shumarov said that someone who sings *kai* is not necessarily a *kaichy*.[41] A real *kaichy* knows traditions, sayings, and blessings and can perform at least one epic from start to finish. Daniel Danzheev agreed that a person who sings *kai* does not automatically become a *kaichy*. Instead, he said, a *kaichy* is someone who can tell an epic tale from the beginning to the end and is recognized by the people as a *kaichy*.[42]

A *kaichy* may be chosen by spirits and can be subject to punishment if errors are made during the epic performance. Emil Terkishev confirmed that there will be punishment from the spirits if a *kaichy* tries to change the structure of the story of the epic.[43] One time he was warned in a dream that he had made a mistake, and the spirits made him sweat repeatedly until he had played the whole epic again from the beginning to the end. However, Kidrash Shumarov, when consulted on this question, replied that he considers it incorrect that the spirits can punish a *kaichy* for making a mistake.[44] Nogon Shumarov reported that one epic singer told him that when the horse is galloping, no one can stop him.[45] The horse must come home, and the hero must finish his mission. This means that it is important to sing the whole epic tale from start to finish. If the epic singer sings only part of the epic during a concert or performance, then the epic singer is obliged to sing the remainder when he comes home, or the spirits will come and punish the singer. Nogon Shumarov also told a story of an epic singer who, after singing epics for seven years, had a vision of one of the heroes from one of the epics he was singing. The hero grabbed the epic singer and told him to sing. The

---

38. Personal interview with Bair Turulanov, Jul. 2022.
39. Personal interview with Nogon Shumarov, Jun. 2022.
40. Personal interview with Emil Terkishev, Jul. 2022.
41. Personal interview with Kidrash Shumarov, Jun. 2022.
42. Personal interview with Daniel Danzheev, Jul. 2022.
43. Personal interview with Emil Terkishev, Jul. 2022.
44. Personal interview with Kidrash Shumarov, Jun. 2022.
45. Personal interview with Nogon Shumarov, Jun. 2022.

hero said that if the singer made a mistake, he would suffocate him. The epic singer then sang the entire tale!

Nogon Shumarov confirmed that although the *kaichy* is not a shaman, he is spiritually stronger than a shaman because he can travel through all three worlds during the epic singing.[46] He may go into a trance during the epic and see all the characters and places in the epic in his vision. During the epic singing, some people from the audience have seen visions and some have experienced healing. Van Deusen comments that shamans and singers of epic tales have much in common, but the latter have more knowledge and are spiritually stronger.[47] Emil Terkishev also confirmed that a *kaichy* is not a shaman, commenting that it is said in Altai that if a *kaichy* wakes up, a shaman or prophet (*jarlikchi*) will not be needed.[48] However, Natalya Enchinova gave her opinion that normally a *kaichy* will be descended from a bloodline that originally included a shaman, and the two are inextricably linked.[49] Daniel Danzheev also commented that the *kaichy* is similar to a shaman, going into a trance and entering the world of the heroes.[50]

The Altai also have a performer of epics known as an *eelü-kaichy*. According to Pegg, the *eelü-kaichy* is referred to as an epic-teller "with spirit," and, chosen by spirits, possesses extrasensory abilities.[51] Pegg writes that Elbek Kalkin is the only surviving *eelü-kaichy* alive today, the son of Aleksei Kalkin (1925–98), now living in Yabogan, Ust'-Kan district.[52] The *eelü-kaichy* can be described as one who has a special contact to the spiritual world. Daniel Danzheev described the *eelü-kaichy* as one who knows the philosophy and the worldview of Altai, which he passes on to the people through the epic tales.[53]

Previously, it was taboo for women to sing *kai* in Altai.[54] Traditionally, the skill was passed on through the family line, from a grandfather to a son to a grandson. When a woman had her monthly period or was pregnant, it was considered physically dangerous for her to sing *kai*. Nogon Shumarov now takes female *kai* students in his *kai* school and says there are female *kai* singers in Altai who sing in the recitative style without the accompaniment

---

46. Personal interview with Nogon Shumarov, Jun. 2022.
47. Van Deusen, *Singing Story*, 92.
48. Personal interview with Emil Terkishev, Jul. 2022.
49. Personal interview with Natalya Enchinova, Jul. 2022.
50. Personal interview with Daniel Danzheev, Jul. 2022.
51. Pegg, "Re-Sounding," 129.
52. Pegg, "Re-Sounding," 129.
53. Personal interview with Daniel Danzheev, Jul. 2022.
54. Personal interview with Nogon Shumarov, Jun. 2022.

of the *topshur*. Emil Terkishev said that a woman can tell tales but cannot sing *kai*, as it is dangerous for her to have any connection to the master of the underworld, *Erlik*.[55] Natalya Enchinova calls herself a poetess rather than a *kaichy*.[56] She considers that a young woman who is able to give birth should not sing *kai*, but an older woman can.

The instrument

The *topshur*, a tiny, two-stringed lute with its nylon strings tuned in a fourth and the upper notes strung above the low note, is typically played to accompany throat singing. The horse's hide and stomach were traditionally used to make the sounding board and the strings, which later became the master-spirit or helper-spirit.[57] The instrument is endowed with a life force of its own, initially transforming into a horse on which the epic teller can ride. It can further adapt and take the form of various inanimate objects, such as a boat, throughout the course of the epic.

Lord entitled his 1960 study of South Slavic oral epic poetry *The Singer of Tales*, emphasizing the significance of the singer who often accompanies his melody with a musical instrument.[58] Epic poetry is an oral tradition that is experienced through hearing, and within its performance lies vocalization.[59] Its effectiveness relies on both the music and the poetry's use of sound. The reverberation from the *topshur* can impact those listening. As per Reichl, "Epic music forms an integral part of living performance, not merely as decoration but as a necessary factor to the communicative event."[60] Reichl notes that, in most epic traditions, melodies tend to be repetitive and composed with a simple monotonous structure.[61] This feature is particularly evident in Altai epic songs. Additionally, when playing the *topshur*, some performers imitate a horse's gallop during the narrative.

Plueckahn noted that epic songs in Mongolian Altai typically include a repeating, descending melody accompanied by a plucked accompaniment on the two-stringed *topshur*.[62] This tune is commonly repeated twice with some minor modifications, at which point the singer pauses to take a breath

---

55. Personal interview with Emil Terkishev, Jul. 2022.
56. Personal interview with Natalya Enchinova, Jul. 2022.
57. Pegg, "Re-Sounding," 130.
58. Reichl, "Singing of Tales," 1.
59. Bunn, "Time as Told," 576.
60. Reichl, *Singing the Past*, 26.
61. Reichl, "Singing of Tales," 2.
62. Plueckahn, "Musical Sociality," 191.

while continuing to strum the *topshur*. To signify the end of one verse and the start of another, two vocal sounds—*oii* and *ee*—are uttered.

Communal nature

In the performance of the Altai heroic epic, singers and performers share a special relationship as they are intertwined in this ceremonial occasion.[63] Participants of the audience are drawn into the performance and take part in the ritual, while the singer relies on his listeners. Bunn remarks that certain patterns, imagery, and poetic effects used by the epic singer not only aid him in remembering his poem but also influence those present, bridging generations and past experiences to evoke fond memories.[64] Daniel Danzheev commented that during the performance, deep emotions of melancholy and joy are called up from the audience.[65]

Reichl highlights that through an epic singing event, both the audience and the *kaichy* are able to enter a world of poetic and musical art.[66] Moreover, the performance affirms a shared cultural heritage between the two parties, as it features their language, traditions, poetry, and music, thus providing entertainment with a deeper purpose.

The occasion, location, and atmosphere

Typically, a designated time is set aside for storytelling, and the atmosphere of the audience may be joyful as it could be an occasion of celebration. This could take place when the seasons change or during the waxing moon.[67] Reichl confirms that historically epics in Central Asia were narrated in the evenings and late into the night. Reichl illustrates a presentation of epic tales among Central Asian populations occurring in a yurt.[68] The singer is placed in a position of honor, opposite to the entrance of the yurt, decorated by ornamental wall hangings and floor rugs. The most important participants of the crowd are seated close to the epic singer, a table filled with food covers the area, and the epic story is accompanied by dining. The performance

---

63. Reichl, *Routledge Revivals*, loc. 2285.
64. Bunn, "Time as Told," 575.
65. Personal interview with Daniel Danzheev, Jul. 2022.
66. Reichl, *Oral Epic*, 54.
67. Pegg, "Altai-Sayan."
68. Reichl, *Singing the Past*, 40.

transpires during evening hours and throughout nightfall after feasting begins.

Emil Terkishev described how in previous times the *kaichy* was invited to people's houses, where he would judge the atmosphere in the house and adjust his performance accordingly.[69] He would analyze any problem present and create in its place beauty and healing. Emil Terkishev said that something magic happens during a performance of *kai*, something that cannot be seen or felt, giving freedom to the person's spirit and opening his potential. The performer sings *kai* and enters the world of ancient times created by these tales. Natalya Enchinova said she has feelings of pride and happiness when she sings *kai*, and after she has finished, she feels pure and healed.[70] In her mind, she travels with the heroes on their journeys. Kidrash Shumarov related that in previous times before radio or television, people would gather from the valleys at the home of the *kaichy* to listen to him, bringing cheese, meat, or other gifts for him.[71] He recalled that often a *kaichy* lived alone and in his experience was lonely or even blind..

The Altai people are known to perform during the hunting season, often in the evening hours around the fire. Through song and storytelling, they attempt to soothe or distract the spirits of the animals they hope to hunt. Kidrash Shumarov confirmed that hunters would take a *kaichy* with them on the hunt, and he would be rewarded afterwards with meat from the hunt.[72]

Bolot Bairshev grew up in the village Kirlik near the region center Ust-Kan, the son of a mountain shepherd.[73] During the holidays he and his father helped care for the sheep. His mother and grandmother played the *shoor* (a recorder-type instrument made from reeds and bamboo), and his uncle played the *topshur* while he listened to them. In the late 1980s began a revival of ethno-music and culture, and Bairshev began to perform on the stage, having learned to play several Altai instruments and to sing *kai*. He does not call himself a *kaichy* but is able to play excerpts from several epics, including *Ochy-Bala*, and is a performer of the genre of *kai*. Bolot Bairshev was the *kaichy* for the 1991 ballet performance of *Ochy-Bala*, the epic that will be described later in this chapter. He describes himself as still learning *kai*. He says that *kai* was sung by his ancestors, who died and left this style of singing for the modern generation, and while the mountains of Altai stand

---

69. Personal interview with Emil Terkishev, Jul. 2022.
70. Personal interview with Natalya Enchinova, Jul. 2022.
71. Personal interview with Kidrash Shumarov, Jun. 2022.
72. Personal interview with Kidrash Shumarov, Jun. 2022.
73. Personal interview with Bolot Bairshev, Jun. 2022.

and guard, the river Katun is flowing, and while the fire is burning in the *ail* (a wooden hexagonal structure), the epic *kai* will continue. In order to perform the epic, Bolot Bairshev said that a special atmosphere is required during the evening, around an open fire, perhaps in an *ail*.

Harrison describes epic performances in the Republic of Tuva, which were conducted by roaming narrators.[74] These storytellers would stay at a nomadic camp for a given amount of time, reciting an epic over multiple nights following the conclusion of daily activities. This typically started around dinnertime when animals were led in and people began to settle down to rest. Niles notes that when these heroic poems are solely used for formal occasions like festivals, it is markedly distinct from their original setting within a domestic yurt.[75]

Schubert comments that, in addition to being poetry and art, heroic epics in Central Asia and the Altai region also had a ritualistic function.[76] Performing epics in a family home or yurt would have a positive impact on that family, protecting them against evil spirits by creating contact with the invisible world and the supernatural forces that rule that world.

Features of Altai epic poetry

Altai epic poetry is noted for its use of a number of narrative units, which can be thought of as highly patterned and formulaic "building blocks" with which the poet constructs his work.[77] In his analysis, Foley examines these kinds of narrative units and gives an inventory of constructions available to the poet, along with phrases, scenes, and story patterns that serve as conventional symbols for traditional meanings.[78] This style of composition is reminiscent of the South Slavic epic poetry studied in greater depth by Parry and Lord, in which typical scenes like the saddling of a horse vary within certain parameters from one performance to another.[79]

The presence of highly structured and formulaic diction in orally composed epic poetry can be explained by its mode of transmission. Generally, the start of an epic is formulaic, likely to emphasize its credibility through successive narration from one storyteller to another.

74. Harrison, "Tuvan Hero," 2.
75. Niles, "Introduction," 261.
76. Schubert, "Research About the Altayn," 2.
77. Reichl, *Routledge Revivals*, loc. 4204.
78. Foley, *Oral Tradition*, 109.
79. Foley, *Oral Tradition*, 111.

Parallelism is a hallmark of epic poetry; often the same idea presented in the first half of a parallel structure is echoed or varied in the second half.[80] In addition, Turkic epic oral poetry employs alliteration to create captivating patterns of sound and meaning. Other stylistic devices such as "summation," where multiple ideas are presented in list form, and hyperbole (e.g., exaggerations such as seven-headed monsters, a stock figure in Altai epics) are also frequently used.

Bunn also mentions onomatopoeia.[81] The cultural poetics of the Turkic peoples, including those of the Altai, are deeply connected to their environment and their land. This is evident in their herding and hunting activities, as well as in their nomadic way of life. All these things give rise to the soundscapes created by the approach of horses, wolves, sheep, wind, and other weather phenomena. In many cases, epic singers strive to capture such sounds through throat singing.

The narrative, words, sound, and music employed in this composition of poetry effectively captivate the audience, enveloping them in the grand narrative and transporting them to a bygone era. This evokes a sense of longing for memories, connections, and personal encounters. The epic singer does not merely convey information but creates a link between past and present for the audience's benefit, conveying wisdom from an ancient story applicable to modern times.[82]

The characters in these epics are widely accepted as cultural archetypes, exemplifying idealized behaviors and emotions.[83] Generally speaking, each figure has a distinct role to play, such as the hero, the opponent, the helper, and the heroine, with the last often being linked to the hero in some way—as his beloved, wife, bride, or sister. It is thought that older shamanistic elements serve as the foundation of Altai oral poetry. Heroes are frequently endowed with shamanistic abilities used against underworld adversaries; shape-shifting and other shamanistic phenomena can also be found, such as horses transforming into stars. The epic tales possess a predictable plotline, formulaic diction, and two-dimensional instead of complex characters.

---

80. Reichl, *Routledge Revivals*, loc. 4194.
81. Bunn, "Time as Told," 558.
82. Bunn, "Time as Told," 580.
83. Reichl, *Routledge Revivals*, loc. 3599.

Memorization or improvisation

Reichl referred to Turkic epic poetry as the "art of memory," highlighting its combination of consistent structure with occasional variation.[84] Foley, meanwhile, termed it an "immanent art."[85] Both Reichl and Foley recognized the oral epic tradition as one based on memorized structures that can be adapted in performance, as also noted by Harvilahti and Kazagacheva.[86]

Niles posits that more experienced and confident performers are capable of partly improvising each rendition of the epic.[87] Consequently, there is no single authentic version of these epics, and the variations that can be created through the imagination of singers are virtually endless. Much of the craftsmanship associated with epic singing and improvisation is honed through apprenticeship under master singers.[88]

The research conducted by Parry and Lord in the early 1960s suggested that Homer was a semiliterate master poet who displayed an impressive ability to combine multiple oral legends into epic poems such as *The Odyssey* and *The Iliad*.[89] They hypothesized that these classical texts must have initially been formed as oral compositions due to the works' many characteristics indicative of stories originally told and retold, rather than written by one person and documented immediately. In their field surveys in the Balkans, Parry and Lord noted resemblances between Homer's epic poems and verbal storytelling experiences in Yugoslavia. It has been found that oral epics often feature patterns, such as formulas and consistent themes, which can help the performer to remember and recite the epic with relative ease. Additionally, improvisation is an important element of these performances. Lord argues that a successful performance relies on the bard's ability to assemble building blocks into a poetic structure rather than simply relying on memorization.[90] According to Ong, who based his work on Parry and Lord's research, distinctive aspects of these epics, such as formulas, themes, vivid imagery, repetition, and larger-than-life characters, can act as tools for memory recall when it comes to reciting the poem.[91]

84. Reichl, *Routledge Revivals*, loc. 269.
85. Foley, *Singer of Tales*, 7–8.
86. Harvilahti and Kazagacheva, *Holy Mountain*, 13.
87. Niles, "Introduction," 256.
88. Reichl, *Routledge Revivals*, 261–270.
89. Parry, *Making*; Lord, *Singer*.
90. Lord, *Singer*, 4.
91. Ong, *Orality and Literacy*, 34.

Schubert argues in her article "An Ode to the Altai Mountains" that epic singers are not simply replicating each other's works but rather are able to bring their own interpretations and artistry to the ode through changes in content, style, and duration.[92] This idea is echoed by Bunn in her discussion of the well-known Kyrgyz epic *Manas*; she believes it would be unlikely to hear two identical versions of *Manas* due to its improvisatory nature.[93] Bunn refers to the poem as being "spun" around these themes and patterns rather than simply consisting of memorized segments, demonstrating their importance, dynamism, and creativity within each new context.[94] As Harvilahti and Kazagacheva put it, "The interplay between the more established, relatively static key-passages and constant, masterful variation is characteristic of a learned performer."[95]

Nogon Shumarov commented that when the epic singer is in a trance, he is able to change the text, improving the text each time.[96] This improvisation can be done only by the most talented epic singers. Emil Terkishev confirmed that every time he sings an epic, it is different, depending on the audience and what they are thinking and feeling.[97] The *kaichy* must listen to his heart. Kidrash Shumarov said that he had learned three different versions of the epic *Altai-Buchai*, but when he sings, he does it in his own way, taking the best from each version and combining them, leaving the main plot unchanged.[98]

The future of kai

Daniel Danzheev said that if *kai* is no longer sung in Altai, the people will no longer exist.[99] With his musical ensemble *Bai-Terek*, he is hoping to inspire the Altai people to live with an understanding of the Altai worldview. Bair Turulanov is involved in helping to revitalize *kai* among Altai young people and thinks that this genre will not disappear from the Altai culture.[100] However, Kidrash Shumarov commented that now there are very few real *kaichy*, nor are there many audiences who actually are prepared

92. Schubert, "Research About the Altayn," 5.
93. Bunn, "Time as Told," 574.
94. Bunn, "Time as Told," 575.
95. Harvilahti and Kazagacheva, *Holy Mountain*, 26.
96. Personal interview with Nogon Shumarov, Jun. 2022.
97. Personal interview with Emil Terkishev, Jul. 2022.
98. Personal interview with Kidrash Shumarov, Jun. 2022.
99. Personal interview with Daniel Danzheev, Jul. 2022.
100. Personal interview with Bair Turulanov, Jul. 2022.

to listen to an entire epic.[101] He recommended having competitions that encourage the young people in the Altai Republic to learn epics and sing them. Emil Terkishev said that a real *kaichy* will be able to create his own epic.[102] He has written his own modern epic, which he described as "given to me from above." He considers this necessary for the Altai people to help them understand the Altai worldview and to lead them into the future. He has performed his new epic twice in Altai, as well publishing it as a booklet, and it was accepted positively by the people.

Conclusion

The Altai oral epics were conducted as shared events, with the *kaichy* combining memorization and improvisation. The delivery of these epic narratives facilitated the sharing and reinforcement of moral values within Altai society. These epic stories showcase artistic elements such as alliteration, addition, repetition, parallelism, and hyperbole. The plot and structure are both predictable in nature. These features assist the *kai* singer in the memorization and the transmission of the texts. In recent years, the presence of *kai* singers in Altai has decreased; however, there is currently a revival of epic stories being performed by young throat singers. This revival appears to be gaining popularity, and it is clear that the epics remain an integral part of Altai culture and are highly significant for understanding its history and people.

    The Altai team decided together that the genre of Altai oral epics was the appropriate genre to use to perform Judg 4–5. One of the main Altai epic tales, *Ochy-Bala*, which is discussed below, is about the land and people of Altai being saved by a heroine warrior, Ochy-Bala, and in this way is similar to the story of Judg 4-5. Although there is a small minority among Altai Christians who consider that throat singing is inappropriate for Scripture material because of its connection to shamanism, overall, it seems that the genre of telling epic stories is culturally suitable for telling the story of Deborah, Jael, and Sisera, with the focus on the two female heroines saving the people of Israel. I analyze *Ochy-Bala* in the next section in order to identify the oral features typical of the Altai epics. Some of these oral features were then used to tell the epic story of Deborah and Jael.

---

    101. Personal interview with Kidrash Shumarov, Jun. 2022.
    102. Personal interview with Emil Terkishev, Jul. 2022.

OCHY-BALA

The epic

Ochy-Bala is one of the Altai heroic epic stories sung by Kalkin, a renowned epic storyteller (*kaichy*) in the Republic of Altai. Babaeva, a primary school teacher, first wrote down the epic *Ochy-Bala* from Aleksey Kalkin in 1949, but this text was lost.[103] The text was rewritten and published in 1951 in Gorno-Altaisk.[104] This epic tells of two heroic sisters, Ochy-Bala and Ochira-Mandi, who are threatened by a hostile lord of the underground world. There are multiple battle scenes in this epic. The English translation used below was prepared at my request by Irena Legovetz from the Russian translation, with certain adaptations done by me.

The introduction

The epic begins with praise of the two-stringed lyre, the *topshur*. The whole epic is then dedicated to the goddess of the mountain, referred to as *palam*, meaning *my child*. The song is performed for this mountain spirit with the wish that the song will have a positive emotional impact on the listeners:[105]

> U-u-u! To pass the long night,
> I'm commencing my epic song—listen, child.
> Oh-oh-oh! To dispel your disturbing thoughts,
> I'll start telling you a poem, child,
> To prolong the morning dawn,
> I'm starting my epic song—so, listen, child,
> To dispel your gloomy thoughts,
> I'll start telling you a poem, child.

After this dedication, the epic transitions to the mythical beginning of time, when no one living was yet alive:[106]

> A long, long time ago,
> When there were no people alive today,
> In the early-early, ancient time,
> When we, the present ones, were not there,

---

103. Harvilahti and Kazagacheva, *Holy Mountain*, 48.
104. Kazagacheva, *Altai Heroic*.
105. Kazagacheva, *Altai Heroic*, 88.
106. Kazagacheva, *Altai Heroic*, 84.

The introduction then continues as the epic singer describes the landscape, the mountains, and the river, praising the beauty of the Altai landscape, using traditional formulas such as the ninety tributaries and the nine mountains:[107]

> *Oh-oh-oh! Clean river with ninety tributaries,*
> *On the bank of a winding river,*
> *Nine identical high mountains,*
> *The settlement of the heroes was discernible.*

Finally, at the end of the introduction, the hero's main activities are described, which include settling her people in an ideal landscape in Altai, where there is plenty of firewood and pasture for the cattle and horses:[108]

> *Where there are [many] pastures, Ochi-Bala let the herds go,*
> *Where there is a lot of dead wood, the people were settled by Ochira-Mandyi.*

Altai is then described as the center of the world, in the middle of which is the brown world mountain with sixty-six sides and seventy-seven slopes with fortresses of gold and silver. It is useful to note the comparison with numbered parallelism in the OT, such as in Prov 6:16, where the sequence *six, seven* does not mean that the seventh item is subordinate or an afterthought but is a rhetorical form indicating that the list provided does not encompass all things falling under a specific category.[109] The Altai mountain covers the eye of the sun and the eye of the moon:[110]

> *Spaciously created my earth—umbilical cord,*
> *Created with open territories my sacred Altai*
> *With sixty-six sacred sides,*
> *With golden-silver stone fortresses,*
> *With seventy-seven sacred sides,*
> *With silver-gold stone fortresses.*
> *A brown mountain that does not burn out from the sun,*
> *Under the sun wriggling,*
> *Closing the sun's eye, she stood there.*
> *Piebald mountain, which does not burn out from the light of the moon,*
> *Bending under the moon,*
> *Eclipsing the eye of the moon, stood.*

---

107. Kazagacheva, *Altai Heroic*, 88.
108. Kazagacheva, *Altai Heroic*, 88.
109. Toy, *Critical and Exegetical*, 127.
110. Kazagacheva, *Altai Heroic*, 90.

These shamanistic images of covering the eye of the sun and the moon are also used in *Ochy-Bala* to describe the palace of the enemy or the speed of the heroine's horse:[111]

> The famous Ochy-Bala
> Turned her steed in that direction
> The eye of the moon dimmed.
> Turned her steed in this direction
> The eye of the sun darkened.

Summary of the plot

The main hero of *Ochy-Bala* is a beautiful and strong female heroine whose eyes are like blue stars, with two black plaits of hair dancing on her shoulders. She is famous for her hunting skills, and she knows the languages of the animals. Epics in Altai featuring female heroines are somewhat unusual, but *Ochy-Bala* is not unique in this regard. Tarasova comments that in the Sakha *olongkhos* (epic stories from Yakutia) female warriors are often featured as the first people to arrive and settle in the Middle World with their sisters, battle horses, and cattle herds.[112] In most of these stories the core of the plot involves enemy attacks on the female warriors. The female warriors are involved in many fights, may travel to the hostile world to search for stolen horses, defeat their enemies, and turn them into slaves. These female warriors are indescribably beautiful and possess incredible physical strength.[113]

In the epic *Ochy-Bala*, Ochy-Bala hears that the bloodthirsty and cruel warrior Kan-Taad'i-Biy and his army, together with his son Ak-D'alaa, have attacked her homeland, Altai. Ochy-Bala fearlessly goes to fight against her enemies and kills Kan-Taad'i-Biy's son Ak-D'alaa. However, Kan-Taad'i-Biy resurrects his son Ak-D'alaa and starts attacking Altai again. Ochy-Bala travels to the valley where Kan-Taad'i-Biy lives in order to discover the secret of his strength, and on the way, she meets many different mythical beasts, including a blue bull, a messenger of Erlik, the enemy from the underworld. She goes to fight him and, following the advice of her horse Ochy-D'eren, turns into a golden eagle and beats him. Thanks to her great intelligence and resourcefulness, Ochy-Bala is able to discover the secret of Kan-Taad'i-Biy's strength, which is found in a nine-sided blue stone, kept in a golden chest.

111. Harvilahti and Kazagacheva, *Holy Mountain*, 99.
112. Tarasova, "Role of Women," 30.
113. Tarasova, "Role of Women," 45.

Taking the stone, Ochy-Bala defeats her enemy and saves her land and her people, after which she turns into a thin moon, and her horse Ochy-D'eren becomes the North Star.

Poetry and oral style

There are a number of key oral-poetic devices characteristic of Altai epics that can be found in *Ochy-Bala*.

Contrast

The principle of contrast is very important in the Altai epics, as the positive hero who has supernatural powers is pitted against the negative characters (the king, the mythological bull, Erlik, D'elbegen, and the snake).[114] In *Ochy-Bala* there are two main characters who stand in opposition to each other. Ochy-Bala is clever and beautiful, and her beauty is compared with untouchable objects such as the sun, the moon, the rainbow, and the stars. Her opposing enemy Kan-Taad'i-Biy is rude, cruel, and cunning, and has become rich through wars and pillage of other peoples. The heroine is called *my daughter* and *my sweet Ochy-Bala*, but Kan-Taad'i-Biy is described as having *bloodshot eyes* and *a black face*, and as a *person who deceives to drink the blood of others*.

Parallelism

Altai epic poetry frequently uses parallelism, where the second line parallels the first. Parallelism may consist of verse couplets or a cluster of verses.[115] Words, which may be synonymous, analogous, or antithetical, are repeated to create a symmetric structure.

> *Кесер келзе—кезе тудар,*
> *Алып келзе—аймай тудар.*[116]
>
> *Keser kelze—keze tudar,*
> *Alyp kelze—aĭmaĭ tudar*
>
> *If a warrior steps up—he will squeeze to death,*
> *If a hero steps up—he will grab an armful.*

---

114. Harvilahti and Kazagacheva, *Holy Mountain*, 8.
115. Harvilahti and Kazagacheva, *Holy Mountain*, 84.
116. Harvilahti and Kazagacheva, *Holy Mountain*, 92.

Morphosyntactic parallelism, the repetition of the same grammatical form in the same syntactical position, is also a common element.[117] This often occurs at the end of parallel verses and is a consequence of the regularity of the structure of the Turkic languages:

> Körgön közi kök cholmondyĭ
> Köörkiĭ poĭy su-altyndyĭ pu kabaktu,
> Kysyl maral pu chyraĭlu
> Tolun aĭdyĭ ėm chyraĭlu
> Solongydyĭ pu kacharlu.[118]

> *Körgön közi kök cholmondyĭ*
> *Köörkiĭ poĭy su-altyndyĭ pu kabaktu,*
> *Kysyl maral pu chyraĭlu*
> *Tolun aĭdyĭ ėm chyraĭlu*
> *Solongydyĭ pu kacharlu.*

> *Her seeing eyes—are like blue stars,*
> *Sweetheart herself, with eyebrows, as if made of gold,*
> *Her face is like a red deer,*
> *Her face is like a round moon,*
> *Her cheeks are like rainbows.*

Also, a group of verses may be connected by the same lexical units being repeated in the same syntactical position in the middle of the verses.[119] This lexical repetition is called *mezodiplosis*:

> Ok jetpeediĭ omogy par,
> Kush jetpeediĭ kurulu par,
> Pazyp polbos paĭym semis malynda kozho,
> Jylyp polbos jylmaĭ semis jylkyda jaba.[120]

> *Ok jetpeediĭ omogy par,*
> *Kush jetpeediĭ kurulu par,*
> *Pazyp polbos paĭym semis malynda kozho,*
> *Jylyp polbos jylmaĭ semis jylkyda jaba.*

> *Not to be reached by an arrow—there are [such] frisky ones,*
> *Not to be caught up by a bird—there are [such] fast ones,*
> *There are so fat ones [in the herds]—they can't walk,*
> *There are so stout ones [in the herds]—they can't move.*

---

117. Harvilahti and Kazagacheva, *Holy Mountain*, 83.
118. Harvilahti and Kazagacheva, *Holy Mountain*, 92.
119. Harvilahti and Kazagacheva, *Holy Mountain*, 83.
120. Harvilahti and Kazagacheva, *Holy Mountain*, 92.

Clusters

Verses are also combined to form clusters, usually consisting of two to ten verses which are thematically related.[121] The epic singer usually sings each cluster in one breath, pausing between the clusters to continue singing *kai* but without words. These pauses signal a marker for a new theme or episode in the epic, and perhaps time for the epic singer to recall the next section. The epic also begins with a specific *kai* introduction, which signals the beginning of the performance. This is a contextual cultural hint, which Harvilahti and Kazagacheva call an *ethnocultural strategy*, indicating to the audience that the traditional performance has begun and creating expectations among the listeners of what will follow.

Rhyme/Meter

Altai epics are written in syllabic verse, a structure primarily dictated by the musical pattern of the epic.[122] In *Ochy-Bala*, the lines are mostly made up of eight or seven syllables (four plus four, or four plus three), but lines of twelve syllables (four plus four plus four) are also common. Together, these measures make up 80 percent of *Ochy-Bala*. Seven-syllabic lines are more frequent in dramatic parts of the epic, such as in the passage depicting Ochy-Bala's battle with her enemy.

Атту-чуллу // Очы-Бала (8)
Ары körÿп // атанды (7)
Айдын köзи // jабылды (7)
Пери (ле) körÿп // пурулды (7)
Кÿнныҥ köзин // пöктöлды (7)[123]

Attu-chullu // Ochy-Bala (8)
Ary körÿp // atandy (7)
Aïdyn közi // jabyldy (7)
Peri (le) körÿp // puruldy (7)
Kÿnnyng közin // pöktöldy (7)

The famous Ochy-Bala,
Turned her steed in that direction
The eye of the moon dimmed
Turned her steed in this direction
The eye of the sun darkened

---

121. Harvilahti and Kazagacheva, *Holy Mountain*, 84–85.
122. Harvilahti, *Holy Mountain*, 78.
123. Harvilahti and Kazagacheva, *Holy Mountain*, 102.

Anaphora

This is the deliberate repetition of the same vowel, syllable, or lexical unit at the beginning of consecutive verses, or across a chain of verses or couplets.[124] Harvilahti and Kazagacheva call this "anaphora," but it is also called "acrostic rhyme," "initial rhyme," "vertical alliteration," and "head-rhyme" by different scholars.

> Ат пажындый алтын кӱӱк
> Анда-мында эдип јадат
> Кой пажындый коҥыр кӱӱк
> Комулдалду јырап јадат.[125]

> *At pazhyndyĭ altyn kÿÿk*
> *Anda-mynda ėdip jadat*
> *Koĭ pazhyndyĭ kongyr kÿÿk*
> *Komuldaldu jyrap jadat.*

> *The size of a horse's head was a golden cuckoo*
> *Here and there she cooed,*
> *The size of a sheep's head, a brown cuckoo*
> *She cooed plaintively.*

Alliteration

Alliteration is very common in Altai epics. This is the repetition of the same vowel, consonant, or syllable at the beginning of two or more words in the same verse:

> Кесер келзе—кезе тудар,
> Алып келзе—аймай тудар.[126]

> *Keser kelze—keze tudar,*
> *Alyp kelze—aĭmaĭ tudar.*

> *If a warrior steps up—he will squeeze to death*
> *If a hero steps up—he will grab an armful.*

---

124. Harvilahti and Kazagacheva, *Holy Mountain*, 82.
125. Harvilahti and Kazagacheva, *Holy Mountain*, 86.
126. Harvilahti and Kazagacheva, *Holy Mountain*, 92.

Epiphora

This is the repetition of the same vowel, syllable, or lexical unit at the end of two or more verses:[127]

> Озо-озо, озодо,
> Отурган калык јок тушта,
> Эрте-эрте, јебрен ӧйдӧ
> Эмди пистер јок тушта,[128]

> *Ozo-ozo, ozodo,*
> *Oturgan kalyk jok tushta,*
> *Ėrte-ėrte, jebren ŏĭdö*
> *Ėmdi pister jok tushta,*

> *A long, long time ago,*
> *When there were no people alive today,*
> *In the early-early, ancient time,*
> *When we, the present ones, were not there,*

Word pairs

There are also frequent word pairs in the epic song, such as ай-кӱн aĭ-kÿn *moon-sun*, which symbolizes *the good world*, or ада-эне ada-ėne *father-mother*, meaning *parents*.[129] Such word pairs are also frequent in normal Altai speech.

Metaphor

Metaphors are also commonly used in descriptions in the Altai epics.[130] Here is an example of an allegorical couplet giving a beautiful physical description of Ochy-Bala and her strength, likening her to pastures where flocks and cattle graze:

> Јарынында јапшары јок, јаан пӱткен,
> Омырткада јок, ӱйеси јок, пӧкӧ пӱткен.
> Пек тен пӱткен пелинге
> Пежен айгыр мал јӱргедий

---

127. Harvilahti and Kazagacheva, *Holy Mountain*, 82.
128. Harvilahti and Kazagacheva, *Holy Mountain*, 82.
129. Harvilahti and Kazagacheva, *Holy Mountain*, 28.
130. Harvilahti and Kazagacheva, *Holy Mountain*, 34.

Ак јадаңдый јардындаа
Алтан ӱӱр кой тургадый.¹³¹

Jarynynda dapshary d̂ok, d̂aan pÿtken,
Omyrtkada d̂ok, ÿiesi d̂ok, pökö pÿtken.
Pek ten pÿtken pelinge
Pezhen aĭgyr mal d͡ÿrgediĭ
Ak d̂adan͡gdyĭ jardyndaa
Altan ÿÿr koĭ turgadyĭ.

From her birth, she is tall, with no prominences in her shoulders
From her birth, strong, in the joints without recesses.
On her back, strong from birth,
The herds of fifty stallions could graze,
On her shoulder blades, as on a white plain,
In sixty (rams) the flocks could stand.

Taboo expressions

Although some taboo words or concepts occur in the Altai epic, they are generally referred to euphemistically. For example, the words *sky* or *heavens* are not used in the Altai epic because they are holy words referring to the *Upper World* where the gods live.¹³² Instead, the word ак-кöк ak-kök *white-blue* is used:

Акка ла јеткен ак сумердыҥ
Алтын пажы јалтыраган,
Кöккö ло јетуен кöк сумердиҥ
Мöҥӱн пажы мысылдаган.¹³³

Akka la d̂etken ak sumerdyn͡g
Altyn pazhy d̂altyragan,
Kökkö lo d̂etuen kök sumerdin͡g
Mön͡gÿn pazhy mysyldagan.

The top of a white, sharp-topped mountain,
Reaching the top of the white (sky), shone with gold,
The top of a blue-peaked mountain,
Reaching up to the blue (sky) it sparkled with silver.

---

131. Harvilahti and Kazagacheva, *Holy Mountain*, 93.
132. Harvilahti and Kazagacheva, *Holy Mountain*, 34–35.
133. Harvilahti and Kazagacheva, *Holy Mountain*, 93.

Epithets

The use of epithets is common, for example in the names of the characters.[134] Also, they are used to describe the idealized appearance of the heroine, frequently using exaggeration to make comparisons:

> Кöргöн кöзи кöк чолмондый
> Кööркий пойы су-алтындый пу кабакту,
> Кысыл марал пу чырайлу
> Толун айдый эм чырайлу
> Солоҥыдый пу качарлу.[135]

> *Körgön közi kök cholmondyĭ*
> *Köörkiĭ poĭy su-altyndyĭ pu kabaktu,*
> *Kysyl maral pu chyraĭlu*
> *Tolun aĭdyĭ ėm chyraĭlu*
> *Solongydyĭ pu kacharlu.*

> Her seeing eyes—are like blue stars,
> A true sweetheart, with eyebrows, as if made of gold,
> Her face is like a red deer,
> Her face is like a round moon,
> Her cheeks are like rainbows.

Another example is a series of verses linked together by epithet nouns (a word or phrase applied to a person or thing to describe an attributed quality often used in place of a name or title) reflecting the ethnocultural background of the Altai epics: the *white livestock*, the *black mountain*, and the poetic use of the word *mist*.[136]

> Ак тумандый ак тар малы[137]

> *Ak tumandyĭ ak tar maly*

> As white mist, the white cattle.

> Ак тумандый ак тар малын,
> Амыр јонын.[138]

> *Ak tumandyĭ ak tar malyn,*
> *Amyr jonyn.*

> As white mist, the white cattle,

---

134. Harvilahti and Kazagacheva, *Holy Mountain*, 35.
135. Harvilahti and Kazagacheva, *Holy Mountain*, 93.
136. Harvilahti and Kazagacheva, *Holy Mountain*, 100.
137. Harvilahti and Kazagacheva, *Holy Mountain*, 89.
138. Harvilahti and Kazagacheva, *Holy Mountain*, 120.

Their peaceable people.

Ат нереези куу тумандый.[139]

At nereezi kuu tumandyĭ.

His heroic steed as a grey mist.

Ат тыныжы чӧйлӱип
Туман полуп кайнады.[140]

*At tynyzhy chöĭlÿip
Tuman polup kaĭnady.*

*The breath of the steeds
was whirling like the mist.*

Hyperbole

Hyperbole is also often used in descriptions of the characters or of nature:[141]

Пек тен пӱткен пелинге
Пежен айгыр мал јӱргедий
Ак јадаҥдый јардындаа
Алтан ӱӱр кой тургадый.[142]

*Pek ten pÿtken pelinge
Pezhen aĭgyr mal d͡ÿrgediĭ
Ak d͡adaṅgdyĭ jardyndaa
Altan ÿÿr koĭ turgadyĭ.*

*On her back, strong from birth,
The herds of fifty stallions could graze,
On her shoulder blades, as on a white plain,
In sixty (rams) the flocks could stand.*

Conclusion: Summary of features to be carried over into the biblical epic

Foley writes that it is important to decode messages in the performative act by recognizing and interacting with the encoded markers embedded in the

---

139. Harvilahti and Kazagacheva, *Holy Mountain*, 120.
140. Harvilahti and Kazagacheva, *Holy Mountain*, 125.
141. Harvilahti and Kazagacheva, *Holy Mountain*, 35.
142. Harvilahti and Kazagacheva, *Holy Mountain*, 93.

performance.¹⁴³ These involve codes (e.g., dialect, dress, and music), figurative language such as heroic similes, parallelism, special formulas (fixed phrases which act as prompts to the audience helping them understand the context), and appeals to tradition (such as a prologue to the song addressed to the musical instrument). All of these have been analyzed above. Here is a list of these features of the Altai epics, and in particular of the Altai epic *Ochy-Bala*, that the Altai OBT team will attempt to use in their Altai epic version of Judg 4–5: contrast, parallelism, clusters, opening of the epic with *kai* singing, musical episodes of *kai* during the epic, rhyme or meter, anaphora, alliteration, epiphora, word pairs, metaphor, taboo expressions, epithets, and hyperbole.

AN EXAMINATION OF ALTAI FOLKLORE AND SONGS

Introduction

In addition to epic stories, there are other genres in the Altai culture which are used to pass on the Altai worldview and culture. The Altai translation team decided to examine some of these genres in order to find appropriate cultural expressions for the three psalms. Folklore is one of the most important parts of the traditional Altai culture.¹⁴⁴ This folklore is made up of many different genres, including blessings, laments, myths, legends, folktales, epics, and of course songs. Harrison notes that in the nearby Republic of Tuva, oral genres include praise songs, blessing songs, tongue-twisters, shamanic chants, stories, metered verse, songs, aphorism, and riddles.¹⁴⁵

Кожоҥ Kozhoṅg Songs

Verbitskiy, who lived in Altai in the nineteenth century, commented that the Altai people "are very inclined to singing and music and are able to improvise."¹⁴⁶ Tyukhtenev classified Altai songs in the following categories: "historical, relating to work, relating to family and life, for weddings, lyrical and romantic, fun, satirical, and for battle."¹⁴⁷

---

143. Foley, *How to Read*, 85.
144. Yenchinov, "*Jangar Song*," 1.
145. Harrison, "Tuvan Hero Tale," 3.
146. Verbitskiy, *Altai Peoples*, 198.
147. Tyukhtenev, *Songs*, 99.

Songs in the culture of the Altai people go back a long way in history and are very connected to their life, their occupation, their worldview, and their origins.[148] Every family unit and tribe had their own songs and their own way of singing and performing them. Altai songs are characterized by singing in unison (where there are two or more voices singing in melody but perhaps one or two octaves apart), chanting, sequence music (the restatement of a motif or melodic passage a higher or lower pitch in the same voice), and by pentatonic harmony, using a five-tone scale. These are often choral and polyphonic (multi-voice) songs, expressing an optimistic and uplifting mood. Through songs it is possible to understand the heart of a people, their lives, their traditions, and their history. The folk songs of the Altai people not only express personal feelings but also the concerns, joys, and woes of the whole people. The Altai folk songs have a deep psychological and pedagogical meaning and exhibit high poetic quality.

Before the revolution, Verbitsky and Radlov spent time researching and collecting Altai folk songs. This material was published in Radlov's 1866 book *Models of Folk Literature of the Turkic Peoples of South Siberia and the Dzungar Steppe*[149] and in Verbitsky's ethnographic collection, *The Altai Peoples*, published in 1893.[150] Anokhin, over the course of thirty years, researched song folklore and made recordings of over five hundred Altai folksongs and eight hundred melodies.[151] In these songs, the theme is often the greatness and beauty of the nature of Altai, its lakes, rivers, and forests. The Altai word кожоҥ *kozhoṅg* [song] probably originates from the word кош *kosh*, meaning *in addition*, *standing near*, or *extra*, reflected also in the structure of the Altai folk songs, which are marked by parallelism and repetition with variation.[152]

Јаҥар кожоҥ Jaṅgar kozhoṅg Jangar songs

There is a special type of song in Altai which is both ritual and ceremonial, known as the *jangar* song.[153] *Jangar* songs are one of the most popular and important genres in Altai. This type of song is used at prayer times, at weddings, festivals, family events, and at other ceremonies where the song itself is part of the ritual. However, they are not sung at funerals. Such a song can

---

148. Katash, "Altai Folk Songs," 1.
149. Radlov, *Models of Folk*.
150. Verbitskiy, *Altai Peoples*.
151. Katash, "Altai Folk Songs," 1.
152. Demchinova, "Collection and Study," 8.
153. Yenchinov, "*Jangar Song*," 1.

be dedicated to the homeland, to parents, to a child, or to the newly married. This type of song usually carries positive emotions and aims to encourage, inspire, and give joy to the people. Pegg and Yamaeva, when discussing *jangar* songs, note that both the text and the style differ according to the ethnicity or dialect of the particular Altai group, or the occasion on which it is performed.[154] Traditionally no instruments are needed, the length is flexible, and the song and the words can be sung spontaneously with some improvisation. The *jangar* song is normally sung by women of middle age or older, and married women will wear an Altai tunic or чегедек *chegedek* while singing the *jangar*.

Traditionally such a song is made up of two four-line verses, and normally the second set of four lines contains elements which repeat the contents of the first set of four lines.[155] This helps to emphasize the point of the song and is also a mnemonic device. This traditional structure can be seen in a *jangar* song composed by Kleshevaya Shima Zakharovna, from the village of Kyrlyk in the Ust-Kan region of the Altai Republic:

Алтын чакы тургажын
Ак-бороны буулайдым,
Албатынын ортодо
Ак јанарды айдадым.
Кумуш чакы тургажын
Кок-бороны буулайдым,
Кооркийлердин ортодо
Кок јанарды айдадым.[156]

Altyn chaky turgazhyn
Ak-borony buulaĭdym,
Albatynyn ortodo
Ak janardy aĭdadym.
Kumush chaky turgazhyn
Kok-borony buulaĭdym,
Koorkiĭlerdin ortodo
Kok janardy aĭdadym.

To the gold hitching post,
I tie the white-grey horse,
Among the people,
I sing a white song.
To the silver hitching post,
I tie a blue-grey horse,

154. Pegg and Yamaeva, "Sensing 'Place,'" 302.
155. Yenchinov, "*Jangar Song*," 1.
156. Yenchinov, "*Jangar Song*," 1.

Among nice people,
I sing a blue song.

The first lines of each four-line verse refer to a well-known traditional symbol of unity, which is the horse hitching post.[157] In Turkic and Altai tradition, the top of the hitching post reaches the upper world, the middle is found in the middle world (the earth), and the bottom of the post reaches down into the underworld. According to Harvilahti, the hitching post is the symbolic center of the world in the Altai epic stories, running through the lower, middle, and upper levels of the earth.[158] The second and fourth lines of each four-line verse use colors as epithets to describe the purity and positivity of the song (the white-grey horse, the white song, the blue-grey horse, and the blue song). In the worldview of the Altai people, the color epithets of white and blue, when used to describe something, show that these things belong to the upper, heavenly world.

The third line of the four-line verses point to the addressees of the song, who are the people.[159] This song, which is addressed to the people, expresses a wish that the people will not forget their culture and their songs and communicates goodwill for the people and protection for them from evil and harm. The author commented that this song should be sung at traditional festivals to the people. The people in the village said that when they sing this song, they normally stand in a half-circle, so that the oldest person, who is familiar with the rituals and folklore, is standing in the center with his face directed towards where the sun rises. It is also important to note that among the singers there should not be anyone who has had a close relative die within the last year, as that makes this person unclean and connected to the world of the dead. The *jangar* song is directed to the upper world, to the gods, and must be pure from all possible pollution.

The *jangar* song can be performed as a solo or in a group, depending on the event or ceremony.[160] However, they are most beautiful and clear when sung by a group, normally of between six to twelve people. Such a group performance gives the participants strength and reinforces the spiritual defenses of a person, their family, and their house. Pegg and Yamaeva, in their observation of Altai rituals, note that the mode of performance of the *jangar* song does encourage a sense of community.[161] The song imparts a sense of unity, of belonging to the Altai people, and reinforces identity.

---

157. Yenchinov, "*Jangar Song*," 1.
158. Harvilahti, "Altai Oral Epic," 221.
159. Yenchinov, "*Jangar Song*," 1.
160. Yenchinov, "*Jangar Song*," 1.
161. Pegg and Yamaeva, "Sensing 'Place,'" 303.

One singer sings a line, which is repeated by another singer, and then is followed by the whole group, like a choir, encouraging everyone to join in. They also play a major role at a traditional Altai wedding and can be sung by someone on a journey on horseback. Such songs should also be sung during the period from the full moon to the half-moon, because when the moon is waning, Altai tradition maintains that evil spirits are more active.

The whole expression *jangar kozhong* has the idea of *making an echo*. The *jangar* song sounds like an echo when it is sung by a group because of the parallelism and repetition. The term *jangar kozhong* may have come about because of the nature of the song.[162]

Personal interviews

In an interview with Aidin Kurmanov, he explained that *jangar* is a festival type of singing, such as during a wedding.[163] *Jangar* songs are sung to bless and praise Altai and to describe the beauty of its nature. The style of singing is like that of a choir with multiple voices. These songs bring unity, as the people form a circle and sway together in a round, almost in a trance. Aidin was of the opinion that this style of Altai singing would be an appropriate genre for Ps 133, where the focus is on unity and community.

Bolot Bairshev describes *jangar* as similar to a choir song, sung normally by older ladies.[164] These songs evoke pride, a sense of gentleness, and a cry of the heart. Nogon Shumarov calls *jangar kozhong* a choral folk song, sung in unison, and often in a canon.[165] Yuri Chendeyev also agreed that *jangar* is a type of folk singing, normally sung by the older generation rather than by the youth.[166] *Jangar* songs are of varying types, often like a lament, but are known for conveying hope for the future. Each region and dialect have their own version and slightly varying melodies and words. Yuri agreed that performing a psalm in the form of *jangar* would be appropriate use of this genre. Nikolay Sergetkishov divided *jangar* into several types: those used at weddings (той јаңгар *toĭ jangar*), prayers used at celebrations (in Russian молебные *molebnye*), and ritualistic ones (in Russian обрядовые *obrĭadovye*).[167] Anatoli Turulanov added to the types laments (сыныт јаңгар *synyt jangar*), those used at festivals (ойын јаңгар

---

162. Demchinova, "Collection and Study," 8.
163. Personal interview with Aidin Kurmanov, Jun. 2022.
164. Personal interview with Bolot Bairshev, Jun. 2022.
165. Personal interview with Nogon Shumarov, Jun. 2022.
166. Personal interview with Yuri Chendeyev, Jul. 2022.
167. Personal interview with Nikolay Sergetkishov, Jun. 2022.

oĭyn jangar), those sung as a duet (cöröш jaнгap *sögösh jangar*), and a choir song (кypee jaнгap *kuree jangar*).[168] Anatoli also agreed that if the psalms were translated as poetry, they could be sung in the style of *jangar*. Natalya Enchinova described *jangar* as given from the Altai land to the people and as an expression of their soul.[169]

Conclusion

The Altai translation team decided that the *kozhong* song was appropriate for all three psalms. The particular type of *jangar* would be used for Ps 133 to reflect its values of unity and harmony.

---

168. Personal interview with Anatoli Turulanov, Jun. 2022.
169. Personal interview with Natalya Enchinova, Jul. 2022.

8

Translating the Texts into Altai

INTERNALIZATION OF JUDGES 4-5 IN PREPARATION FOR ORAL TRANSLATION

Introduction

Before starting the process of oral translation with the Altai team, I decided it would be beneficial for me personally to internalize and retell Judg 4–5. The internalization by the exegete of the relevant passages is a crucial step in the process of oral translation and performance. This description of the internalization of Judg 4–5 can serve as a model for internalization of the psalms as well as for other passages. In order to do this, I asked for help from a small group of people who are familiar with the process and techniques of internalization, and we met several times over Zoom. This group did the internalizing and retelling of the passage with me.

Plan for internalization

In consultation with the group, the following steps were followed:

1. A facilitator was selected to monitor the group discovery.
2. Ahead of time, the facilitator considered the intersections of Judg 4–5 with contemporary life in terms of themes, motifs, and archetypes and selected one among these which fitted the situation in Altai. The

participants were asked to craft their own stories on this topic, which they then shared in pairs, recorded, and sent to each participant to listen to.

3. In the group, the facilitator collected key images, words, phrases, and anything expressing poignant impact from the participants' stories.
4. The group listened to Judg 4–5. The facilitator arranged for one person to tell it or read it out loud.
5. The group discussed key images, words, phrases, and expressions of poignant impact from Judg 4.
6. The group listened again and discussed the characters (what they say and do, roles, responsibilities, motivations, and emotions).
7. The group discussed the context: setting, people groups and histories, geography, politics, etc.
8. The group listened again to Judg 4 and recreated the plotline together.
9. The group identified the Most Important Thing (MIT) and determined where it features in the story.
10. Individually, the participants did an image-building exercise (everyone drew their own storyboard and then shared them with the group).
11. They practiced telling the story in small groups (either in breakout rooms or individually).
12. They gathered feedback and revised their tellings.
13. The group discussed difficult terms or concepts and looked for options for translation.
14. The group discussed rhetorical devices in the text and how to account for them in the tellings.
15. The individuals practiced, practiced, practiced.
16. As a group, they discussed discoveries that happened during embodiment and the choices each person made in performance, such as word selection, reordering, intonation, pausing, etc.
17. Several tellers were recorded performing Judg 4. The reason several tellers are used is that each storyteller will have his or her own way to tell the story. Unlike in drama, a storyteller shares the story from his or her own authentic self and does not take on the role or identity of a character.

Session 1

Initially we met as a team of five people. We were told beforehand by the facilitator to come with stories on a theme, genre, motif, or archetype that intersects with the story in Judg 4–5. This was intended to help the team probe their own story forms, rich language, cultural values, and rituals so as to identify cultural matches and mismatches with the ANE cultures. In this case, we were asked to come with stories on the theme of female heroines, and we had a discussion about the character traits that made these women heroines and any commonalities or surprises. Two participants told about female Christians who have continued doing ministry in heroic circumstances, someone shared from a film they had seen, another a scene from American history, and the final participant about a lady who had acted as a prostitute during a war in order to help win the battle by delaying the enemy leader. It was noted that this final story has parallels with Jael in the story of Judg 4, who commits murder in order to save the Israelites from Sisera.

In this session we also completed the initial phase of internalization. This included listening to the story, experiencing the story afresh, and sharing the impact of any vivid images, any senses that were provoked, and any intersection with our own stories. This worked well to encourage broad discussion and to note the parts of the story that we decided to explore in further detail later. The facilitator retold Judg 4, and we all talked about key images, words, or phrases and their poignant impact. There was a discussion about the gruesome nature of the killing, done with instruments readily available to Jael. We also talked about the actions of Jael in treating Sisera like a child by giving him milk to induce sleep and covering him with a blanket, the unwillingness of Barak to go into battle without Deborah, and the repetition of tree imagery and the significance of mountains and valleys. A comparison was made of Jael to Rahab in Josh 2. Rahab was a prostitute who used what was available to hide the spies from a sense of collaborating with their brave mission. In Judg 4, the tribal chief's wife, who was presumably well respected, uses her coverings to seduce Sisera, a coward who was the general of a dictator's army. As homework, before the next session, we were asked to divide the chapter into sections, to find the Most Important Thing (MIT) of the story, and to draw a storyboard (see Appendix 11).

Session 2

We met for the second session with the same team of five. Initially, we listened again to a second telling of the story by the facilitator and then had a discussion about the different characters who play a role in this story. There was a long debate about Jael—whether her killing of Sisera was premeditated or not and what might have motivated her actions. It was generally thought that the murder was opportunist and that having induced Sisera to sleep, Jael took the opportunity to kill him with the tools that conveniently lay by. She was contrasted with the cowardly Sisera, who had run away from the battle scene on foot. There was also a discussion of Barak's timidity and the fact that he wanted the reassurance of having Deborah the prophet with him to go into battle. The facilitator had asked us to think about the MIT in the story during the week. It was generally agreed that God's saving Israel through the actions of women was particularly important, given similar stories before and after this one in the book of Judges that highlight God's saving Israel through unusual heroes, such as Ehud, Gideon, or Samson.

I showed the group my prepared story board (see Appendix 11) and did a retelling of the first part of the story of Judg 4:1–5, which introduces all the characters. We spent some time thinking about how to relay in English the idea that God sold the Israelites into the hands of Jabin, king of Canaan, in verse 2. One suggestion included, "God gave power to Jabin, king of Canaan, over the Israelites." We were instructed to practice retelling the story before the next session and to ask feedback questions to improve our story, including:

- What did I leave out?
- What did I add?
- What did I change?

For an audience that is less familiar with the story, the following questions will provide helpful feedback:

- What was confusing about my story?
- What do you think was the MIT in my story?
- What images stood out from my story?

Another idea that emerged was to put together a physical map, because of the significance of geography in the story of Judg 4. This would involve creating a tabletop map with geographical features and then using sticks or pencils moving around the map to show events as they transpire throughout the story. Standing around this tabletop map gives opportunities to talk about distances between the main places. It also provides the chance to discuss implied issues such the difficulty of travel or other important features in the area where the story took place. These may be issues that impact the story but which may not be obvious to the Altai participants, since their part of the world is not similar to the Middle East. It would be a worthwhile investment of time to create such a map, as it could make the movements of a story easier to memorize and retain. In addition, the team could "jump back into" the map when they work in later sessions to internalize other stories, and the map could be used to address any geographical confusion. Such a map would mean that whenever there is movement in the stories, it would be possible to move around the physical map together. However, this proved impossible to do on Zoom.

Session 3

In this final session for chapter four, for most of the time, the participants shared their own retellings of Judg 4. We had a discussion on the importance of *hand* in this story, as the Israelites are *delivered* or *sold* into the *hand* of their enemies (verse 2) or the promise that God will deliver the enemy into the Israelites' *hand* (4:2, 7, 9, 14), an expression which appears multiple times throughout the book of Judges. Jael also takes up small tools in her hands and uses these to murder the enemy.

It was decided for the following session to move on to Judg 5. We were asked as homework to divide Judg 5 into sections, to try to think of a song that Judg 5 reminded us of, and to internalize Judg 5:24–31 (Jael and Sisera) for a retelling next time.

Adjustments to the translation after performance

After my retelling of Judg 4, I decided to emphasize the expressions using *hands* more in this chapter, and I adapted my translation to be ready for a final performance. For example, the original translation of verse 2 read, *And the Lord turned them over to Jabin king of Canaan, who reigned in Hazor*, and this is now changed to *And the Lord sold them into the hands of Jabin king of Canaan, who reigned in Hazor*. I also changed the translation in verse 7, changing it from *I will give you victory over him* to *I will give him into your hands*. In addition, I adapted the translation in verses 9, 14, and 24.

I also decided to add the words *former judge* before Ehud's name in verse 1, to make it clearer to the audience who Ehud was, as this performance of chapters 4 and 5 of Judges is taking place without any context of what has happened beforehand. After discussion with the internalization team, I also decided to change *Harosheth Haggoyim* to *Forest of the Nations*.

Session 4

We began this session by listening to the facilitator's retelling of Judg 5:23–31. This retelling was not particularly poetic but was given in very clear and colloquial English.

We spent some time discussing the powerful image of Sisera falling and lying at the feet of Jael, which has sexual connotations but also portrays the image of subjugation and defeat. We noticed the difference between the prose narrative and the poetic rendering of the death of Sisera, observing that probably the poetic song version adapted the truth to some extent as hyperbole under the image of the total subjugation of Sisera.

We were asked whether we sympathize with Sisera as a mother waiting for her son to come. However, as we explored this section in more detail, including some of the more grotesque imagery that Sisera's mother uses, we became less sympathetic and identified what we thought was a mocking tone from the editor. We then listened to another member's retelling, which was noted as being less colloquial but more poetic than the previous retelling.

Session 5

There were only two people for session five, and each person gave a retelling of Judg 5:1–11. This session was done against the background of the invasion of Ukraine by Russia in February 2022, and some of the lines in this section were difficult to say in light of the scenes in the news, such as:

> *My heart is with Israel's governors,*
> *with the willing volunteers among the people.*
> *Bless the Lord.*

This affected our emotions and understanding of these passages. We discussed the dramatic nature of the Lord's theophany and the identification of Deborah as *mother of Israel*, rather than as judge or prophet. We decided to prepare the final section for the next session (Judg 5:12–23).

Session 6

This time two of the four participants had prepared their readings of Judg 5:12–23. Mine was a poetic reading, translated from the Hebrew. The other participant's reading was largely based on the NLT and was more understandable but less poetic. One listener commented that my reading was too fast, and so it was hard to digest because the text is so dense.

We discussed verse 13, including how to translate לְאַדִּירִים *(to the) nobles* and בַּגִּבּוֹרִים *as/against warriors*, and whether these terms are both referring to the Israelites, to the Canaanites, or to a mixture. We also looked at a map, drawn by one of the participants and discussed the location of the tribes that responded and those that did not.

Session 7

One other participant and I had prepared our own retellings and recordings of Judg 4–5 for the team to watch. Between session 6 and session 7, I travelled to Altai and translated Judg 4–5 with the Altai translation team. In this session, I shared with the internalization team the process and my observations of how the Altai team had translated these chapters.

Performer-researcher reflections on the text performed

One member of the group did a retelling of Judg 4 (see Video 1). She used many facial expressions and varying hand gestures during the telling, as well as pauses and changes of pace. Her emotions also ranged between excitement, frustration, shock, and aggression. In chapter 4 she reordered the passage slightly, placing verse 11 with the parenthetical information about Heber the Kenite slightly earlier in the text after verse 9b, so as not to break up the battle narrative.

This group member also did a retelling of Judg 5 (see Video 2). She made use of her whole body, looking up into the heavens to describe how the stars came to fight against Sisera, looking down during the description of Sisera falling at Jael's feet, looking left and right during naming of the tribes, and reaching with her hands for the tent peg and hammer. She employed different tones of voices, such as praise for the tribes that rallied to help in the battle and rebuke for those who did not. She used hand gestures to show the clouds pouring down water, the winding roads, and to call Deborah and Barak to arise. She also varied the emphasis in her voice for such phrases as *not a shield or a spear was seen* or *dedicated ones from the people of Israel*, making use of intonation to stress certain words and phrases. The pace was also varied, faster during the description of the rallying of the tribes but slower during the scene when Jael prepares to kill Sisera.

I used the translator's oral performance notes, which I had already prepared, and the voice prosody notes to help prepare for this retelling or performances of these chapters. I tried to use some hand gestures and embodiment (for example, looking down), voice transitions because of many emotional changes in this passage, pace changes, and intonation and stress on various words (see Video 3 and Video 4).

Conclusion

The process of internalization was significantly harder for the poetic section of chapter 5 as compared to the narrative of chapter 4, and I had to rely heavily on memory during the retelling. However, this process of internalization and performance of chapter 4 and 5 helped me to intimately understand and personally interact with the characters and events of this chapter. The discussion in the group around the emotions of the characters and the key terms was beneficial, and the preparation for the retelling itself forced me to internalize the passage and to embody it more completely. The process gave me a new temporal and dynamic understanding of the text and of the location of the episodes in the sequence of the story. For exegetes, internalizing and embodying the passage and performing or reciting it aloud in groups or individually will substantially deepen their exegesis and will also enhance later oral translation and performance with the translation team. The exegetical adviser will then be able to modify their initial exegesis and performance notes with the assistance of the observations obtained in this phase. If this internalization and embodiment can be done with a team, this process is even more effective.

TRANSLATING PSALMS AS SONGS

Introduction

This section investigates how to translate psalms as songs and is included here as preparatory to an account of the translation of the chosen biblical passages with the oral translation team. Cousins observes that psalms are particularly appropriate for a study linked to BPC, because they are communal and performative, and they express their theology using imagery and poetry.[1] She notes that there have been few studies using performance criticism to study the psalms, even though they are inherently performative

---

1. Cousins, "Pilgrim Theology," 1.

and were intended to be used for performance by future faith communities.[2] This is one of the reasons why I chose the three psalms for this research.

Psalms 1, 100, and 133 as songs

Zogbo and Wendland note that the chances for a successful transfer of a poetic text from the Bible into the RL are high if the function of poetry in the RL is the same or similar to that of the function of poetry in the SL.[3] The subject matter being addressed and the goal of speaking must correspond or overlap, at least to some extent. Boerger gives ten principles for sung Scripture translation.[4] Her first principle is to represent SL genres by RL genres. In the case of the psalms, this means translating biblical poetry as poetry and using a suitable RL song form or genre to represent the psalm. When performing a psalm today, the context of the performance must also be considered.[5] The biblical context would have been different, but the communicative message of the psalm and the effect it creates on the audience and their response should be similar.

In the case of Ps 1, the subject matter is wisdom, and the goal of speaking is to instruct and inspire the listeners in the way of wisdom. For Ps 1 the Altai translation team chose a didactic and inspirational style of song, which aims to teach and reflect the morals of the Altai community and to motivate the Altai people towards certain community values.

Psalm 100 is a praise psalm, highlighting the characteristics of the Lord as a reason for praising him. This will be performed as a celebratory song in the Altai language using traditional Altai instruments and dance.

The subject of Ps 133 is unity, and the communicative purpose is to inspire and motivate the listeners to a common goal. The Altai *jangar* folklore song is normally sung in unison and is intended to edify and encourage the Altai people when they are in a community gathering. The element of unity in the *jangar* song is emphasized by the fact that the song is normally accompanied by a ring dance where the participants link arms and move slowly in a circular movement and by the echoing of the lines of the song by the chorus.

---

2. Cousins, "Pilgrim Theology," 68.
3. Zogbo and Wendland, *Hebrew Poetry*, 62.
4. Boerger, "Freeing Biblical Poetry," 183.
5. Dickie, "Using Psalms," 55.

The oral-lyrical method

The method of translating the psalms recommended by Salisbury, and the one that I used in this research, is the oral-lyrical method, which involves composing songs orally with poetic effects from exegetically correct explanations and then making translations from them.[6] Using the oral-lyrical methodology means that poetic elements will be included in the song and translation from the beginning of the process rather than the team attempting to add them later. The translation will thus be more appealing to the receptor audience, drawing them into the message of the song or poem. The translation will be more expressive, communicating the correct intended emotional meaning for the psalms and impacting the hearers in ways that the original editors intended. The psalm will also be more persuasive, achieving its central communicative purpose.

Steps to translate the psalms as songs

Initially it is necessary to form a talented team, including poets, musicians, and translators, and then to run a psalms workshop, where the team is trained in the oral-lyrical method and attempts to translate using this method.[7] It is important that during the workshop, the translation team has fun, is left feeling energized, and that there is a positive and creative atmosphere.[8] Zogbo adds that the workshop should have an unpressured, interactive environment, with a positive team spirit and plenty of group interaction.

Salisbury suggests the following steps for the translation team.[9] The exegete or TA initially does a linguistic and literary analysis of the psalm, including the genre, its poetic features and functions, any textual or exegetical issues, key terms, unfamiliar concepts for the receptor audience, implicit background knowledge, and its performance context. The exegete should also study the psalm as a whole and its overall impact. The translation team then listens to the psalm in different translations, especially paying attention to the structure and poetic peaks of the poem. After this, the team internalizes the psalm, and the exegete leads the team through its analysis. The team, made up of songwriters and poets, then compose orally one or more poems or songs attempting to convey the same meaning and impact as for

6. Salisbury, "Translating the Psalms," 2.
7. Salisbury, "Translating the Psalms," 11.
8. Zogbo, "From Scripture to Song," 10.
9. Salisbury, "Translating the Psalms," 10–12.

the original audience, focusing on naturalness and poetic effects. The team then chooses the best draft of a natural combination of all the pre-drafts. The team compares this draft to three or four other translations in related languages and can modify the psalm keeping to exegetical accuracy, assessing any changes for accuracy against loss of poetic effect. The final step is a redraft in which the song is converted into an accurate translation. The draft should then be played for the community, and any community feedback should be taken into account before continuing with the translation of other psalms. It is important to get the community involved throughout the whole process.

Conclusion

The psalms were originally composed to be sung, which is why they have been chosen for this research. Most applications of BPC have been to the NT, except for some studies on the prophets in the OT. Doan and Giles express that the performance way of thinking and communicating is "just beneath the surface" of the OT and propose that BPC can be applied throughout the OT, being particularly appropriate for the psalms.[10] Brueggemann describes this act of embodiment as "worldmaking," a term adopted by Cousins, by which she means reshaping the understanding of the world by those who participate in the performance of the psalms.[11] The next sections of this chapter will describe the process of translating Judg 4–5 and Pss 1, 100, and 133 into Altai using the method of OBT with the Altai translation team.

TRANSLATION OF THE BIBLICAL PASSAGES INTO ALTAI

Introduction

The following sections of this chapter describe the internalization and oral translation process used by the Altai oral translation team to translate the chosen biblical passages.

---

10. Doan and Giles, *Twice Used Songs*, 14–15, 18.
11. Brueggemann, *Israel's Praise*, 160.

Translation of Judges 4 into Altai

Internalization, exegesis, and translation

Before the process of internalization of Judg 4 began, I, as TA, had done extensive research on this chapter, outlined in chapter 5 above, as well as my personal process of internalization described earlier in this chapter. The Altai OBT team had already been working together closely for over two years, so close relationships had been formed, and open communication and trust were already in place. This meant that the team did not need to spend time getting to know each other before the process of internalization began. It was noted in chapter 3 that the internalization process fosters group work and participatory learning, which was the process I wanted to use during the internalization of Judg 4.

The Altai OBT team began by listening to Judg 4 in Russian, the LWC. The team listened to the passage initially in two translations, the Synodal translation (1876/1994) and the Contemporary Russian Version, 2nd edition (CRV2, 2015). I then gave a general introduction to the book of Judges in narrative form and an overview of the book of Judges, and we had a discussion on the themes and context of the whole book of Judges. We looked in particular at how chapter 4 fits into this context. The team read in detail about Ehud in chapter 3 in order to understand the context more fully. The team then listened to Judg 4 again, this time using the New Russian Translation, and identified the important characters that feature in the chapter. The team then listened to Judg 5 and spent some time discussing the genre of both passages, comparing the prose and poetry accounts of the same event. The translators spent some time making comparisons of the genre and content of Judg 5 with some of the Altai epic stories that tell of heroes saving their people and, in particular, stories with female heroines.

I led the team through the story charts, internalization notes, and exegetical notes, discussing the questions and answers with them orally. The team then spent some time initially identifying key terms and difficult concepts, such as *judge, prophet, palm tree, tent peg*, and the phrase *give into their hands*. One of the team members retold Judg 4 in the Altai language, describing the main content of the passage and the order of the events as they occur. At this stage the team also relayed the story in pictorial format (see Appendix 12) and performed an amateur drama (see Video 5), in order to engage with and experience the passage more fully. These are two popular techniques OBT teams can use in order to imagine and internalize the passage more effectively, and they are the two techniques most frequently used by the Altai team.

One of the translators expressed emotion about how the Altai people might react to this passage when they hear it in their own language. Some of her questions touched on the topic of how people may view God as a result of this passage, especially hearing the description of the brutal murder of Sisera. I then led the team in a devotion on Judg 4 discussing what they like and did not like in the passage, what characteristics of God and of people can be understood from the passage, and what can be taken away as an individual application.

The translation team then reached the third stage of internalization, when they began to draft the passage in the receptor language of Altai. The team discussed the characters in more detail, describing each one and what emotions they may have felt during these events. At this point they also used the oral and performance notes prepared on this chapter and added their own ideas and thoughts to these.

For this oral translation, the team chose to make certain information more explicit in the text, partly due to the fact that the audience is listening to the text rather than reading it and also because the team was preparing the translation of Judg 4–5 separately from the rest of the book of Judges. Examples of this more explicit oral approach are in the first verse, where a description of Ehud as a judge in Israel is added, and in verse 7, where the team described the valley of Kishon as sometimes flowing with water to reflect the fact that this river is not permanent. The oral team translated several phrases quite freely, including adding a description of the town *Harosheth Hagoyim* as *the town where the worshipping of handmade idols took place*.

Key terms

There was a long team discussion about which Altai word to use for *judge*, and the team decided on јаргычы *jargychy* rather than јайзаҥ *jaĭzaṅ*, even though the latter had been used in a previous translation of the book of Ruth. A јайзаҥ was a political and religious leader of an Altai clan in the past, but the Altai team decided that this word could not be applied to a woman, despite the fact that in ancient Israel it also probably would have been shocking for Deborah to be called a judge. In the context of Deborah's story, the team decided to use јаргычы *jargychy* [judge].

The word נְבִיאָה nevi'ah was translated јарлыкчы *jarlykchy*, which has already been adopted in the Altai NT as a key term for *prophet*. The Altai-Russian Dictionary defines this word as "a religious messenger, a Burkhanist priest who uses both shamanic and Buddhist attributes in this practice."[12] Burkhanism or *Ak Jang* [The White Faith] was a new religious movement in Altai that grew in the beginning of the twentieth century. It exists today as a variation of Altai folk religion, and а јарлыкчы is one who receives messages from God.

Translation of Judges 5 into Altai

Internalization, exegesis, and translation

The Altai team began their exegesis and internalization of Judg 5 by listening to their translation of Judg 4 in order to remember the context and the events of the story and then by listening to Judg 5 in Russian (the LWC) several times in different translations (Synodal and the New Russian Translation). In the same way as I did during my own personal internalization process of Judges, the team divided the chapter into three sections (5:1–11c, 11d–23, and 24–31), and began with the final section contrasting Jael and Sisera's mother (5:24–31).

The team then spent some time discussing and internalizing 5:24–31, first contrasting the murder event in the prose scene in chapter 4 with the same event in chapter 5. One of the translation team members found it difficult to understand why the murder is praised in this story and told in so much detail in chapter 5. It did not seem to her to correspond with Christian ethics. This discussion was especially poignant in light of the events of the Russia-Ukraine war, which was going on at this time in March 2022. Despite this, the team also talked about the fact that in the Altai epics, victory is always praised, and the murder of the enemy is celebrated in great detail. The team also discussed the idea of producing an Altai epic from this passage that would be performed around Altai, and one of the team members had the idea of using shadow theater as an accompaniment to the throat singing of the epic.

In order to internalize the passage, the team used the techniques of retelling, some drama, and a lot of oral discussion around the characters and their emotions. In agreement with the research done on internalization, they found that in the case of chapter 5, storyboarding did not particularly help because the scenes are descriptive and poetic, rather than narrative and chronological.

The oral translation team made certain implicit information more explicit, for example, in verse 4 the phrase баатыр кептӱ бу Бойың *baatyr*

---

12. Chumakaev, *Altai-Russian Dictionary*, 190.

keptü̂ bu Boĭyn͡g [He himself like a warrior hero], portraying the image of the Lord marching out into battle by explicitly comparing him to an Altai warrior hero. Other examples are using the word јаргы [judge] to clarify the identity of Shamgar in verse 6, Sisera's death being described in verse 27 as тыны кыйылган *tyny kyĭylgan* [his spirit departed], and the wise ladies who are referred to as calming Sisera's mother down in verse 29. Another example is in verse 18 with the addition of the phrase Ӧлӱмге удура коркыбай барган *Ölumge udura korkybay bargan* [unafraid they went to the death].

Occasionally the oral translation has also used variety in verbs or descriptive phrases to make the translation more poetic, such as in verse 3 Кайраканга кожон͡гдоорым, Оны мактап ойноорым *Kaĭrakanga kozhon͡gdoorym, Ony maktap oĭnoorym* [To the Lord I will sing, praising him I will play]; in verse 5 ан͡ду туулар кыймыктаган *an͡gdu tuular kyĭmyktagan* [the mountains covered with animals shook]; in verse 7 келбенчем *kelbenchem* [until I came] and чыкпанчам *chykpancham* [until I rose up]; and in verse 26 with a variety of Altai verbs used for *struck*. In verse 10 the oral translation has used a traditional Altai word токум *tokum* [saddle blanket], јайзан͡дар *jaĭzan͡gdar* meaning *tribal chieftains* in verse 13, and куру калган *kuru kalgan* [empty-handed] in verse 19.

In verses 5, 21, 22, 25, and 28, the Altai rhyming scheme utilized by the oral translation team is clearly visible and audible. In verse 21 the final two lines are poetically expressed in Altai, with rhyming verbs at the end position:

Тыным мениҥ, ичкери!
Ийде алынып, јӱтки!

Tynym meniŋ, ichkeri!
Iĭde alynyp, juĭtki!

My spirit move forward!
Take strength, strive on!

In verse 22 the Altai team attempted to add the onomatopoeic sound of the horses' hooves in the verse by using т multiple times in Аттар *Attar*, тибирти *tibirti*, and туйгактары *tuĭgaktary*. The team decided that in verse 25, as in the Hebrew, it would be possible to front the word for *water* and *milk* in the Altai sentence, to give these a special emphasis. Чӧӧчӧй *chòòchòĭ* is an Altai word meaning *drinking cup*, which is given to the guest of honor during a feast. Айрак *aĭrak* is a sour milk product considered a delicacy in Altai, and this word sounded more poetic in the Altai sentence than чеген *chegen*, which is a synonym also meaning *sour milk*. In verse 28 the direct speech of Sisera's mother rhymes in Altai and is poetic, ending in the two similar phrases: *Why are they not visible? Why are they not audible?*

> Оныҥ јуучыл абралары нениҥ учун кӧрӱнбейт?
> Абра тегелик табыжы нениҥ учун угулбайт?
> *Onyng juuchyl abralary nening uchun körünbeït?*
> *Abra tegelik tabyzhy nening uchun ugulbaït?*

The team had decided to draft this chapter directly into poetry using the oral-lyrical method rather than translating it as text and then turning it into poetry. This was in order to retain more of the oral poetic effects. The team found the process of translating Judg 5 orally extremely difficult. In the end they opted for oral drafting and then writing their draft on a whiteboard, so they could see the poetic expression more clearly. Using the whiteboard, the team then juggled around the words and concepts to put it mostly into free rhyme in the Altai language. The time available was limited (we were restricted to one week), and if there had been unlimited time available, the team may have been able to translate completely orally. However, in this case oral drafting was used.

Translation of Psalm 1 into Altai

Internalization, exegesis, and translation

The Altai translation team and I attended a seminar about singing the psalms, teaching the oral-lyrical method of translating the psalms and about Hebrew poetry in general. The Altai translation team listened to Ps 1 initially in two different Russian translations (CRV2 2015 and Synodal 1876/1994) and discussed the structure of the psalm. The team spent time internalizing the psalm using actions before beginning to translate and simultaneously compose the song.

In verse one, three different words for sinners were used by the oral translation team—*those who do evil deeds*, *sinners*, and *mockers*. Initially the team chose the phrase *those who do bad deeds*, but changed this to *those who do evil deeds*, as that provided alliteration in Altai in the first two words Калју кылыктулалардыҥ *Kalju kylyktulalardyng*.

Overall, the OBT team attempted to make a poetic rendering of Ps 1 (for the final recording after testing, see Video 6). Lovelace, comparing the OBT's version of Ps 1 with a written version in Altai, comments, "It is clear, however, that the oral translation of Ps 1 is composed like poetry. That is, couplets in the oral translation tend to be the same or similar metrical length, and they exhibit rhyme and iambic cadence more regularly than the written draft."[13]

In the song version, verse 6 is also recited rather than sung. Then the singers return to verse 3 and repeat that verse, finally ending with the phrase Кайраканнаҥ алкышту *Kaĭrakannaṅg alkyshtu* [blessed from the Lord], which was at the end of verse 1.

Translation of Psalm 100 into Altai

Internalization, exegesis, and translation

The Altai translation team listened to the psalm initially in two different Russian translations (CRV2 2015 and Synodal 1876/1994) and discussed the structure of the psalm. They noted the use of the seven imperatives and the reasons for praise in verses 3 and 5, and they discussed the central truth in verse 3. The team spent time internalizing the psalm using actions. Then the team translated and simultaneously composed the song, with both the translators and the musicians present.

The oral translation team ended up with a free dynamic translation, in order to fit the words of the psalm into the melody (see Video 7 of a rehearsal and Video 8 of the final recording). For example, they added *great* to *the Lord* in verse 5, and *We (are) his creation* in verse 3. They modified some concepts in order to adjust the song to the Altai culture, such as not comparing people to sheep but using *shepherd* instead and changing *gates* and *courtyard* to *door* and *house*. The song form repeats the first verse at the end of the song, forming a frame around the poem.

Translation of Psalm 133 into Altai

Internalization, exegesis, and translation

I led the team through an exegesis of Ps 133. We talked about the metaphors of the oil and the dew and the importance of these in Hebrew culture. The team listened to several Russian translations of the psalm, before attempting an oral-lyrical translation of this psalm as a worship song in Altai.

The team also agreed on using the genre of *jangar* song, and so each line was sung initially by the leader of the group and then repeated by the rest of the group in *jangar* style. Since the *jangar* genre emphasizes unity, it was regarded as an appropriate genre for this psalm (see Video 9 and

---

13. Lovelace, "Comparison," 2.

Video 10). The team used some poetic license in the translation in order to express the meaning in a song format according to the Altai *jangar* style, for example, in adding серүүн эзин-јыбардый *seruün ėzin-jybardyĭ* [cool wind-breeze] in verse 3.

It would be interesting to do more field research on how proper nouns and names are understood in Altai and their importance in the culture. This is an excellent example of the question of alterity and how it is possible to retain the alterity while making the oral translation intelligible and attractive to the audience.[14] Naudé and Miller-Naudé conclude that "performance translation provides one way to recreate the alterity of ancient oral texts in a meaningful way to modern readers and hearers."[15] One possibility in this psalm is to contextualize the terms by adding a descriptive phrase such as "Aaron, the priest of God's people" or "Mount Zion, where the Lord dwells," etc. With regard to the proper nouns, the team initially removed the proper nouns to reduce foreignization in this worship song and to focus instead on making the song appropriate and understandable in the local culture. The aim of the translation of Ps 133 as a worship song is to reinforce the idea of the unity of God's people, both through the content of the psalm but also by using the local genre and dance of *jangar*. However, the consultant emphasized that accuracy to the original biblical text was also an important consideration, even in these shorter poetic passages, and recommended using the proper nouns. Perhaps in the future one idea is to have more than one oral version: one as a worship song and one as an oral translation of Scripture.

CONCLUSION

In this chapter I have described my own personal internalization and embodiment of Judg 4–5, which proved essential to the process of exegesis. I then discussed how to translate psalms as songs, concluding that psalms are particularly appropriate for BPC. Next, I described in detail the oral translation process of the biblical passages as carried out by the Altai team. The following chapter describes the twelve performances in Altai and the response of the audiences.

---

14. Makutoane et al., "Similarity and Alterity."
15. Naudé and Miller-Naudé, "Alterity, Orality," 310.

9

Altai Performances

INTRODUCTION

The Altai team and I decided to do two live rehearsals followed by ten full concerts, some in Gorno-Altaisk and some in other regions of Altai. After the two rehearsal concerts, the audiences made recommendations which were implemented in the subsequent concerts. To watch the performance of the second rehearsal concert and discussion afterwards, see Video 11 in the bibliography.

FIRST REHEARSAL CONCERT

Performance

The first of the two rehearsal concerts took place on Sunday, January 25, 2023, in Gorno-Altaisk, in the church of the pastor, Alexander Li. There were eleven members of the audience who participated in answering the questions after the concert.

Yuri Chendeyev, one of the musicians and a local pastor, gave a brief introduction to the concert in the Altai language. There were five musicians who took part in the concert: Aidin Kurmanov, Mergen Chenkurov, Larisa Baina, Ayas Chendeyeva, and Yuri Chendeyev. The concert started with a greetings song in Altai to welcome people to the concert. Then Aidin gave a short verbal introduction to the Altai epic tale of Judg 4–5. While Aidin was singing the epic, on the screen in the background were shown the words to the epic tale in Altai, accompanied by contextualized illustrations drawn by the Altai artist of the story of Judg 4–5. The performance of the epic tale lasted twenty-two minutes.

The epic tale was followed by the performance of Pss 1, 133, and 100. During Ps 133 two of the performers performed the *jangar*-style dance on stage, linking arms and swaying to demonstrate unity. The team ended their performance with Ps 150. The whole concert lasted an hour. On the table to the right of the stage, we had planned that there would be objects from the Altai culture relating to the story of Judg 4–5: an Altai bottle used for holding water or other drinks (such as that perhaps used by Jael to give a drink to Sisera), a horse's saddle, a tent peg, and a wooden hammer. Unfortunately, at the first rehearsal concert it was not possible to place these objects on the stage.

There were some recommendations from the audience after the first concert:

- To put the objects on the stage during the performance.
- To put the words of the psalms also on slides during the performance.
- To give an introduction before the singing of the epic tale, telling people about the story of Deborah and not assuming that people know this story beforehand.
- To give a short introduction explaining the themes of the psalms.

SECOND REHEARSAL CONCERT

The second of the two rehearsal concerts took place on Sunday, January 22, 2023, in Pastor Gera Mundusov's church in Gorno-Altaisk. There were ten members of the church who took part in answering the questions after the concert.

This time, the performers agreed that Aidin's epic tale performance of Judg 4–5 would be the first item in the program, following the short introduction. Aidin was sitting on stage when the concert started, with the objects, such as the saddle and the bottle, placed near to him in full sight of the audience. Aidin began with an introduction to the song of Deborah in Judg 4–5, explaining that he would perform this story through throat singing, in the style of an Altai epic. Aidin performed the epic, which lasted just over twenty-one minutes. This was followed by an introduction by Yuri, who explained the names of each of the national instruments in the Altai language and talked about how the psalms had been translated and put to music. The group began with their performance of the traditional Altai greeting song, followed by Ps 1. Yuri did not give a verbal explanation of the theme of the psalm, and the words of the psalm were not shown during the performance. This was followed by a performance of Ps 133 and Ps 100. The group ended the performance with Ps 150, preceded by a short introduction. The whole concert lasted fifty-four minutes.

There were some recommendations after the second rehearsal concert from the audience:

- To give a fuller introduction before the singing of the epic tale about the plot of the story of Deborah.
- To give a fuller introduction before the singing of the psalms about the theme of the psalms.
- To show the words of the psalm on the slides in Altai during the performance.
- One lady asked for the text for the epic tale to be on the screen behind the performance in Russian as well as in Altai.

FIRST FULL PERFORMANCE

The first of the ten full performances took place in the town of Gorno-Altaisk on Saturday, January 28, 2023, in Pastor Gera's church. There was an audience of twenty-five people, ten of whom took part in the focus group questions after the concert. The concert began this time with the Altai epic performance, prefaced by a short introduction to the song of Deborah and the plot of Judg 4–5. This was intended to help orient the audience to the performance and deepen their understanding. The visual objects (a saddle, an Altai bottle, a large wooden tent peg, and a bow and arrow) were placed in front of the epic tale singer on the stage in full view, and the audience's attention was drawn to these during the introduction. This was followed by the greetings song in Altai and then Pss 1, 133, 99, and 150. This time, each psalm had a short verbal introduction explaining the theme and the content, and the words of the psalms were displayed on a slide behind the performers. As a result, at times the audience was able to join in singing. The audience were also encouraged to get up and link arms and sway during the performance of Ps 133, in keeping with *jangar* style, reflecting the moves of the two female dancers on the stage. Some of the audience members were clapping and dancing during the praise psalms.

SECOND PERFORMANCE

The second concert performance was on Sunday, February 5, 2023, at Pastor David's church in Gorno-Altaisk. This performance was done in the same format as the first performance. There were about fifteen members of the audience, ten of whom took part in the focus group questions after the performance.

THIRD PERFORMANCE

The third concert took place on Friday, February 24, 2023, in the regional center of Kosh-Agach, in the local evangelical church building. This time Aidin, the throat singer himself, did an introduction before the singing of the epic tale, telling the audience about the story of Deborah and explaining the meaning of the objects on the stage. There were about fifteen people present at the concert. Mergen Chenkurov, one of the musicians, introduced each of the psalms, explaining the theme of the psalm to the audience.

FOURTH PERFORMANCE

The fourth concert took place in the regional center of Kosh-Agach on Saturday, February 25, 2023, in the village of Kukure, in the local administrative building. There were ten people present at the concert.

FIFTH PERFORMANCE

The fifth concert took place in the regional center Kosh-Agach on Sunday, February 26, 2023, in a Pentecostal church. There were sixteen people present at the concert.

SIXTH PERFORMANCE

The sixth concert was in the regional center of Shebalino in the local Pentecostal church on Friday, March 10, 2023, the leader of which was Pastor Slava Li. There were about twenty people present.

SEVENTH PERFORMANCE

The seventh concert was in the regional center of Onguday on Saturday, March 11, 2023, in a local church that meets in an Altai *ail* (the traditional wooden hexagonal house of the Altai people). There were about seventeen people there.

EIGHTH PERFORMANCE

The eight concert was in the Church of Truth in Gorno-Altaisk on Sunday, April 2, 2023, with Pastor Slava Han. There were over thirty people present.

NINTH PERFORMANCE

The ninth concert was in the regional center of Onguday on Friday, April 7, 2023, in the Pentecostal church lead by Pastor Ailan Tazov. There were fourteen people present. In this concert the team also added a song that they had previously translated from an animated video about the story of Joshua.[1]

TENTH PERFORMANCE

The tenth concert was in the regional center of Ulagan on Saturday, April 8, 2023, in the Pentecostal church, lead by brother Aimrak Tadirov. There were thirteen adults present.

AUDIENCE COMMENTS

After each concert, the audience members were invited to discuss the performances, share their responses, and propose suggestions for improvement. Most audience members used Russian during these discussions, although some spoke Altai. The discussions were recorded, translated, and transcribed by Rasul Kudachinov. The following comments are taken from these transcriptions:
What were your impressions of the concert?

- Mind-blowing, excellent impressions.
- I really enjoyed it.

---

1. This animated video can be found at http://www.altai-obt.ru/?page_id=102.

- We do not need to go to the theater; the theater is here with us.
- I loved the Altai costumes and instruments.
- Through the translation of these psalms and stories into the Altai language, it is great to see the praise of the Lord by these musicians in their own language. We are very pleased that the Altai translation team are doing these concerts.
- We give the concert full marks.
- It was very pleasurable, especially for our soul, to hear something completely new. I think that it would cause a great interest for someone who did not know anything about the Bible, I think they would hear this and want to find out more.
- It was very good, especially the psalms.
- It was very useful to have the words of the epic on the slides. It made the Bible stories close to our hearts to hear it in the Altai language. It's very good for the youth in Altai to hear such a performance.
- The translation was very good quality. It was very joyful to hear.
- It was very beautiful to listen to and inspiring because it was all in Altai, especially the sounds of nature.
- I really liked the Altai concert. It helped me to get into the Altai spirit and feel at home with the Altai language.
- It was really interesting. It was the first time I've heard a story through throat singing.
- I really enjoyed it. It was very beautiful.
- Hurray, we thought it was excellent!
- I received great pleasure from the concert, and I did not see any mistakes. It was my impression that all of the performers were musicians. I had very good impressions and it was all over too quickly.
- I was happy that God was worshiped at this concert, and I felt unity here among the people. It was very powerful that God's word was performed in the Altai language and using the Altai style of throat singing, and I was happy to sing psalms from the Bible in the Altai language. I enjoyed it very much and I felt unity deep in my spirit.
- I am very thankful for this great project, and I am very impressed with the costumes and with this musical group of performers. You are very talented, and we expect more and more of you. We hope you will tour around the Altai Republic and even around the world.

- With regards to throat singing, I have studied this style of Altai music, and I know it very well. There is nothing wrong with this style and to praise God using this Altai style is a very good thing indeed. Anybody should be able to praise God in their own language using their own culture, so I consider this concert to be a good beginning. I had heard one of the psalms before, and I'm still singing it in my head.
- Your costumes are very beautiful.
- My eyes were swollen from crying because it was so wonderful, and my heart was beating fast.
- I felt the Altai spirit at the concert.
- I have very good and positive impressions. I liked the concert very much, especially the costumes, and I wanted to join in the singing myself (at first quietly and then I joined in the singing loudly). This is a great concert to perform around the Altai Republic to show the Altai people.
- The voices were strong, and the melodies were very joyful. My heart tried to come out of my body, and I felt like the whole earth was shaking. I liked it very much.
- It improved my mood a lot.
- I am very proud that such a concert from the Bible is being shared around Altai. This will help to promote the Altai culture and language.
- This concert was something new for the Altai people. The songs were very interesting. I have never heard such music as this before.
- This was the first time we had had such a concert in our village. It was great to see God being praised on different instruments. The youth were very interested to hear it, and people's hearts opened to hear the message.
- I wanted to cry because I was so touched by the concert.
- We were surprised by the quality of this performance. The ensemble needs to take this concert to the different clubs in villages in our area. We really want others to see this as well.
- Our mood was lifted by the concert.
- We were overjoyed by the concert, and our hearts were very happy. I joined in when I could with the singing.
- We are waiting now for the next concert.
- It really touched my heart.

- There were new instruments, such as the hooves and the horn. It sounded brilliant.
- The concert became more and more interesting as it went on. It was not boring.
- It was great to see many Altai national instruments.
- I was inspired and invigorated. I didn't even want to move but just to listen.
- We noticed the sounds of the horses and the birds.
- You should perform this concert at the major Altai festivals.
- My expectations were exceeded. It was unexpected.
- It is so exciting that you are traveling around Altai and spreading his word and opening the eyes of the people to understand that God is for the Altai people. Many Altai people think that God is Russian, but this performance, and especially the *jangar* and throat singing, will reach the hearts of the Altai people. Please do not stop traveling around Altai and showing this concert everywhere.
- I was proud that this was from my culture and language. It was so pleasant and wonderful to hear. I want to bring my friends to hear this concert and to take part in some way as well. I would like you to do more concerts and to perform in more places.
- It would be great to involve the youth more in this concert.
- We loved the voices and the translation.
- Our expectations were met, and we wished it had been longer.
- It really lifted our mood.
- The songs help to unite people.
- It entered my spirit very deeply.
- The concert brought truth, joy, and love.
- You need to take these concerts out to the Altai villages.
- I enjoyed the first and the last psalm; I wanted to cry during it.
- We liked the translation of the psalms into Altai; it was inspiring.
- The program was too short. You need to translate more psalms and do a longer performance. The concert exceeded all my expectations.

- We were amazed by the concert. It was a great time. We are very proud of the translators, and the music was very well composed to fit the words.
- The songs are very joyful, and we wanted to dance. They were optimistic melodies which lifted our mood.
- We felt joyful, and our mood was lifted.
- We are proud that we have such a rich Altai culture and language.
- Psalm 1 would be a very appropriate psalm to perform for a non-Christian audience.
- Normally the throat singing praises the lyre, but in this context, we liked it when the throat singing was used to praise God. Our attitude changed after the concert and now we have started to like the throat singing better and playing on Altai instruments.
- We felt joy and were encouraged to do more singing in this style and in the Altai language.
- I did not accept it before, but this time I was able to accept it and wanted to start to learn to play myself on these instruments. The concert encouraged me to wear my Altai clothing more often.
- We felt unity and harmony during Ps 133 and the *jangar* style.
- It really hit our spirits because it was in our own Altai language.

What did you think of the throat singing epic performance of Judges 4–5?

- It was a bit difficult to understand. We did not know the story of Deborah in the first place, so it was hard to understand from the epic tale. It would be better if we knew the story in a bit more detail before the epic tale. However, the concert inspired me to go and read this passage and this book of the Bible in more detail.
- It being performed by throat singing made it seem like our own, our own Altai story. I started by reading the words on the slide of the first epic tale, and then I stopped reading and started to understand the throat singing epic on my own, without the help of the words. The words were very clear and understandable. I would like to hear more of the Bible through this method of the Altai epic tale in the future. We don't listen to throat singing very often, and so we need to get used to this style, and then we will understand it more easily.
- I liked the throat singing epic tale very much indeed.

- Indeed, it feels like "our own." At first, I did not understand, but the words on the slide helped me.
- I really liked it. I could understand all the words and really liked the music. Doing it in this way makes it accessible for our people.
- I really liked it, and it was close to my heart. It was hard at first to understand, but the words helped me on the slides, and then I started to understand automatically without the words. I really enjoyed it.
- It is a style that is close to our people and our hearts and so many will enjoy listening to this. Among my relatives there were throat singers, like my father, my father-in-law, and my uncle, so I understand very well.
- I don't normally like throat singing, but I could understand because I could see the words on the screen, and it became easier to listen. In some places I didn't know the Altai words, but I could see them on the screen and understand.
- I did not understand the first half, but then I opened the Bible and followed the story in Russian and that helped me understand it. Once you get into the story, then it is easier to understand; it's like going into a trance.
- I enjoyed it very much, but it's important to understand what the stories are about in Russian first.
- I honestly found it a bit difficult to understand. I need to spend more time reading the Bible and learning my own language. It really affected my spirit in a deep way.
- If we listen to God's word in the throat singing style, it enters our hearts in a different way, as if directly from God, from "the other side." The Altai person is created, so that understanding comes directly to the heart and the soul if it is delivered through throat singing.
- Sometimes I was confused by the sounds the throat singer made.
- It was difficult for me to listen to. It would be easier if I heard it every day.
- I liked that you are bringing the word of God in the Altai language to the Altai people.
- I liked the throat singing, and I liked the psalms as well (Ps 1 in particular was very well structured musically). I liked how you stopped, and then people started to clap in the pause, but then you started to play again.

- I liked it and the sound of the throat singing. I couldn't understand all the words, but it was nice to listen to.
- I had positive impressions. For me the throat singing was fifty-fifty because it wasn't easy to understand, but I loved the use of Altai instruments and costumes.
- I liked it, especially the throat singing.
- I liked the greeting song, especially at the beginning. The throat singing was not totally clear to me, but I still liked it.
- I liked the last song, which was Ps 150, and the throat singing epic the best.
- I was very impressed by the quality of this concert and the translation. However, the throat singing was not really for me.
- I enjoyed the fact that you put the Bible stories in the form of an epic tale. The text was visible, and the pictures were available, and so I could understand what was being sung. Without the text and pictures, it would have been much more difficult to understand.
- We are the Altai Telengit people, and I grew up from childhood among throat singing. Near our fire in the center of our house my father sang using throat singing, and we were nearby listening and felt in some kind of "trance," and we also sang Altai songs using ethnic instruments such as the Altai flute. It was interesting and magical. Our father taught us this, and from an early age I have been able to throat sing. Sometimes I was told not to do this because I was a woman, and they said that I would bring a curse on myself. However, still I find myself throat singing sometimes. I then studied the Bible, and I was very happy sometimes to sing Christian songs using throat singing together with another Altai performer. For me, today, hearing this Altai group, it was very pleasant to hear this, and my soul rejoiced to hear this harmony of voices and instruments. I will try to come again to more concerts. If we sing Christian songs using throat singing, people will be healed and people will rejoice. I wish this as well for other Turkic peoples.
- I enjoyed the epic poem from Judges 5 about the heroic deeds of the prophetess Deborah. In the Christian epic the team included certain stylistic moments from the traditional throat singing Altai epics. Some people say that the throat singing is not pure, but we know that nothing was created by Satan. Satan can only steal. The use of Altai national instruments and throat singing in this concert helps people to understand that this was all created by God and encourages us to

use these forms without fear, because through this God is praised and our culture is returned to the Altai people. Altai is the language of our heart. I also liked the fact that the epic did not contain the normal praise of the mountains and the Altai nature but was based on a story from the Bible. When I heard the epic for the first time today it was like I had a revelation, earth and heaven opened and it became light, and I understood the words of the Bible. I saw before me all the nations and tribes, and I wanted to dance. It was great and a very good-quality translation.

- When the throat singing was going on, it was hard for Russians to understand. It would be good to have the Russian text alongside the Altai, if possible, please. It's clear that God has given a gift to the person who translated this text and put it to music, and it was a very harmonious performance of Deborah's song.

- The pictures helped make it understandable for a wider audience.

- When I listened to other performances of throat singing before, I imagined that demonic spirits were involved. However, today, when I heard the story from the Bible through epic singing, I was very surprised. I understand that God gives us the possibility through different ways to bring his truth and stories to the Altai people.

- When the throat singing normally begins (and I am a throat singer myself), people start to get bored and move around after five minutes. But today, people listened well, and I was very surprised that they listened for so long.

- It was great to have the words on the screen, which helped keep people's attention.

- People were surprised that the voice of the throat singer stayed fresh and strong all the way through the whole performance. Here in the village, there are children who are learning throat singing, and they were fascinated to see this performance.

- It's the first time I have heard throat singing in person. Before I have only heard it on television, but I enjoyed it very much.

- I never thought I would hear throat singing in the church. I thought it would not go together very well with church activities. So, this was new for me.

- I enjoyed the throat singing and felt that I had entered a new world. I thought it was not possible to sing like this in the church, but then I realized that if a Christian sings, it's OK. It depends on what reasons we are doing this. God gave us all these instruments, and it is good to use them to praise him.

- We really enjoyed the throat singing, it was not too long and the fact that it was a Bible story was very interesting. I don't understand Altai very well, but the words on the screen really helped.
- It was very clear and expressed the meaning of the biblical text very well.
- I did not understand all the Altai words, but it still touched me a lot when I heard it.
- I love throat singing because I am from a shaman family, so I am very familiar with this style. Today this throat singing was the best I have heard, and I was so impressed and had the feeling of joy that I was flying in the clouds. I have seen a lot in my life, but today you really surprised me by the quality of the throat singing.
- I don't think we will find people in Altai who did not like this performance.
- Throat singing is like a spiritual doctor for us.
- We all grew up on the Altai epic stories about the heroes, and I really enjoyed the throat singing version of Deborah. Your translation of the story of Deborah into an Altai epic story was very original, and it will be very well liked by the Altai people. I enjoyed it very much indeed.
- My favorite Altai epic in my childhood was *Maadai-Kara*, but now I don't know the Altai language very well. I would have liked a parallel text in Russian of the story of Deborah and the psalms.
- I find it a bit difficult to understand and keep up with the words on the screen, and I liked the psalms better.
- I wondered if we were moving away a bit from God's word and trying to mix the Bible too much with local culture.
- I especially enjoyed the throat singing.
- I enjoyed the epic tale, and it was useful that we could see the text on the screen at the same time.
- It would be good to do more performances using throat singing from different parts of the Bible, like the parables of Jesus and his acts of healing, casting out demons, and teaching from the New Testament, and this would have a great effect on the audience. The throat singer would pray and perform, and this would touch the hearts of non-Christians. I

would suggest putting the throat singing performance after the psalms and to do a longer program. You should take this concert to all the churches in Altai, to festivals, to youth meetings, to seminars, and conferences.

- I really appreciated the blessing at the end of the throat singing tale about Deborah.
- In my childhood I didn't really like the throat singing, and I found it a bit hard to listen to and understand. However, the fact that the words were on the screen helped, and there weren't any words I did not know in the translation. You could also print the words and give them out to people, so it would be easier to follow along.
- The question was discussed of whether the whole Bible could be presented by throat singing. I think it would be very appropriate for the young Altai men. We should mix the Bible and throat singing, and it will be a great presentation.
- I fell asleep during the throat singing.
- We liked the throat singing. It was a good translation and a good performance without mistakes. The pictures and the text on the screen helped us to understand. Often throat singing is hard to understand, so this helped us.
- We felt the word of the Holy Spirit during the throat singing ministering to our hearts.
- God has given the Altai people this gift of throat singing, and we should use it.

How did you find the singing of the psalms in the Altai language?

- We often sing using the piano and the guitar, but in this concert, it was really nice to see the Altai instruments and hear the Altai language being used. It was very joyful and very interesting, and I enjoyed it very much.
- I was touched today by the fact that the whole concert was in the Altai language. The Altai epic tale touched me to the center of my heart, and it woke me up spiritually. When I listened to the psalms in my own language, I realized they were written for my Altai people. If we continue to sing the psalms in the Altai language, it will make a very great impression on the Altai people.

- It was very beautiful, and we enjoyed listening to the instruments and our own language. You need to take this concert around the Altai Republic. It's so great that you are doing this concert free. Please can you make recordings of these psalms so that we can sing along to them at home? We think people will receive healing as they listen to this concert.
- I loved the singing of the psalms. I wrote down all the words and will go through them again at home.
- I felt very joyful during the singing of Psalm 150, that God has created us, and we can praise him on all these instruments.
- I don't know the Altai language very well, but when you started to sing Psalm 1, I felt very emotional and cried, even though I didn't understand the words very well. The atmosphere was very moving.
- The concert helped us understand the Bible more clearly. People open up their hearts more easily when they hear songs than if we asked them to read the Bible itself. It's easier for people to remember what they see and hear than what they read. It makes a bigger impression on people.
- I noticed the experiences and worries of real people are written about in the psalms, who are asking help from God and also praising God with joy.
- I have never read the psalms in the Bible in Altai because they are not translated yet in a written form. It's the first time we have heard them, and it felt very close to us hearing them in our own language and set to our own style of music.
- Someone who has never read the Bible will understand more easily in this way through the songs. If someone has read the psalms, this will be confirmation when they hear these songs. The hearing and singing will complement each other very well.
- We enjoyed Psalm 133 particularly, with the *jangar* melody and dance. At all the Altai celebrations, the *jangar* style is the most popular. It was fascinating to see God's word performed using this style. *Jangar* is often used at weddings or when a baby is one year old.
- The singing of the psalms helped make them more alive and relevant.
- It was very beautiful to hear the psalms in the Altai language, especially Psalm 133. It was the first time we have heard them in our language.

- We very much enjoyed Ps 133 done in the *jangar* style. The translation really expressed the text well.
- I never imagined before that it would be possible to sing the psalms in the Altai language. I loved especially the melody of Ps 1. It was a very "Altai" modern melody, and we can sing this in church if we have the melody and the words. It was maybe a bit more happy than normal Altai songs, which make you want to cry. It felt like Altai spiritual music, and it was easy to pray and join in during the songs. These psalms will reach the heart of the Altai people.
- We loved the costumes, which made the story and the psalms come alive.
- We loved the use of the Altai instruments (especially the hooves), and this is great for young people who have not seen the use of them before.
- I also very much liked the *jangar* melody of Psalm 133.
- The psalms were all about different themes. Psalm 150 was about worshiping God on many different instruments, and we saw that today in reality.
- We started to understand Psalm 1 in more depth after this performance. However, we are worried that our children will not understand.
- When I first heard Psalm 150 (before this concert), I could not get it out of my head! It's great when these words from the Bible are circling around your head!
- It's brilliant news for us that you are translating the psalms as songs.
- We want to learn the psalms and sing them ourselves.

What is the difference between reading the text and hearing/seeing the performance in this way?

- It was like being in a theater. I loved it. You are the first people who have attempted to translate the Bible into Altai and perform it in this way.
- Even without the pictures, it is good to listen to the story and get into it. It was helpful to have the contextualized pictures, and this helped us imagine the story and understand what was happening. It is easier to understand the Bible story through song.

- We couldn't understand all the words of the psalms, so it is important also to read the Bible yourself and understand it, and then the performance will be easier to understand.

- It was good to experience the Bible in a new way. It would be a very interesting and easier way to present the Bible to non-Christians in Altai. It would be great to have more Bible stories available in this style.

- I think it might be difficult for non-Christians to understand without more Bible context.

- The psalms can be listened to as songs while doing something else.

- When I first heard Altai worship in the Altai language, I was drunk, but it touched my heart straight away, and I became sober immediately. Now I see that God is touching people's hearts through this concert in the Altai language. I think this is a great way for God to touch the hearts of the Altai people and reach the Altai people. God will open the hearts of people through the psalms.

- I enjoyed it, and if a non-believer heard this, he would think that this God is for the Altai people, rather than just for the Russians. If I had heard this originally when I didn't know God, this would be easier for me to understand than in Russian.

- I think that faith comes from hearing, so a non-believer hearing this would become interested in the Bible stories. I think the throat singing is a good style to use to present the Bible.

- I enjoyed it very much, and the presentation of the Bible stories in the Altai language suited me very well. I did not understand everything.

- The Altai language is disappearing, and our children do not speak the language well anymore. You are doing a great work translating the Bible into Altai and using local styles to present it to us and help renew the language.

- Of course, both are important, but the concert helped give new impressions.

- The story of Deborah became more understandable than before.

- When I heard the story of Deborah and realized how as a woman she gained a victory for her people, I was deeply touched and inspired that a woman can be such an important person in society.

- It may depend on the person. For me, it is easier to just read the Bible.

- I am used to watching videos and films more than reading, so for me the concert was easier to understand and gave me a fuller picture of the Bible stories and themes. For me I remember things that I watch better than what I read.
- I agree. It's easier for me to listen than to read on my own.
- In this concert the texts were understandable in a new way. In this way it's possible to reach the listener in a different way than normal and from a new perspective.
- It was very rhythmic. It seems to me that it is easier to understand the Bible in this way than if one is just reading it. One can remember the words and receive new insights and knowledge through such a performance. I felt unity among the people in the concert. Thanks to these songs and this music, the people were touched and received the message.
- The fact that it was in our Altai language helped us to understand the truths in a deeper way.
- Through the performance we were able to enter into the story with more energy, and it engages all parts of our brain and our emotions.
- If we just give the Bible to someone to read, this person may not understand why he should read it and will not be interested in it. If it is accompanied by music, pictures, and costumes, he will have a greater understanding of what is written.
- The translation into Altai helped us understand the meaning of the text better and be able to enter into it in a deeper way.
- Through singing and praise, it is possible to understand God's truths better than if we just read them.
- I was very happy to hear worship and God's word in the Altai language and that a team is working on translating the Bible into the Altai language. I want to wish this group all the best in their continued translation work.
- Yes, I realized how little we value our own language and our own culture and musical melodies. This was such a blessing to hear these musical pieces in our own language. We really liked the costumes, the music, and the words, and it reminded us that we are in fact Altai people. We are used to speaking in Russian, but this brought us back to our roots. The Altai are beautiful people with a unique and wonderful language.

- It helped us understand the meaning of the psalms better. This was true especially during Psalm 133 and when we swayed and sang together. I understood that God loves the Altai people very deeply. I would like others to hear this song as well.
- Before I have looked for worship and songs in the Altai language, but I couldn't find any. Today it was great to hear this for the first time in the Altai language. At the moment in our church, we sing in Russian. Please, can you put this recording on the internet, so we can sing these songs and psalms in the future?
- Yes, when the words of the Bible are sung, it seems closer in your heart, and you can remember it for longer.
- We understood that God is a God of the whole world, and all the nationalities of the world can worship him with their own language and their own instruments.
- The costumes were very beautiful and helped demonstrate the Altai culture. The children were interested to see the Altai national instruments and see how they are played. I myself only saw this today for the first time.
- Also, when we all stood up and swayed during Psalm 133, it was very moving. However, our *jangar* here in Kosh-Agach is slightly different than that melody. In every region the *jangar* melody is slightly different in style.
- We learned today about the great talent of the Altai people, who are able to express themselves through songs, throat singing, and *jangar*. I was very touched by what I heard and loved the atmosphere of the concert. In this way we will win the heart of the Altai people, through these songs and using their own genres. Many people will start to think about God through these concerts. People often say that we believe in a Russian God, but your concert demonstrates that God is also for the Altai people through the costumes, music, and instruments.
- In particular we noticed the Altai instruments and we enjoyed that one of the singers was imitating bird noises during some of the psalms. We saw some of these Altai instruments played for the first time today, such as the hooves.
- The costumes were beautiful and even noble.
- The melodies were very attractive.

- We are happy that our culture is alive and being celebrated and that through our culture we can praise God.
- I was a bit frightened when I saw someone playing the shaman drum in the concert, but then I realized that we can also use these instruments to praise God and receive joy and freedom.
- I was very interested to see the objects on the stage during the throat singing performance. We see the tent peg, the hammer, and the bottle which Jael offered to Sisera. It helped us to visualize the performance and made us ask questions afterwards.
- I thought at first that the drum could only be used by shamans, but when I saw it used here in worship and for the psalms, I was convinced that this is a good idea. Psalm 150 says that we can use all instruments to worship God.
- The costumes and instruments worked very well together to create an impression on the listeners. The illustrated contextualized pictures also helped us understand the story.
- It was a joy to hear the different Altai national instruments, which express what is written in the psalms.
- The costumes were very beautiful.
- It helped us understand the biblical texts more clearly. When we read it's not so clear, but when we heard it today, it made a big impression on us. The music made it very approachable and understandable, and the psalms were opened for us in a new way today with a deeper meaning.
- It was very different to when we just read. It was great to hear the tune and be able to hear the psalms set to music.
- It was pleasing to see the worship of God using Altai national instruments.
- The Altai costumes were beautiful and inspiring.
- The costumes and dances were very familiar to me, and we also use this in our church. A person understands the biblical themes better through performances and presentations.
- I was very encouraged by what I heard today. We are living in an environment where our children are starting to forget the Altai language. It is very hard for our Altai people to understand the Bible as it is, but this presentation helps our people to understand this truth and

- to open their hearts and ears. It will be easier for them to understand using Altai instruments and the local genres.
- I looked at the words of the songs, and they are very appropriate, and the music fit very well to the words, and it was pleasing to listen to. I noticed how the throat singer played on the *topshur*, and I felt that we were entering into a dialogue and fellowship with God. I was sure that God was very happy and was maybe even crying. The worship on the Altai musical instruments was brilliant and very powerful.
- The physical objects helped add to the atmosphere of the performance.
- It was much better to see the performance than a video.
- We loved the costumes, the music, and the physical objects on the stage, which made the stories and the biblical themes come alive.
- During the concert you expressed the words very clearly.
- The costumes were very beautiful and the instruments rich, and some of them we hadn't even seen before. A big thank you to you.
- The concert was good for the heart. It raises the question about the youth and children in Altai who do not know our language very well now. We hope that these performances will raise the understanding of our people about our language and culture.
- I wasn't sure about the use of the Altai drum, which is normally associated with shamanism. And then I understood that all instruments are God's instruments and can be used to worship him.

What did you learn about people, the word, and God from the texts you heard?

- We understood from the singing of the psalms that it is important that a person rejoices in the Lord.
- It helped me understand that I am an Altai person because I was able to listen to the Bible in my own language and see people performing in national costumes and playing national instruments.
- We are happy that the Altai people, if they hear this concert, will turn to God and think more about him.
- It is important to listen and obey the word of God and respect God.
- We learned more about God and that it is important to worship him. We learned that God accepts everyone. We praise God through our culture and our Altai culture.

- It's important to understand that our talents and gifts all come from God and can be used to sing and play for him.
- It was translated so well, and the music was so good. It was very rich and joyful, and we are proud of this effort.
- I learned that God loves all peoples, and we can worship him in our own language and using our own culture.
- We need to praise God with joy.
- It will help the older generation come to know God better using this concert format. It will really help those who love the Altai traditions and language to accept the word of God better and easier. It will soften their hearts.
- Of course, it was more interesting and easier to listen and understand the Bible truths when presented in this way. When a person hears, rather than reads, his imagination is switched on, and it helps him understand the message better.
- The only negative was that I have an association with shamanism, especially during the throat singing session. I am not used to worshiping God in this way, but I understand that it's not important which style or instrument you use to worship God (you can even use the shaman drum to do this).
- Everyone is unique, but God has given us unity, and we each can express ourselves differently, but we are still one body.
- A play is written to be seen on the stage and not to be just read, and so this performance makes the Bible come alive in a new way and engages our brain completely.
- We are happy that your group is translating the Old Testament and making it accessible to the people through the local Altai styles of music and performance.
- Today I received a blessing from God and grace. I realized that you must take this concert around all the Altai villages to bless the Altai people.
- We need to pray more and praise God.
- We understand that God is strong, he is good, and he loves us and defends us.
- We understood that people must praise the Lord, keep his law and not break it, and be righteous.

- We need to be brave and joyful in doing God's deeds and fear the Lord.
- In the first psalm when they sang about people who mock, God rebuked me, and I realized that this was about me. I need to be more careful about the people I spend time with.
- I understood that the Altai people are in God's hands.
- We saw that God is really alive and with us.
- We realized that we can worship God in many different languages. God is multifaceted and amazing. It made a big impression on me that we could worship God in the Altai language.
- God is great and loves each one of us in Altai.
- I realized that today God is everywhere and all-knowing.
- God cares for us, and we felt his love today through this performance.
- We felt that God was very close to us during the concert.
- Through hearing the word of God today in this way our faith has become stronger.
- Psalm 1 made a big impression on me, both the words and the melody. I could listen to it many times. I understood that the wicked person cannot stand with the righteous, and they were contrasted. Some of the Altai words stopped me and made me think deeply.
- I was impressed by the song from the Deditos film in Altai about Joshua on the theme of me and my family serving the Lord, and I began to think about my family. It gave me hope that my family will also serve the Lord.

Were there any words or phrases you did not understand in the translation and which you would want to change?

- The text in the throat singing and the psalms went by too fast for us to judge. Psalm 1 was translated especially well.
- We were worried that the children would not understand кутук *kutuk* [well; water source] and also терек *terek* [poplar].

CONCLUSIONS

The comments by the focus groups about the concerts in general were overwhelmingly positive. Overall impressions included "mind-blowing," "amazing," "joyful," "exceeding all expectations," and "too short." Everyone agreed that the quality and beauty of the hand-made Altai costumes contributed to the overall impression of the concert. Showing the Altai texts on the screen during the performance helped the audience to understand the content of the biblical passages, especially during the throat singing Altai epic of Judg 4–5. The purpose of the physical objects on stage was not always initially understood by the audience, but once explained, people realized how they were relevant. Many people commented on their enjoyment of the use of different Altai national instruments, some people seeing them for the first time. There was some confusion occasionally about the use of the Altai drum, which is linked to shamanism in the Altai culture, but, overall, the opinion was that it is allowable to use this instrument in worship and Christian performance.

The reaction to the psalms was also very positive, and there were no negative comments. It should be noted that because the comments were shared in person (in the presence of the performers and other members of the OBT team), it may be that people's responses were biased towards the favorable. People found the psalms joyful, inspiring, and encouraging to listen to, and in some comments people mentioned how they and other audience members had joined in by dancing, clapping, and singing. The response to the epic tale was more varied but was more positive in the regions of Altai that are more remote and farther away from the main town, where Russian is spoken frequently. It was said frequently that the Altai epic tale based on the story of Deborah is appropriate for non-Christian audiences, and it was suggested that more epic tales should be produced based on passages from the New Testament and especially the life of Jesus. The audiences were in agreement that they came to a deeper understanding of the biblical passages and themes through the multimedia presentation. It was sometimes difficult for the audiences to draw personal conclusions from the performances about what they had learned about God, themselves, or the world, perhaps because the question was difficult to understand. However, some conclusions were drawn on these themes.

One recommendation—that the Russian translation should be provided alongside the Altai texts, especially for the epic tale—was unfortunately not implemented in time for the remainder of the concerts. There was another recommendation after the last two concerts that the Altai text should be provided either on paper or by phone for the audience to follow along. However, I wondered if this would distract from watching and experiencing the actual performance. It was decided by the team and me to add one more specific question concerning the translation after the final two concerts, asking if the audience would suggest any changes to specific words or phrases. Following the final concert, the comments of the audience on the terms in Ps 1 кутук *kutuk* [well; water source] and also терек *terek* [poplar] were discussed by the translation team. The team decided that кутук [well; water source] would be difficult to replace but that терек [poplar] could be changed back to агаш [agash tree], which was in fact the term used in the initial draft. This may be an Altai word that people are more familiar with than терек [poplar].

The multimodal performances were appreciated greatly by almost all the audiences. The lyrics, the musical syntax, and the associated visual and multimodal cues all worked together in the Altai performances to effectively convey the meaning of Scripture to the Altai audiences. In my final chapter, I provide an overview of my research and conclusions, and I make recommendations for further study and implementation in the field of orality and performance in BT.

10

Conclusions

INTRODUCTION

In this book I have been seeking to address the following research question: How should one design a performance based on the oral translation of biblical texts into the Altai language, taking into account the traditional cultural genres? Using an integrated approach that includes the complex interplay of discussions about orality in the world today, orality and literacy in the Bible, and also Biblical Performance Criticism, I have designed a model for performing orally translated texts using traditional local genres. This model, founded on the functional theory of translation, together with aspects of complexity theory, multimodality, and hospitality theory, highlights principles that are relevant for other OBT teams seeking to translate orally and perform biblical passages.

THE MODEL

Exegetical and performance study

The first step was to do a detailed study of Judg 4–5 and Pss 1, 100, and 133. I translated these passages into English from the original Hebrew. This included a linguistic and literary analysis of these passages, including their genre, poetic features and functions, textual and exegetical issues, key terms, unfamiliar concepts for the receptor audience, implicit background knowledge, and their performance context. I prepared oral performance notes for the translation team, along with a story-chart.

Personal performance

Simultaneously with step one, together with a storytelling group, I prepared a retelling of Judg 4–5 in the English language, so that I myself would be able to embody this passage. I used Agnew's Embodied Performance Analysis method to feed performance interpretation back into my translation and oral performance notes.

Research into local genres

Together with the Altai translation team, I conducted research into local genres in order to find the most appropriate match for the passages to be performed. This included interviews with Altai throat singers and musicians, as well as research into one particular Altai epic, *Ochy-Bala*.

Internalization and translation process

I then led the Altai translation team, together with local musicians and poets, through the exegesis and internalization of Judg 4–5 and of Pss 1, 100, and 133. This included using the principles of internalization drawn from the survey results with nine OBT translation teams and an OBT trainer and endorsed by them.

Trial performances

The Altai translation team did two initial exploratory performances of these passages in order to assess the impact on the Altai community and be able to let the audience feedback influence the translation and performance choices for the future.

Performances

After incorporating some of the audience feedback and recommendations into the concert from the exploratory performances, the Altai translation team prepared a final series of performances to be shown around the different regions of Altai.

Evaluation

The translation team and I evaluated the performances, based on feedback from ten audiences, and again used the feedback to modify the original translation and potential future performances.

SUB-QUESTIONS

In this book I also have addressed the following sub-questions:

- How does the process of internalization influence the method of OBT, distinguishing it from written BT?
- How can the method of OBT be used to translate genres other than prose narrative?
- How and when should the process of extralinguistic exegesis take place during the OBT process?
- How can the oral features of local poetry, in a particular context, be incorporated into an oral poetic translation of a biblical text?
- What is the most useful way to create notes for the oral performance of an orally translated text, including extralinguistic and paralinguistic features?
- How can the response to the oral performance be incorporated back into the oral translation process and become part of the process of translation?

I will now look at the answers to each of these sub-questions in turn:

How does the process of internalization influence the method of oral Bible translation, distinguishing it from written Bible translation?

Internalization is a key component of the OBT process. Internalization was enjoyable for the Altai oral-preference community because it utilized their preference for collective and participatory learning. A larger group was preferable, made up of people who already know and trust each other, combined with working in a stress-free environment (in the Altai team there were six people, including three musicians). The emphasis was on complete understanding of the passage, helping the team to mentally reconstruct the scene in the passage and to access their tacit linguistic knowledge. The team began by listening to the passage several times. In breaks between listening, the team shared stories on a theme similar to that of the passage and discussed devotional questions.

I led the team through the three parts of internalization, which are experience, exposure, and engagement, using a combination of internalization techniques in order for the process to be most effective. Frequent but timed repetition enabled the translators to remember the material more permanently. There were Altai poets and musicians present during the whole process, who together translated the passages poetically into the target language.

Internalization, although fun, is tiring, and the team required sufficient rest and needed a sufficient length of time to internalize the longer passages of Judg 4–5. The team practiced retelling the passages to each other, which helped them to adapt and correct the stories naturally. I was familiar with voice prosody issues, and voice prosody considerations were included in the training, the exegesis, testing, and consultant stages of this translation project.

How can the method of oral Bible translation be used to translate genres other than narrative?

The internalization process was most successful with the narrative passage in Judg 4. When traditional internalization techniques did not work for the non-narrative passages, the conversational discovery of meaning was used. This was especially useful during the translation of Judg 5. For the non-narrative genres, the internalization process was considerably more difficult and took a longer time, and to some extent the team had to rely on memorization and the use of the whiteboard, particularly during the translation of the poetry in the three psalms and in Judg 5.

Recommendations for teams wanting to translate non-narrative genres

For teams wanting to translate non-narrative genres, the TA will need to take more time to research the passage and the genre and think through appropriate methods of internalization. Increased training is needed for OBT teams on non-narrative translation that is specific to various biblical genres. When a team internalizes poetry, more time and effort are required. Traditional methods of internalization may not work for non-narrative genres, and it may be necessary to use the conversational process of discovery, more rote memorization, and the whiteboard to write down phrases. One possibility is that after the team internalization, each member of the team proposes their own poetic rendition of the verses, and the team then chooses the most effective version, perhaps even mixing and matching different options.

How and when should the process of extralinguistic exegesis take place during the oral Bible translation process?

I (the TA) orally discussed exegetical information with the team during the initial process of internalization, with a focus on the emotions of the characters. This was particularly useful in the Judges story, as a way to analyze the characters of Deborah, Jael, Barak, and Sisera and in discussing the likely attitudes and emotions of the editors of the psalms. It was found that emotional exegesis is most effectively done during the internalization process. This can be done by reconstructing a range of possible emotions for the characters involved and choosing those that are most appropriate. There needs to be greater emphasis and training on this topic during OBT training and consultancy.

How can the oral features of local poetry, in a particular context, be incorporated into an oral poetic translation of a biblical text?

A key factor in this process is the initial analysis of local genres in the target language and culture. This includes analyzing target-language songs and other genres and identifying their poetic features. Based on this analysis, the translation team can then decide which local genres might be appropriate for an oral poetic translation of a biblical text.

What is the most useful way to create notes for the oral performance of an orally translated text, including extralinguistic and paralinguistic features?

Extralinguistic and paralinguistic performance notes that I had designed for the OBT team in the form of tables helped them in this process and these are recommended for use by future OBT teams.

How can the response to the oral performance be incorporated back into the oral translation process and become part of the process of translation?

The Altai team conducted two initial experimental performances outside the group and received feedback, which was then used to adapt the future performances. There was also feedback after the final performances, which was fed back into the translation of Ps 1. Where possible, performance should be used as a step in the OBT process because it provides many opportunities for increased Scripture engagement and community involvement in the translation process.

SUMMARY AND REFLECTION

In summary, I recommend the model presented in this book for exegetical advisors, for OBT teams, and for those producing a performance based on the oral translation of biblical texts into a local target language. It will benefit the exegetical advisor initially to do extensive research and exegesis on the passage or passages, including the less frequently used steps of creating a story chart, particularly for a prose passage, and preparing, for their team's use, performance and extralinguistic notes on the passage. If these extralinguistic notes on frequently translated biblical books can be prepared for OBT teams in advance, this would be of great assistance to OBT teams worldwide who would like to experiment with performance. Simultaneously, the depth and impact of this exegesis for those of us who are exegetical advisors will be greatly enhanced by internalizing and embodying the passage ourselves and doing a performance or retelling individually or in a group. Observations gathered from this last step will help the exegetical advisor then adjust his or her initial exegesis and performance notes. If this internalization and embodiment can be done with a team, this process is even more effective.

The second recommended step is research into local genres in the target culture. In Altai culture, this included research by the translation team into oral epic stories, in particular one epic story, and into the *jangar* style of singing. If poetic features from these genres can be identified and used in the performance of the orally translated text, there is a greater likelihood that the translation and performance will be acceptable and accessible to the local audience.

When the team is ready to begin orally translating the passage, the exegetical advisor should lead the team in a process of internalization, including analyzing the range of possible emotions of the characters and of the editor of the passage. This internalization should follow the best practices for internalization, as summarized in the results of the OBT survey. These include using a larger group of people if possible, employing a range and combination of different internalization techniques appropriate to the local culture and team and to the genre of the passage, the addition of the conversational discovery of meaning if necessary, the use of devotional questions to help the translators integrate the passage with their personal experience, a stress-free environment with frequent breaks, and repetition of the retelling of the passage. Prior to commencing their work with the OBT team, the exegete, translation team, and consultant should be trained in issues of voice prosody, which should be a component of the translation and internalization process from the beginning. If the OBT team is translating a non-narrative genre, they should be aware that the process of internalization will be more difficult and require more time, so alternative techniques may need to be used.

Performance is an optional extra step in the OBT process. In some cases, it may be that time restrictions and finances do not allow for this extra step, but where possible, if done, it will positively influence the exegesis and translation of the passage. Feedback from the performances or retellings can be used to revise the original translation and will lead to a greater understanding of the passage on the part of the translators. In this way, performance in itself contributes to the process of exegesis and translation. In the Altai project, response and feedback by the audience to initial performances was "fed back" into the translation loop.

LIMITATIONS

I was not able to do extensive in-depth research on the topic of internalization. My research was carried out during the time of the COVID-19 global pandemic and the resultant widespread lockdown periods, during which people had restricted movement and opportunities to meet each other face-to-face. Only nine OBT teams and one OBT trainer were interviewed, in sessions conducted by teleconference or solicited through written responses, rather than in person, as was originally planned. I had hoped to observe several OBT teams doing the process of internalization, but this was not possible.

My research was able to cover two genres, one narrative passage and then several poetic passages, but I was unable to research at length using the process of OBT for other genres such as laments, epistles, or proverbs. For my personal embodiment and retelling of the texts, I was able only to internalize Judg 4–5 and not the three psalms.

The actual performances around Altai were limited to ten with a combined audience of approximately two hundred people. Community testing was conducted with around thirty to forty members of the Altai community.

RECOMMENDATIONS FOR FUTURE RESEARCH

I would recommend that going forward, more research be conducted on the process of internalization and especially its use in relation to a wider variety of genres. Such research would help trainers learn how to coach future OBT teams in translating non-narrative genres. It would also contribute to the debate regarding the feasibility and the desirability of translating the whole Bible using the OBT process, or whether there are certain genres for which this method is unsuitable. Similarly, I would recommend more in-depth research on extralinguistic exegesis and, in particular, more study on the area of how emotions should be factored into translation and performance.

The majority of BPC research has focused on the NT so far, with some work having been done on the psalms and the prophets. More research needs to be done on how to construct performances of OT texts in locally appropriate genres.

ORIGINAL CONTRIBUTIONS OF KNOWLEDGE TO THE FIELD

In the introduction of this book, I listed five areas in which my research has provided an original contribution to this field. First of all, I was also able to do a detailed study on the process of internalization, including a summary of interviews with OBT teams around the world. The practice of personally embodying and performing the text was an aid to the exegetical process and is recommended for exegetes and consultants involved in OBT. The conclusions above from this research will help OBT teams, their trainers, exegetes, and consultants understand the process of internalization and embodiment, and how to do these in the most effective way.

Secondly, in preparation for this book and for the doctoral dissertation upon which it is based, I researched how to translate genres other than narrative using OBT. I compared the experiences of OBT teams around the world who have attempted to translate poetry orally, and I made recommendations for those OBT teams who plan to translate biblical poetry orally in the future.

Thirdly, the need for guidance on extralinguistic exegesis is becoming increasingly relevant for OBT and sign language translation. My extralinguistic notes for performances or retellings with extralinguistic and paralinguistic features are a useful tool for future OBT and sign language teams.

Fourthly, this research examined how to design a performance based on an orally translated text in a local culture. I investigated and observed the use of Altai oral epics in the history and culture of the Altai people and decided, with the Altai translation team, which poetic features of the Altai epic poems can perform the same function as the features of orality in the biblical text. The Altai translation team then created the performance, incorporating multimodal methods of presentation. This can serve as a guide for OBT teams who would like to follow a similar process of creating a performance from an orally translated text.

Finally, I analyzed the value of feedback from performance in the translation loop. Currently in OBT, feedback on the translation is provided via the stages of peer review and community review, but there are few teams who have experimented with the idea of using performance as a way of getting additional community feedback. The feedback gained from the two initial performances and then the final ten performances was invaluable in contributing to the final translations of our passages.

My research uniquely contributes to the existing body of knowledge on the topic of OBT. The topics of internalization, extralinguistic exegesis, and doing OBT with non-narrative genres are particularly relevant for OBT teams, trainers, exegetes, and consultants around the world. The idea of using performance as part of the translation process is a key aspect of the relatively new and expanding field of BPC. My research on performance of OT texts in local genres also adds to the wider body of knowledge on BPC.

On the topic of OBT and internalization, my research adds new information about the best practices of OBT and especially about the process of internalization, based on my survey results among OBT teams. My work on extralinguistic exegesis contributes significantly to current research by providing examples of notes that can be prepared for OBT teams on emotional exegesis. My record of the Altai translation team's experience working with non-narrative genres, as well as the survey on this topic among OBT teams, expands upon existing knowledge of this topic. Little work has been done thus far on producing performances from OT texts. My work on the prose and poetry story of Judg 4–5 is exciting and unique in producing and analyzing such a performance and in using audience feedback to refine the translation itself. As Gravelle says, "For Scripture to be truly embodied, it must be experienced."[1]

---

1. Gravelle, "Meaning Making," 6.

Appendix 1

Story chart for Judges 4

This story chart is used in OBT to help the translators orally understand the structure and peak of the story. This story chart is based on five major elements of stories: plot, conflict (the tension that drives the story forward to a conclusion), setting (the details of time and place in which a story occurs), characters (the people of the story), and theme (the main idea of the story).[1] The chart assists the translators in understanding the plot details, discussing the characters and identifying the main point in the narrative.

---

1. Andrews and Andrews, *Teaching the Classics*, 5.

Appendix 1

Figure 1: Story chart for Judges 4

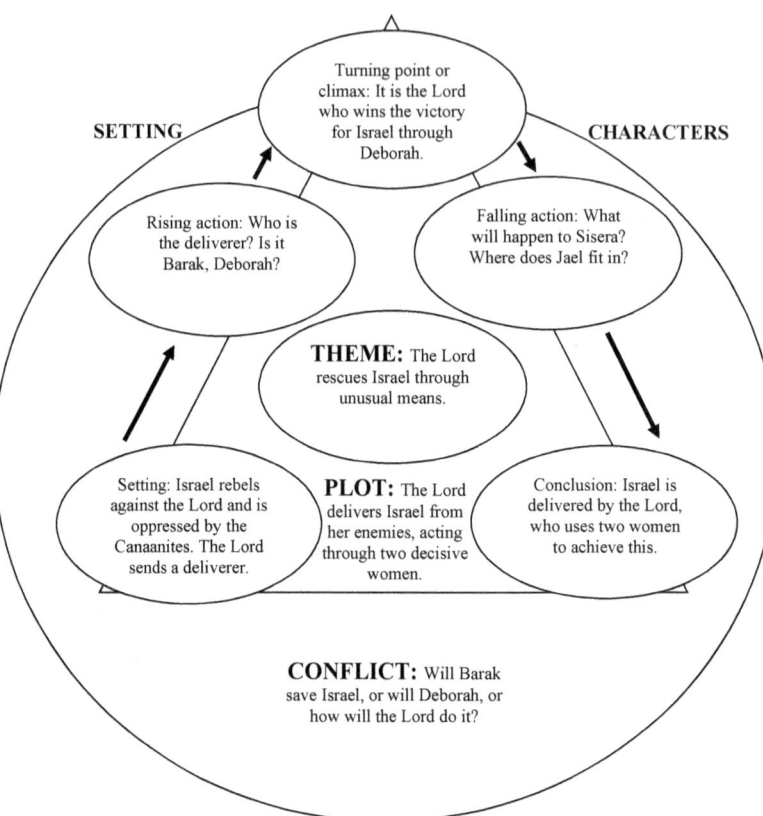

Appendix 2

Translators' oral notes for Judges 4

In response to the need of OBT teams for more guidance in the area of emotional exegesis, I have prepared notes for OBT teams on the passages included in my research. These OBT notes include analysis of the structure, themes, and the peak of the passage, as well as observations on the passage's intended impact, including imagery, emotions and senses, performance features and evidence for them, and performance ideas that can be adapted according to the receptor culture. If the translation team is preparing their own performance, they will need to discuss which ideas are appropriate for their own cultural context. Some ideas might need to be adapted, and new ones may need to be added.

Table 3: Translators' oral notes for Judges 4

Hebrew	Author's Translation	Passage Structure and Themes	Character Speaking	Emotion and Rationale	Ideas for Performance
וַיֹּסִ֙פוּ֙ בְּנֵ֣י יִשְׂרָאֵ֔ל לַעֲשׂ֥וֹת הָרַ֖ע בְּעֵינֵ֣י יְהוָ֑ה וְאֵה֖וּד מֵֽת	4:1 The Israelites continued to do evil in the eyes of the Lord. Now Ehud had died.	Judg 4:1–3 is an introduction to the prose account.	Narrator	Negative emotion, because the cycle of Israel's disobedience begins again.	Slight tone of frustration and inevitability.

Hebrew	Author's Translation	Passage Structure and Themes	Character Speaking	Emotion and Rationale	Ideas for Performance
וַיִּמְכְּרֵ֣ם יְהוָ֗ה בְּיַד֙ יָבִ֣ין מֶֽלֶךְ־כְּנַ֔עַן אֲשֶׁ֥ר מָלַ֖ךְ בְּחָצ֑וֹר וְשַׂר־צְבָאוֹ֙ סִֽיסְרָ֔א וְה֥וּא יוֹשֵׁ֖ב בַּחֲרֹ֥שֶׁת הַגּוֹיִֽם׃	4:2 And the LORD sold them into the hand of Jabin king of Canaan, who reigned in Hazor. The commander of his army was Sisera, who was living in Harosheth, the forest of the nations.		Narrator	Negative emotion. Harosheth Haggoyim (Forest of the Nations) may conjure up the image of the "nations" fighting against the not-yet-unified tribes of Israel.	Ominous tone
וַיִּצְעֲק֥וּ בְנֵֽי־יִשְׂרָאֵ֖ל אֶל־יְהוָ֑ה כִּ֣י תְּשַׁ֤ע מֵאוֹת֙ רֶֽכֶב־בַּרְזֶ֣ל ל֔וֹ וְה֗וּא לָחַ֞ץ אֶת־בְּנֵ֧י יִשְׂרָאֵ֛ל בְּחָזְקָ֖ה עֶשְׂרִ֥ים שָׁנָֽה׃	4:3 Then the Israelites cried out to the LORD for help, because Sisera had 900 iron chariots and had oppressed the Israelites cruelly for twenty years.		Narrator	Emphasis. This verse shows the extent of the pressure from the enemies, and the desperate state of the Israelites.	Emphasis on nine hundred iron chariots and twenty years. Hand gestures for "cried out" (hands cupped round mouth, for example). Pause showing end of section verses 1–3.

Translators' oral notes for Judges 4

Hebrew	Author's Translation	Passage Structure and Themes	Character Speaking	Emotion and Rationale	Ideas for Performance
וּדְבוֹרָה֙ אִשָּׁ֣ה נְבִיאָ֔ה אֵ֖שֶׁת לַפִּיד֑וֹת הִ֛יא שֹׁפְטָ֥ה אֶת־יִשְׂרָאֵ֖ל בָּעֵ֥ת הַהִֽיא	4:4 Now Deborah, a female-prophetess, the wife of Lappidoth, was judging Israel at that time.	Judg 4:4–10 has the theme of God's agent of deliverance. 4:4–5 — the prophetic agent.	Narrator	Positive emotion. The audience recognizes in the cycle of disobedience and salvation that Deborah could be the deliverer of Israel this time.	A more optimistic tone to start this section.
וְ֠הִיא יוֹשֶׁ֨בֶת תַּֽחַת־תֹּ֜מֶר דְּבוֹרָ֗ה בֵּ֧ין הָרָמָ֛ה וּבֵ֥ין בֵּֽית־אֵ֖ל בְּהַ֣ר אֶפְרָ֑יִם וַיַּעֲל֥וּ אֵלֶ֛יהָ בְּנֵ֥י יִשְׂרָאֵ֖ל לַמִּשְׁפָּֽט	4:5 She used to sit under the palm of Deborah between Ramah and Bethel in the hill country of Ephraim, and the Israelites came up to her to ask for justice.		Narrator		

Hebrew	Author's Translation	Passage Structure and Themes	Character Speaking	Emotion and Rationale	Ideas for Performance
יְהוָה אֱלֹהֵי־יִשְׂרָאֵל לֵךְ וּמָשַׁכְתָּ בְּהַר תָּבוֹר וְלָקַחְתָּ עִמְּךָ עֲשֶׂרֶת אֲלָפִים אִישׁ מִבְּנֵי נַפְתָּלִי וּמִבְּנֵי זְבֻלוּן	4:6 She summoned Barak, Abinoam's son from Kedesh in Naphtali and said to him, "Hasn't the Lord, the God of Israel, commanded you, 'Go, gather your men at Mount Tabor, taking 10,000 from the tribe of Naphtali and the tribe of Zebulun.	4:6–7 — the commissioning of Barak.	Narrator, Deborah and the Lord	Authority. The mountain here symbolizes a place where God meets with his people and has victory.	Deborah's voice is commanding, with two imperatives — "go" and "gather." It would be possible to have the Lord's voice here, one of authority, to the end of verse 7. Hand gestures summoning Barak and pointing upwards to Mount Tabor.
וּמָשַׁכְתִּי אֵלֶיךָ אֶל־נַחַל קִישׁוֹן אֶת־סִיסְרָא שַׂר־צְבָא יָבִין וְאֶת־רִכְבּוֹ וְאֶת־הֲמוֹנוֹ וּנְתַתִּיהוּ בְּיָדֶךָ:	4:7 And I will bring Sisera, the general of Jabin's army, to meet you by the river Kishon with his chariots and his troops, and I will give him into your hand.'"		The Lord		

Translators' oral notes for Judges 4

Hebrew	Author's Translation	Passage Structure and Themes	Character Speaking	Emotion and Rationale	Ideas for Performance
וַיֹּאמֶר אֵלֶיהָ בָּרָק אִם־תֵּלְכִי עִמִּי וְהָלָכְתִּי וְאִם־לֹא תֵלְכִי עִמִּי לֹא אֵלֵךְ	4:8 Barak said to her, "If you will go with me, I will go, but if you will not go with me, I will not go."	4:8 — the hesitation of Barak.	Narrator and Barak	Tension. Barak seems hesitant.	Barak's tone is faltering, perhaps with a pause at the beginning. Hand gestures indicating refusal.
וַתֹּאמֶר הָלֹךְ אֵלֵךְ עִמָּךְ אֶפֶס כִּי לֹא תִהְיֶה תִּפְאַרְתְּךָ עַל־הַדֶּרֶךְ אֲשֶׁר אַתָּה הוֹלֵךְ כִּי בְיַד־אִשָּׁה יִמְכֹּר יְהוָה אֶת־סִיסְרָא	4:9a And she said, "I will surely go with you. Nevertheless, because of the way you are going about this, the glory will not be yours, for the Lord will sell Sisera into the hands of a woman."	4:9a — the promise of God's presence.	Narrator and Deborah	Authority. Emphasis.	Deborah's voice is firm and certain. Emphasis on the phrase "over to a woman"

Hebrew	Author's Translation	Passage Structure and Themes	Character Speaking	Emotion and Rationale	Ideas for Performance
וַתָּקָם דְּבוֹרָה וַתֵּלֶךְ עִם־בָּרָק קֶדְשָׁה וַיַּזְעֵק בָּרָק אֶת־זְבוּלֻן וְאֶת־נַפְתָּלִי קֶדְשָׁה וַיַּעַל בְּרַגְלָיו עֲשֶׂרֶת אַלְפֵי אִישׁ וַתַּעַל עִמּוֹ דְּבוֹרָה	4:9b-10 Then Deborah got up and went with Barak to Kedesh. And Barak summoned Zebulun and Naphtali to Kedesh, and 10,000 men followed him. Deborah also went up with him.	4:9b-10 — the call to arms.	Narrator	Emphasis.	Emphasis on "Deborah" in the last sentence. Hand gestures showing summoning. Pause to show end of section verses 4–10.
וְחֶבֶר הַקֵּינִי נִפְרָד מִקַּיִן מִבְּנֵי חֹבָב חֹתֵן מֹשֶׁה וַיֵּט אָהֳלוֹ עַד־אֵלוֹן בצענים אֲשֶׁר אֶת־קֶדֶשׁ	4:11 Now Heber the Kenite had moved away from the Kenites, the descendants of Hobab, Moses' father-in-law, and had pitched his tent as far away as the terebinth in Zaanannim, which is near Kedesh	4:11–22 has the theme of God's gift of deliverance. 4:11 — the complication in the plot Possible re-ordering—this verse could go after 9b and before 9b-10, so that the mobilisation of the army and then the attack are together.	Narrator	Emphasis.	"Now" introduces an unexpected new person, in the form of an aside. Stress on "Heber the Kenite," introducing a new and significant character.

Hebrew	Author's Translation	Passage Structure and Themes	Character Speaking	Emotion and Rationale	Ideas for Performance
וַיַּגִּדוּ לְסִיסְרָא כִּי עָלָה בָּרָק בֶּן־אֲבִינֹעַם הַר־תָּבוֹר׃ 13 וַיַּזְעֵק סִיסְרָא אֶת־כָּל־רִכְבּוֹ תְּשַׁע מֵאוֹת רֶכֶב בַּרְזֶל וְאֶת־כָּל־הָעָם אֲשֶׁר אִתּוֹ מֵחֲרֹשֶׁת הַגּוֹיִם אֶל־נַחַל קִישׁוֹן׃	4:12–13 When Sisera was told that Barak, Abinoam's son, had gone up to Mount Tabor, Sisera each chariot of his, (equaling) 900 chariots of iron and all the men who were with him, from Harosheth, the forest of the pagans, to the river Kishon.	4:12–16 — the defeat of the enemy army.	Narrator	Negative emotion. Sisera summons his chariots and troops.	Ominous tone.

Hebrew	Author's Translation	Passage Structure and Themes	Character Speaking	Emotion and Rationale	Ideas for Performance
וַתֹּאמֶר דְּבֹרָה אֶל־בָּרָק קוּם כִּי זֶה הַיּוֹם אֲשֶׁר נָתַן יְהוָה אֶת־סִיסְרָא בְּיָדֶךָ הֲלֹא יְהוָה יָצָא לְפָנֶיךָ וַיֵּרֶד בָּרָק מֵהַר תָּבוֹר וַעֲשֶׂרֶת אֲלָפִים אִישׁ אַחֲרָיו	4:14 And Deborah said to Barak, "Go! For this is the day in which the Lord has given Sisera into your hands. Isn't the Lord marching out before you?" So, Barak went down from Mount Tabor with 10,000 men following him.		Narrator and Deborah	Authority.	Deborah is decisive. Hand gestures indicating "go!"
וַיָּהָם יְהוָה אֶת־סִיסְרָא וְאֶת־כָּל־הָרֶכֶב וְאֶת־כָּל־הַמַּחֲנֶה לְפִי־חֶרֶב לִפְנֵי בָרָק וַיֵּרֶד סִיסְרָא מֵעַל הַמֶּרְכָּבָה וַיָּנָס בְּרַגְלָיו	4:15 When Barak attacked, the Lord threw Sisera, all his chariots and his army into a panic before Barak. Sisera got down from his chariot and fled away on foot.		Narrator	Action and pace change.	Excited tone, increased pace.

Hebrew	Author's Translation	Passage Structure and Themes	Character Speaking	Emotion and Rationale	Ideas for Performance
וּבָרָ֞ק רָדַ֣ף אַחֲרֵ֤י הָרֶ֙כֶב֙ וְאַחֲרֵ֣י הַֽמַּחֲנֶ֔ה עַ֖ד חֲרֹ֣שֶׁת הַגּוֹיִ֑ם וַיִּפֹּ֞ל כָּל־מַחֲנֵ֤ה סִֽיסְרָא֙ לְפִי־חֶ֔רֶב לֹ֥א נִשְׁאַ֖ר עַד־אֶחָֽד׃	4:16 And Barak pursued the chariots and the army to Harosheth, the forest of the pagans, and all the army of Sisera fell by the sword; not even one was left.		Narrator	Emphasis.	Intonation stresses, "not even one was left."
וְסִֽיסְרָא֙ נָ֣ס בְּרַגְלָ֔יו אֶל־אֹ֥הֶל יָעֵ֖ל אֵ֣שֶׁת חֶ֣בֶר הַקֵּינִ֑י כִּ֣י שָׁל֗וֹם בֵּ֚ין יָבִ֣ין מֶֽלֶךְ־חָצ֔וֹר וּבֵ֕ין בֵּ֖ית חֶ֥בֶר הַקֵּינִֽי	4:17 But Sisera fled away on foot to the tent of Jael, the wife of Heber the Kenite, for there was peace between Jabin the king of Hazor and the house of Heber the Kenite.	4:17–22 — the assassination of the enemy leader.	Narrator	The information about Jabin and Heber is parenthetical, an aside.	Use a "by the way" tone.

Hebrew	Author's Translation	Passage Structure and Themes	Character Speaking	Emotion and Rationale	Ideas for Performance
וַתֵּצֵא יָעֵל לִקְרַאת סִיסְרָא וַתֹּאמֶר אֵלָיו סוּרָה אֲדֹנִי סוּרָה אֵלַי אַל־תִּירָא וַיָּסַר אֵלֶיהָ הָאֹהֱלָה וַתְּכַסֵּהוּ בַּשְּׂמִיכָה	4:18 And Jael came out to meet Sisera and said to him, "Stop and rest, my lord. Stop and rest with me. Don't be afraid." So Sisera stopped to rest in her tent, and she put a rug over him.		Narrator and Jael	Tension.	Jael's voice is comforting and seductive. Hand gestures luring Sisera.
וַיֹּאמֶר אֵלֶיהָ הַשְׁקִינִי־נָא מְעַט־מַיִם כִּי צָמֵאתִי וַתִּפְתַּח אֶת־נֹאוד הֶחָלָב וַתַּשְׁקֵהוּ וַתְּכַסֵּהוּ	4:19 And he said to her, "Please give me a little water to drink, for I am thirsty." So, she opened a goatskin container of milk and gave him a drink and covered him.		Narrator and Sisera	Tension. The imagery evokes the idea of Jael treating Sisera as a small child, tucking him up in bed and giving him milk.	Sisera's request is in a polite tone, and maybe sounding hoarse. Hand gestures showing thirst.

Translators' oral notes for Judges 4

Hebrew	Author's Translation	Passage Structure and Themes	Character Speaking	Emotion and Rationale	Ideas for Performance
וַיֹּאמֶר אֵלֶיהָ עֲמֹד פֶּתַח הָאֹהֶל וְהָיָה אִם־אִישׁ יָבוֹא וּשְׁאֵלֵךְ וְאָמַר הֲיֵשׁ־פֹּה אִישׁ וְאָמַרְתְּ אָיִן	4:20 And he said to her, "Stand at the entrance to the tent, and if anyone comes and asks you, 'Is there a man here?' say, 'No.'"		Narrator and Sisera	Authority. Sisera here again is in charge.	Sisera's tone is more commanding.
וַתִּקַּח יָעֵל אֵשֶׁת־חֶבֶר אֶת־יְתַד הָאֹהֶל וַתָּשֶׂם אֶת־הַמַּקֶּבֶת בְּיָדָהּ וַתָּבוֹא אֵלָיו בַּלָּאט וַתִּתְקַע אֶת־הַיָּתֵד בְּרַקָּתוֹ וַתִּצְנַח בָּאָרֶץ וְהוּא־נִרְדָּם וַיָּעַף וַיָּמֹת׃	4:21 But Jael the wife of Heber took a tent peg in one hand and a hammer in the other. Then she went softly to him and drove the peg into his temple until it went down into the ground while he was lying fast asleep from exhaustion. So, he died.	The climax or peak of the passage.	Narrator	Tension and suspense. The hands that have just given milk to Sisera and put a cover over him now grab weapons to murder him.	The first line builds suspense. The beginning of the second line as Jael approaches should be said quietly. "Drove the peg into his temple until it went down into the ground" has a brutal force. Hand gestures showing Jael's actions—driving the peg.

Hebrew	Author's Translation	Passage Structure and Themes	Character Speaking	Emotion and Rationale	Ideas for Performance
וְהִנֵּ֤ה בָרָק֙ רֹדֵ֣ף אֶת־סִֽיסְרָ֔א וַתֵּצֵ֤א יָעֵל֙ לִקְרָאת֔וֹ וַתֹּ֣אמֶר ל֗וֹ לֵ֣ךְ וְאַרְאֶ֔ךָּ אֶת־הָאִ֖ישׁ אֲשֶׁר־אַתָּ֣ה מְבַקֵּ֑שׁ וַיָּבֹ֣א אֵלֶ֔יהָ וְהִנֵּ֤ה סִֽיסְרָא֙ נֹפֵ֣ל מֵ֔ת וְהַיָּתֵ֖ד בְּרַקָּתֽוֹ	4:22 Meanwhile, Barak had been pursuing Sisera. Jael went out to meet him and said to him, "Come here and I will show you the man you are searching for." So he went in to her tent, and there was Sisera lying dead, with the tent peg in his temple.	Abrupt change of scene.	Narrator and Jael	This change of scene is an attention-grabber for the audience. Excitement.	Abrupt change of scene to Barak can be reflected by some surprise in the narrator's voice. There could be a pause before the climax, "and there was Sisera lying dead." Shocked tone. Hand gestures as Jael summons Barak and shows him the body. Pause here to mark end of section verses 11–22.

Hebrew	Author's Translation	Passage Structure and Themes	Character Speaking	Emotion and Rationale	Ideas for Performance
וַיַּכְנַ֣ע אֱלֹהִ֗ים בַּיּ֤וֹם הַהוּא֙ אֵ֣ת יָבִ֣ין מֶֽלֶךְ־ כְּנַ֔עַן לִפְנֵ֖י בְּנֵ֥י יִשְׂרָאֵֽל׃ וַתֵּ֜לֶךְ יַ֤ד בְּנֵֽי־יִשְׂרָאֵל֙ הָל֣וֹךְ וְקָשָׁ֔ה עַ֖ל יָבִ֣ין מֶֽלֶךְ־כְּנָ֑עַן עַ֚ד אֲשֶׁ֣ר הִכְרִ֔יתוּ אֵ֖ת יָבִ֥ין מֶֽלֶךְ־כְּנָֽעַן׃	4:23–24, God defeated Jabin the king of Canaan before Israel. And Israel's hand became stronger and stronger against Jabin the king of Canaan, until they destroyed him.	4:23–24 has the theme of God's gift of security. This is an editorial summary.	Narrator	End of section. Positive emotion.	Said with some satisfaction.

Appendix 3

Story chart for Judges 5

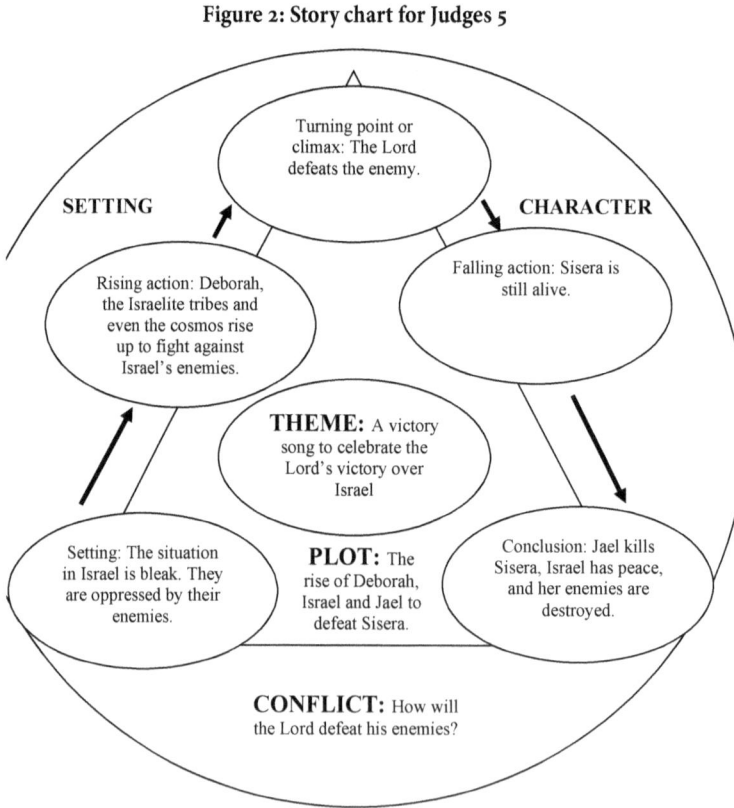

Figure 2: Story chart for Judges 5

Appendix 4

Translators' oral notes for Judges 5

In response to the need of OBT teams for more guidance in the area of emotional exegesis, I have prepared my own notes for OBT teams on the passages included in my research. These OBT notes include analysis of the structure, themes, and the peak of the passage, as well as observations on the passage's intended impact, including imagery, emotions and senses, performance features and evidence for them, and performance ideas that can be adapted according to the receptor culture. If the translation team is preparing their own performance, they will need to discuss which ideas are appropriate for their own cultural context, which might need to be adapted, and new ones they may want to add.

Table 4: Translators' oral notes for Judges 5

Hebrew	Author's Translation	Passage Structure and Themes	Character Speaking	Emotion and Rationale	Performance Ideas
וַתָּשַׁר דְּבוֹרָה וּבָרָק בֶּן־אֲבִינֹעַם בַּיּוֹם הַהוּא לֵאמֹר	5:1 Then Deborah and Barak Abinoam's son sang on that day:	5:1 — Introduction.	Narrator	Optimistic emotion.	Upbeat tone.

Hebrew	Author's Translation	Passage Structure and Themes	Character Speaking	Emotion and Rationale	Performance Ideas
בִּפְרֹעַ פְּרָעוֹת בְּיִשְׂרָאֵל בְּהִתְנַדֵּב עָם בָּרְכוּ יְהוָה שִׁמְעוּ מְלָכִים הַאֲזִינוּ רֹזְנִים אָנֹכִי לַיהוָה אָנֹכִי אָשִׁירָה אֲזַמֵּר לַיהוָה אֱלֹהֵי יִשְׂרָאֵל	5:2 *Because the leaders of Israel took charge and the people volunteered, bless the Lord.* 5:3 *Hear, O kings,* *pay attention, you rulers,* *I will sing to the Lord,* *I will make music to the Lord, God of Israel.*	5:2–3 — Stanza 1: call to praise God.	Deborah	Optimistic emotion.	This is a rousing call. Emphasis on "bless the Lord." Hand gestures around the ears could show a summons to listen. Verse 3 could have music starting in the background. The verse has a rhythmic feel and enthusiastic tone. The emphasis is on "I." A slight pause to mark the end of the stanza.

Translators' oral notes for Judges 5

Hebrew	Author's Translation	Passage Structure and Themes	Character Speaking	Emotion and Rationale	Performance Ideas
יְהוָה בְּצֵאתְךָ מִשֵּׂעִיר בְּצַעְדְּךָ מִשְּׂדֵה אֱדוֹם אֶרֶץ רָעָשָׁה גַּם־שָׁמַיִם נָטְפוּ גַּם־עָבִים נָטְפוּ מָיִם הָרִים נָזְלוּ מִפְּנֵי יְהוָה זֶה סִינַי מִפְּנֵי יְהוָה אֱלֹהֵי יִשְׂרָאֵל	5:4–5 O Lord, when you came down from Seir, when you marched from the land of Edom, the earth shook, the heavens poured, the clouds poured down water. The mountains quaked before the Lord, the One of Sinai, before the Lord, the God of Israel.	5:4–5 — Stanza 2: the introduction of the Lord.	Deborah and Barak singing together? Or Deborah on her own.	Optimistic tone. There is the impact of the sound of marching, thunder, and the motion of the earth shaking and the mountains quaking. There is imagery of seeing God in tremendous acts of nature. The general motion is downward, as if from on high to earth. This conjures up a sense of victory and God's sovereign power.	"O" in the English translation adds an exclamatory tone. This is a celebratory announcement from Deborah, with a tone of awe describing the theophany. Emphasis on "One of Sinai" as a divine title. Could be accompanied by the sound of marching, thunder and the earth shaking. The performer could look up at the mention of the clouds and the heavens. A slight pause to mark the end of the stanza.

Hebrew	Author's Translation	Passage Structure and Themes	Character Speaking	Emotion and Rationale	Performance Ideas
בִּימֵי שַׁמְגַּר בֶּן־עֲנָת בִּימֵי יָעֵל חָדְלוּ אֳרָחוֹת וְהֹלְכֵי נְתִיבוֹת יֵלְכוּ אֳרָחוֹת עֲקַלְקַלּוֹת חָדְלוּ פְרָזוֹן בְּיִשְׂרָאֵל חָדֵלּוּ עַד שַׁקַּמְתִּי דְּבוֹרָה שַׁקַּמְתִּי אֵם בְּיִשְׂרָאֵל יִבְחַר אֱלֹהִים חֲדָשִׁים אָז לָחֶם שְׁעָרִים מָגֵן אִם־ יֵרָאֶה וָרֹמַח בְּאַרְבָּעִים אֶלֶף בְּיִשְׂרָאֵל	5:6–8 In the days of Shamgar, son of Anath, in the days of Jael, the roads were abandoned; travellers kept to winding paths. Village life ceased, ceased in Israel, until I, Deborah arose, arose a mother in Israel. When they chose new gods, war came to the city gates, and not a shield or spear was seen among the forty thousand in Israel.	5:6–8 — Stanza 3: the emergence of Deborah.	Deborah	Negative emotion. There is a sense of loss of hope and verve in the abandoned roads and ceasing of village life. There was no fighting spirit when the war came. It is a contrast to God's tremendous presence in the last verses, when they chose other gods and God's presence is not felt or seen. Positive emotion. Deborah names herself a mother, not a prophetess or judge. It is the banner of a woman, the bearer of new life. This is followed again by negative emotion.	Deborah describes Israel's crisis in a depressed tone. A rise occurs at the point of "until I, Deborah arose, arose a mother in Israel," which is optimistic. Again, the tone is depressed in the final section. The performer could use hand gestures to show the emptiness and the winding paths. Intonation could emphasize "not a spear or shield." A slight pause to mark the end of the stanza.

Hebrew	Author's Translation	Passage Structure and Themes	Character Speaking	Emotion and Rationale	Performance Ideas
לִבִּי לְחוֹקְקֵי יִשְׂרָאֵל הַמִּתְנַדְּבִים בָּעָם בָּרֲכוּ יְהוָה רֹכְבֵי אֲתֹנוֹת צְחֹרוֹת יֹשְׁבֵי עַל־מִדִּין וְהֹלְכֵי עַל־דֶּרֶךְ שִׂיחוּ מִקּוֹל מְחַצְצִים בֵּין מַשְׁאַבִּים שָׁם יְתַנּוּ צִדְקוֹת יְהוָה צִדְקֹת פִּרְזֹנוֹ בְּיִשְׂרָאֵל	9 My heart is with Israel's governors, with the willing volunteers among the people. Bless the Lord. 10 You who ride on tawny donkeys, sitting on your saddle blankets, and you who travel on the road – pay attention! 11 Listen to the sound of the water distributers at the watering places, there they tell of the righteous acts of the Lord, the righteous acts of his villagers in Israel.	5:9–11c — Stanza 4: a call for praise for the Lord's righteous acts.	Deborah	Positive emotion. This is the rousing speech of the "people's" leader. First it focuses on the people who answered the call and then connects them to the Lord. There are the righteous acts of the Lord and righteous acts of his villagers, who previously had "no life" but are now doing the Lord's acts.	Deborah's tone is proud in verse 9, and then there is the repeated call to "Bless the Lord." In verses 10 and 11 Deborah's tone is enthusiastic and motivating, delivered to the audience. A slight pause to mark the end of this stanza.

Hebrew	Author's Translation	Passage Structure and Themes	Character Speaking	Emotion and Rationale	Performance Ideas
אָז יָרְדוּ לַשְּׁעָרִים עַם־יְהוָה	11d Then they went down to the gates, the people of the Lord.	5:11d-18 — Stanza 5: a recitation of Israel's righteous actions. 11d is an introduction to the next section.	Narrator	Movement. The people of Israel are now named as the people of the Lord! God is on their side!	If the whole poem is being read by Deborah, then this line should be, too. If there are different characters, this line could be read by the narrator. A tone of anticipation as the people of Israel moves down to begin the battle.
עוּרִי עוּרִי דְּבוֹרָה עוּרִי עוּרִי דַּבְּרִי־שִׁיר קוּם בָּרָק וּשֲׁבֵה שֶׁבְיְךָ בֶּן־אֲבִינֹעַם	12 Awake, awake, Deborah, awake, awake, sing a song! Arise, O Barak, take away your captives, O son of Abinoam.		Chorus	Multiple voices/chorus. This is a call to sing praises for impending victory!	This is a rousing call to battle to both Deborah and Barak. It could be said by Deborah to herself and Barak, but it could also be said by a chorus.

Hebrew	Author's Translation	Passage Structure and Themes	Character Speaking	Emotion and Rationale	Performance Ideas
אָז יְרַד שָׂרִיד לְאַדִּירִים עָם יְהוָה יְרַד־לִי בַּגִּבּוֹרִים	13 Then down came the survivors to the nobles, The people of the Lord marched down to me against the mighty ones.		Deborah	This is a majestic image of God's survivors doing God's deeds against the more powerful enemy.	Majestic tone.

Appendix 4

Hebrew	Author's Translation	Passage Structure and Themes	Character Speaking	Emotion and Rationale	Performance Ideas
מִנִּי אֶפְרַיִם שָׁרְשָׁם בַּעֲמָלֵק אַחֲרֶיךָ בִנְיָמִין בַּעֲמָמֶיךָ מִנִּי מָכִיר יָרְדוּ מְחֹקְקִים וּמִזְּבוּלֻן מֹשְׁכִים בְּשֵׁבֶט סֹפֵר וְשָׂרַי בְּיִשָּׂשכָר עִם־דְּבֹרָה וְיִשָּׂשכָר כֵּן בָּרָק בָּעֵמֶק שֻׁלַּח בְּרַגְלָיו	14–15a *From Ephraim, their root in Amalek, Following you, Benjamin, with your peoples; From Machir marched down the commanders, and from Zebulun those who bear the commander's staff. The chiefs of Issachar came with Deborah, Issachar was faithful to Barak, Rushing after him, into the valley.*	14–18 is the roll call of the Israelite tribes.	Deborah	Positive emotion. Deborah is naming the heroes.	Deborah's tone is one of praise for Ephraim, and the highest praise is for Issachar at the end. Emphasis on the names of the tribes.

Translators' oral notes for Judges 5

Hebrew	Author's Translation	Passage Structure and Themes	Character Speaking	Emotion and Rationale	Performance Ideas
בִּפְלַגּוֹת רְאוּבֵן גְּדֹלִים חִקְקֵי־לֵב לָמָּה יָשַׁבְתָּ בֵּין הַמִּשְׁפְּתַיִם לִשְׁמֹעַ שְׁרִקוֹת עֲדָרִים לִפְלַגּוֹת רְאוּבֵן גְּדוֹלִים חִקְרֵי־לֵב	15b-16 Among the clans of Reuben, There was much searching of heart. Why do you remain among the sheepfolds, To listen to the pipe playing for the flocks? Among the clans of Reuben, There were great searchings of heart.		Deborah	Negative emotion. Deborah is chiding those who waivered in joining the call to act as the Lord's people.	Here, her tone is one of disappointment and rebuke.
גִּלְעָד בְּעֵבֶר הַיַּרְדֵּן שָׁכֵן וְדָן לָמָּה יָגוּר אֳנִיּוֹת אָשֵׁר יָשַׁב לְחוֹף יַמִּים וְעַל מִפְרָצָיו יִשְׁכּוֹן	17 Gilead stayed beyond the Jordan, And Dan, why did he stay with the ships. Asher sat still at the coast of the sea, He settled down by his harbours.		Deborah	Negative emotion. Deborah is shaming those who did not join by calling out their names.	A continuation of the rebuke in an exasperated tone.

Hebrew	Author's Translation	Passage Structure and Themes	Character Speaking	Emotion and Rationale	Performance Ideas
זְבֻלוּן עַם חֵרֵף נַפְשׁוֹ לָמוּת וְנַפְתָּלִי עַל מְרוֹמֵי שָׂדֶה	18 Zebulun is a people who despised their lives even unto death, Naphtali too on the heights of the field		Deborah	Positive emotion. This is painting the picture of bravery of those who did march nobly and mightily to do the Lord's deeds.	A tone of special honor.
בָּאוּ מְלָכִים נִלְחָמוּ אָז נִלְחֲמוּ מַלְכֵי כְנַעַן בְּתַעְנַךְ עַל־מֵי מְגִדּוֹ בֶּצַע כֶּסֶף לֹא לָקָחוּ	19 The kings came, they fought, Then fought the kings of Canaan, At Tanach, by the waters of Megiddo, They took no silver as plunder.	5:19–23 — Stanza 6: a description of the battle	Deborah	Excitement. The repetition of kings of Canaan may be pointing the blame on the king and not on the warriors.	There is excitement in Deborah's voice, reflected in the shortness of the phrases.
מִן־שָׁמַיִם נִלְחָמוּ הַכּוֹכָבִים מִמְּסִלּוֹתָם נִלְחֲמוּ עִם־סִיסְרָא	20 The heavens fought, The stars from their paths fought against Sisera.		Deborah	Suspense. Imagery of divine interference against Sisera and the Canaanite kings.	Dramatic, building tension. Performer could look up at the heavens and the stars.

Translators' oral notes for Judges 5

Hebrew	Author's Translation	Passage Structure and Themes	Character Speaking	Emotion and Rationale	Performance Ideas
נַ֤חַל קִישׁוֹן֙ גְּרָפָ֔ם נַ֥חַל קְדוּמִ֖ים נַ֣חַל קִישׁ֑וֹן תִּדְרְכִ֥י נַפְשִׁ֖י עֹֽז	21 The torrent of Kishon, it swept them away The ancient torrent, the torrent of Kishon. March on, my soul, in strength!		Deborah	Positive emotion. This is lauding the Lord's mighty act of nature against Sisera and his warriors and a call to not grow weary.	The last line is a spontaneous outburst from Deborah.
אָ֥ז הָלְמ֖וּ עִקְּבֵי־ס֑וּס מִֽדַּהֲר֖וֹת דַּהֲר֥וֹת אַבִּירָֽיו	22 Then hammered the heels of the horse With the galloping, galloping of his steeds.		Deborah	Sound play.	Emphasize alliteration and onomatopoeia.
א֣וֹרוּ מֵר֗וֹז אָמַר֙ מַלְאַ֣ךְ יְהוָ֔ה אֹ֥רוּ אָר֖וֹר יֹשְׁבֶ֑יהָ כִּ֤י לֹֽא־בָ֙אוּ֙ לְעֶזְרַ֣ת יְהוָ֔ה לְעֶזְרַ֥ת יְהוָ֖ה בַּגִּבּוֹרִֽים	23 'Curse Meroz,' said the Lord's messenger, 'Curse, O curse its inhabitants, for they did not come to the help of the Lord, to the help of the Lord against the mighty.'		Narrator and the Lord's messenger.	Negative emotion.	The tone is one of rebuke. Emphasis on "curse." Slight pause at the end of the stanza.

Hebrew	Author's Translation	Passage Structure and Themes	Character Speaking	Emotion and Rationale	Performance Ideas
תְּבֹרַךְ מִנָּשִׁים יָעֵל אֵשֶׁת חֶבֶר הַקֵּינִי מִנָּשִׁים בָּאֹהֶל תְּבֹרָךְ	24 Most blessed of women is Jael, the wife of Heber the Kenite, Of tent dwelling women most blessed.	5:24–27 — Stanza 7: Sisera's death.	Deborah	Positive emotion.	Tone of praise. Emphasis on "blessed" at the beginning and the end of the verse.
מַיִם שָׁאַל חָלָב נָתָנָה בְּסֵפֶל אַדִּירִים הִקְרִיבָה חֶמְאָה	25 He asked for water and she gave him milk, She brought him curds in a princely bowl.		Deborah	Suspense/tension.	The tone is one of mounting suspense. There is some irony in the second phrase.

Hebrew	Author's Translation	Passage Structure and Themes	Character Speaking	Emotion and Rationale	Performance Ideas
יָדָהּ לַיָּתֵד תִּשְׁלַ֔חְנָה וִֽימִינָ֖הּ לְהַלְמ֣וּת עֲמֵלִ֑ים וְהָלְמָ֤ה סִֽיסְרָא֙ מָחֲקָ֣ה רֹאשׁ֔וֹ וּמָחֲצָ֥ה וְחָלְפָ֖ה רַקָּתֽוֹ	26 Her hand reached for the tent peg Her right hand for the workman's hammer She struck Sisera a blow, She crushed his head She shattered and pierced his temple.		Deborah	Change of pace.	The pace should be slow in the first two lines, before the climax which is the murder of Sisera. The second pair of lines should be said dramatically and brutally. The emphasis is on the quick succession of the four verbs. Performer could show the reaching for the tools.

Hebrew	Author's Translation	Passage Structure and Themes	Character Speaking	Emotion and Rationale	Performance Ideas
בֵּין רַגְלֶיהָ כָּרַע נָפַל שָׁכָב בֵּין רַגְלֶיהָ כָּרַע נָפָל בַּאֲשֶׁר כָּרַע שָׁם נָפַל שָׁדוּד	27 *Between her feet he sank, he fell, he lay. Between her feet he sank, he fell. Where he sank, there he fell, dead!*		Deborah	Change of pace.	Pauses between "he sank, he fell, he lay" in the first line. Same in second line. The performer could look down. The climax is on the final word, "dead." Short pause at the end of the stanza.

Hebrew	Author's Translation	Passage Structure and Themes	Character Speaking	Emotion and Rationale	Performance Ideas
בְּעַד הַחַלּוֹן נִשְׁקְפָה וַתְּיַבֵּב אֵם סִיסְרָא בְּעַד הָאֶשְׁנָב מַדּוּעַ בֹּשֵׁשׁ רִכְבּוֹ לָבוֹא מַדּוּעַ אֶחֱרוּ פַּעֲמֵי מַרְכְּבוֹתָיו	28 Through the window she peered, the mother of Sisera looked out through the lattice, Why is his chariot taking so long to arrive? Why is the clattering of his chariots taking so long?	5:28–30 — Stanza 8: Sisera's mother waiting for his return.	Narrator and Sisera's mother	Negative emotion.	If Deborah is not saying the whole poem, then the narrator could say the first lines here. A sudden change in scene—the first line is said with nervousness and suspense. The two rhetorical questions could be said by Sisera's mother. She is distraught. The performer could raise hands in the air for the rhetorical questions: "Why?"

Appendix 4

Hebrew	Author's Translation	Passage Structure and Themes	Character Speaking	Emotion and Rationale	Performance Ideas
חַכְמוֹת שָׂרוֹתֶיהָ תַּעֲנֶינָּה אַף־הִיא תָּשִׁיב אֲמָרֶיהָ לָהּ	29 Her wisest ladies answer her Indeed, she repeats her words to herself,		Narrator		
הֲלֹא יִמְצְאוּ יְחַלְּקוּ שָׁלָל רַחַם רַחֲמָתַיִם לְרֹאשׁ גֶּבֶר שְׁלַל צְבָעִים לְסִיסְרָא שְׁלַל צְבָעִים רִקְמָה צֶבַע רִקְמָתַיִם לְצַוְּארֵי שָׁלָל	30 Are they not finding and dividing the spoil? One girl, two girls for every man. Spoils of dyed cloth for Sisera Spoils of dyed cloth embroidered Two pieces of dyed cloth embroidered for the neck as spoil.		Chorus of ladies—could be one woman's voice or several voices saying different lines.	Negative emotion.	The whole answer is a rhetorical question. The first line is reassuring. The second is in a coarse tone. The last lines emphasize the luxury of the plunder and are heartless and even boastful.
כֵּן יֹאבְדוּ כָל־אוֹיְבֶיךָ יְהוָה וְאֹהֲבָיו כְּצֵאת הַשֶּׁמֶשׁ בִּגְבֻרָתוֹ	31 So, may all your enemies perish, the Lord, But those who love him be like the rising of the sun in its might.	5:31a — Stanza 9: the conclusion of the poem.	Deborah, or this could be song by a chorus	Positive emotion.	An official tone giving praise to the Lord. Short pause at the end of the section.

Hebrew	Author's Translation	Passage Structure and Themes	Character Speaking	Emotion and Rationale	Performance Ideas
וַתִּשְׁקֹט הָאָרֶץ אַרְבָּעִים שָׁנָה׃	32 Then the land had peace for forty years.	5:31b — final conclusion.	Narrator	End of scene.	Summary tone.

Appendix 5

Story Chart for Psalm 1

Figure 3: Story chart for Psalm 1

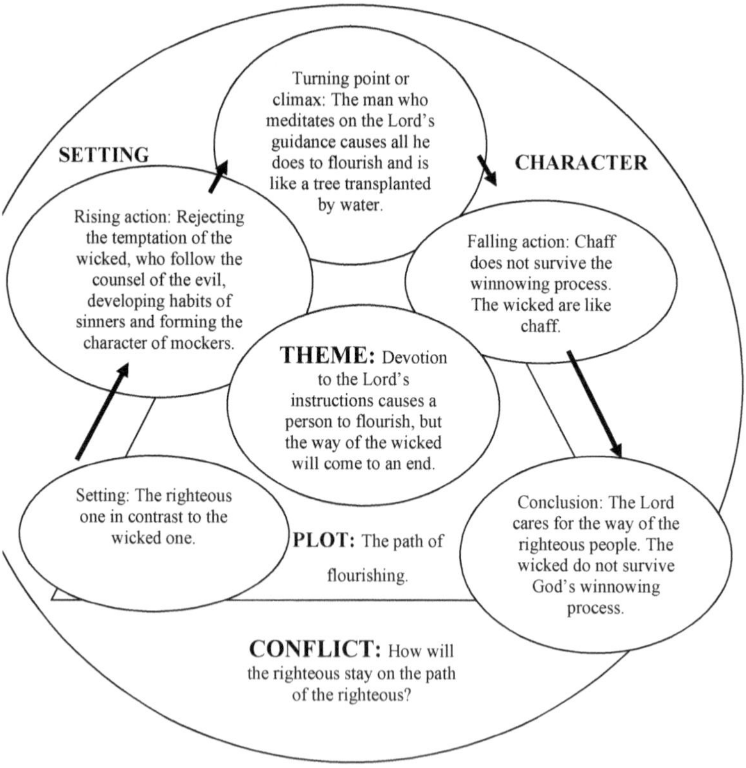

- **SETTING**
- **CHARACTER**
- **Turning point or climax:** The man who meditates on the Lord's guidance causes all he does to flourish and is like a tree transplanted by water.
- **Rising action:** Rejecting the temptation of the wicked, who follow the counsel of the evil, developing habits of sinners and forming the character of mockers.
- **Falling action:** Chaff does not survive the winnowing process. The wicked are like chaff.
- **Setting:** The righteous one in contrast to the wicked one.
- **THEME:** Devotion to the Lord's instructions causes a person to flourish, but the way of the wicked will come to an end.
- **Conclusion:** The Lord cares for the way of the righteous people. The wicked do not survive God's winnowing process.
- **PLOT:** The path of flourishing.
- **CONFLICT:** How will the righteous stay on the path of the righteous?

Appendix 6

Translators' Oral Notes for Psalm 1

In response to the need of OBT teams for more guidance in the area of emotional exegesis, I have prepared my own notes for OBT teams on the passages included in my research. These OBT notes include analysis of the structure, themes, and the peak of the passage, as well as observations on the passage's intended impact, including imagery, emotions and senses, performance features and evidence for them, and performance ideas that can be adapted according to the receptor culture. If the translation team is preparing their own performance, they will need to discuss which ideas are appropriate for their own cultural context, which might need to be adapted, and new ones they may want to add.

Appendix 6

Table 5: Translators' oral notes for Psalm 1

Hebrew Text	Author's Translation	Passage Structure and Themes	Character speaking	Emotion and Rationale	Performance Ideas
אַשְׁרֵי־הָאִישׁ אֲשֶׁר ׀ לֹא הָלַךְ בַּעֲצַת רְשָׁעִים וּבְדֶרֶךְ חַטָּאִים לֹא עָמָד וּבְמוֹשַׁב לֵצִים לֹא יָשָׁב	1:1 Happy is the one who does not follow the advice of the wicked, does not stay on the path of sinners, and does not sit in the company of mockers,	Verses 1–3 describe the truly righteous person. This verse is arranged in a parallel triplet.	Narrator all the way through	Positive emotion—admiration. Here is admiration for the one described, and the wicked are considered evil. The ultimate purpose is to provoke the audience to join in admiring this person and to want to be like him themselves.	Upbeat tone and exclamation of admiration. Facial expression of admiration.

Hebrew Text	Author's Translation	Passage Structure and Themes	Character speaking	Emotion and Rationale	Performance Ideas
כִּי אִם בְּתוֹרַת יְהוָה חֶפְצוֹ וּבְתוֹרָתוֹ יֶהְגֶּה יוֹמָם וָלָיְלָה	1:2 *But who delights in the Lord's teachings, and he meditates on his word, day and night!*	Here are two parallel positive lines, the second developing the thought in the first. כִּי אִם *but* introduces the first contrast.		Continuation of positive emotion—admiration of the one who ends up so confident in life and has peace and security. Here is an emotional attachment to the Torah. He determines to delight in it and devotes himself to study. This provokes interest in the hearer about how he can be so admired.	Assertion and tone of awe.

Hebrew Text	Author's Translation	Passage Structure and Themes	Character speaking	Emotion and Rationale	Performance Ideas
וְֽהָיָ֗ה כְּעֵץ֮ שָׁת֪וּל עַֽל־פַּלְגֵ֫י מָ֥יִם אֲשֶׁ֤ר פִּרְי֨וֹ ׀ יִתֵּ֬ן בְּעִתּ֗וֹ וְעָלֵ֥הוּ לֹֽא־יִבּ֑וֹל וְכֹ֖ל אֲשֶׁר־יַעֲשֶׂ֣ה יַצְלִֽיחַ	*1:3 That person is like a tree planted by streams of water, Which produces fruit in its season, And its leaf withering away, And all which he does prospers.*	There is loose parallelism here, but the simile of the tree is dominant here.		Positive emotion—awe. Provokes the hearer to desire to be like this tree and so to devote himself to the Lord's instructions. This admired one is desirable in every way: productive, healthy, beautiful and prosperous. This is the first peak of emotional intensity in the psalm.	Tone and facial expressions of awe. Short pause at the end of this section.

Hebrew Text	Author's Translation	Passage Structure and Themes	Character speaking	Emotion and Rationale	Performance Ideas
לֹא־כֵן הָרְשָׁעִים כִּי אִם־כַּמֹּץ אֲשֶׁר־תִּדְּפֶנּוּ רוּחַ	1:4 *Not so the wicked! Instead, they are like chaff that the wind blows away.*	Verses 4–5 have the wicked as their subject.		High contrast and reversal of prior attitudes. There is no admiration for the wicked, who are useless, a failure and to be truly despised. לֹא־כֵן *not so* and כִּי אִם *instead* introduce the point of contrast. 4a Negative emotion—disgust. This is an attempt to dissuade the audience from wanting to be like these people and to make them shudder at their fate. Contrast to verses 1–3. 4b Assertion—the chaff will not survive the winnowing process, and neither will the wicked.	Disgust in voice and facial features for the transient wicked. Exclamation of woe. Tone emphasizes the contrast between the wicked and the righteous of verses 13. Emphasis in intonation on "the chaff" in contrast to "the tree" above.

Hebrew Text	Author's Translation	Passage Structure and Themes	Character speaking	Emotion and Rationale	Performance Ideas
עַל־כֵּן ׀ לֹא־יָקֻמוּ רְשָׁעִים בַּמִּשְׁפָּט וְחַטָּאִים בַּעֲדַת צַדִּיקִים	1:5 So, the wicked cannot withstand the judgement, Nor can sinners join in when the righteous gather.	עַל־כֵּן so, again introducing contrast. These lines are in synonymous parallelism.		An assertion by deductive reasoning. The wicked are like chaff and the righteous are like grain, so the wicked will end up entirely separated from the righteous. These paths cannot be combined. Negative emotion—condemnation.	Judging tone. Short pause before the final conclusion in verse 6.

Translators' Oral Notes for Psalm 1

Hebrew Text	Author's Translation	Passage Structure and Themes	Character speaking	Emotion and Rationale	Performance Ideas
כִּי־יוֹדֵעַ יְהוָה דֶּרֶךְ צַדִּיקִים וְדֶרֶךְ רְשָׁעִים תֹּאבֵד	1:6 Surely, the Lord watches over the way of the righteous, but the way of the wicked leads to destruction.	Generalizing summary in a final antithetically parallel couplet. The subject of verse 6 is God.		Negative emotion in final line—rejection. The Lord is intimately involved with the righteous but disregards the wicked, who perish. The audience realized that this is a divinely instituted reality which cannot be challenged, and the hearer is inspired to devote himself to the path of the righteous. This is the second peak of emotional intensity in the psalm.	Tone of rebuke in final line.

Appendix 7

Story chart for Psalm 100

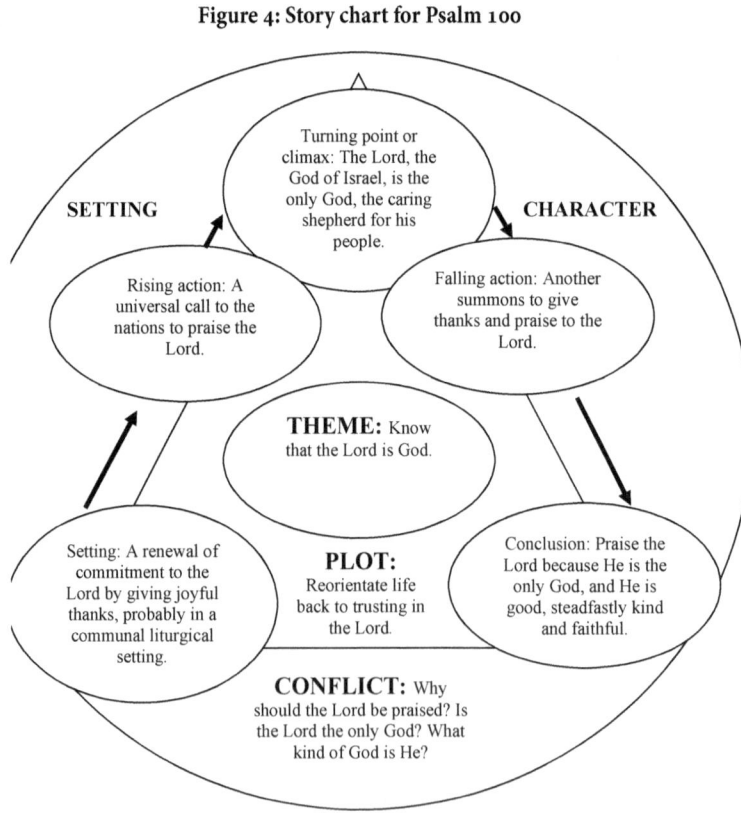

Figure 4: Story chart for Psalm 100

Appendix 8

Trcnslators' Oral Notes for Psalm 100

In response to the need of OBT teams for more guidance in the area of emotional exegesis, I have prepared my own notes for OBT teams on the passages included in my research. These OBT notes include analysis of the structure, themes, and the peak of the passage, as well as observations on the passage's intended impact, including imagery, emotions and senses, performance features and evidence for them, and performance ideas that can be adapted according to the receptor culture. If the translation team is preparing their own performance, they will need to discuss which ideas are appropriate for their own cultural context, which might need to be adapted, and new ones they may want to add.

Table 6: Translators' oral notes for Psalm 100

Hebrew Text	Author's Translation	Passage Structure and Themes	Character speaking	Emotion and Rationale	Performance ideas
מִזְמוֹר לְתוֹדָה	A thanksgiving psalm.		Narrator speaks from start to finish.		

Appendix 8

Hebrew Text	Author's Translation	Passage Structure and Themes	Character speaking	Emotion and Rationale	Performance ideas
הָרִיעוּ לַיהוָה כָּל־הָאָרֶץ	100:1 Shout for joy to the Lord, all the earth.	Stanza 1 (verses 1–3) gives a call to praise (1–2) and a reason to praise (3). Verse 1 contains a monocolon.		Positive emotion—an exclamation of joy!	Arms in the air or other bodily posture indicative of joy.
עִבְדוּ אֶת־יְהוָה בְּשִׂמְחָה בֹּאוּ לְפָנָיו בִּרְנָנָה	100:2 Worship the Lord with gladness, Come before him with ringing shouts of joy.	Verse 2 contains a bicolon.			
דְּעוּ כִּי־יְהוָה הוּא אֱלֹהִים הוּא־עָשָׂנוּ וְלֹא אֲנַחְנוּ עַמּוֹ וְצֹאן מַרְעִיתוֹ	100:3 Know that the Lord is God, He has made us, and we are his, We are his people and the sheep of his pasture.	This is a tricolon and contains internal parallelism in 2b and 3a.			Short pause at the end of this stanza.
בֹּאוּ שְׁעָרָיו בְּתוֹדָה חֲצֵרֹתָיו בִּתְהִלָּה הוֹדוּ־לוֹ בָּרְכוּ שְׁמוֹ	100:4 Enter his gates with thanksgiving And his courts with praise; Give thanks to him and praise his name.	Stanza 2 (4–5) gives a call to praise (4) and reason to praise (5).			

Hebrew Text	Author's Translation	Passage Structure and Themes	Character speaking	Emotion and Rationale	Performance ideas
כִּי־ט֣וֹב יְ֭הֹוָה לְעוֹלָ֣ם חַסְדּ֑וֹ וְעַד־דֹּ֥ר וָ֝דֹ֗ר אֱמוּנָתֽוֹ	100:5 For the LORD is good, His loyal love endures forever, his faithfulness continues through all generations				

Appendix 9

Story chart for Psalm 133

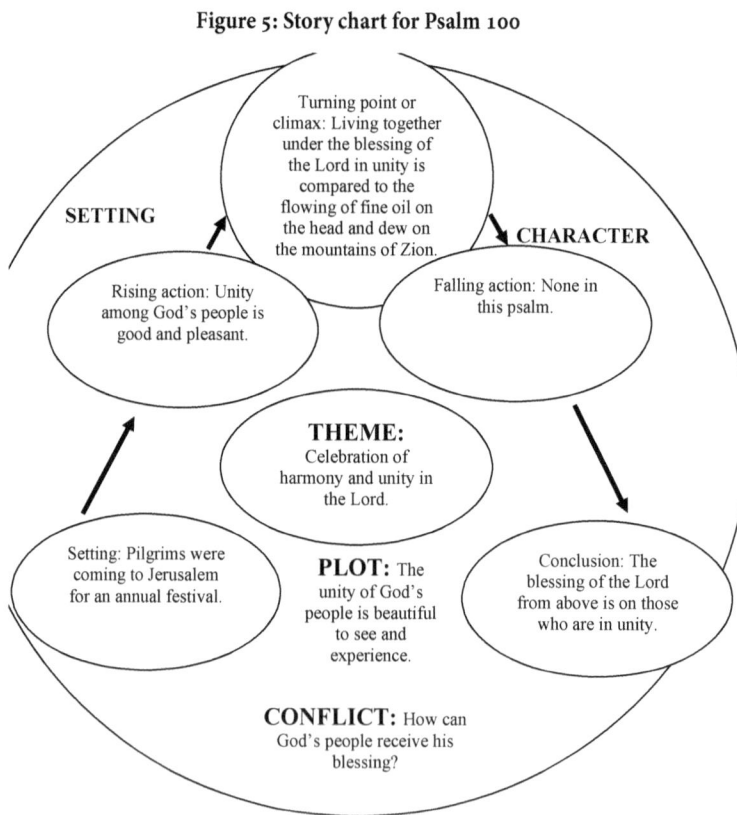

Figure 5: Story chart for Psalm 100

Appendix 10

Translators' Oral Notes for Psalm 133

In response to the need of OBT teams for more guidance in the area of emotional exegesis, I have prepared my own notes for OBT teams on the passages included in my research. These OBT notes include analysis of the structure, themes, and the peak of the passage, as well as observations on the passage's intended impact, including imagery, emotions and senses, performance features and evidence for them, and performance ideas that can be adapted according to the receptor culture. If the translation team is preparing their own performance, they will need to discuss which ideas are appropriate for their own cultural context, which might need to be adapted, and new ones they may want to add.

Table 7: Translators' oral notes for Psalm 133

Hebrew Text	Author's Translation	Passage Structure and Themes	Character Speaking	Emotions and Rationale	Performance ideas
שִׁיר הַמַּעֲלוֹת לְדָוִד	A Song of Ascents. Of David.	This is the title of the psalm.	Narrator speaks from start to finish.		

Hebrew Text	Author's Translation	Passage Structure and Themes	Character Speaking	Emotions and Rationale	Performance ideas
הִנֵּה מַה־טּוֹב וּמַה־נָּעִים שֶׁבֶת אַחִים גַּם־יָחַד	133:1 How good and pleasant it is When God's people live together in unity!	Verse 1 is the first of three sections. Verse 1 has two lines.		Positive emotion. Emphasis.	Strong exclamatory statement of joy! Short pause.
כַּשֶּׁמֶן הַטּוֹב ׀ עַל־הָרֹאשׁ יֹרֵד עַל־הַזָּקָן זְקַן־אַהֲרֹן שֶׁיֹּרֵד עַל־פִּי מִדּוֹתָיו	133:2 Like precious oil poured on the head, Running down on the beard—Aaron's beard, Running down onto the collar of his robe.	Verse 2–3a is the middle section with the figurative images. Verse 2 has three lines.		Emphasis	Hand motions to the head or hand motions flowing down. Motion to imaginary beard on face or robe. Possible sound effects of running liquid. Short pause.
כְּטַל־חֶרְמוֹן שֶׁיֹּרֵד עַל־הַרְרֵי צִיּוֹן כִּי שָׁם ׀ צִוָּה יְהוָה אֶת־הַבְּרָכָה חַיִּים עַד־הָעוֹלָם	133:3 Like the dew of Mount Hermon Running down on Mount Zion. For there the Lord has promised his blessing—life for evermore.	Verse 3b is the final section and climax of the poem. Verse 3a has two lines and verse 3b has two lines.		Change of pace. Emphasis.	Short pause after 3a. Pace slows down for final couplet in 3b. The word "promised" is more forceful.

Appendix 11

Illustrations of Judges 4 for internalization

I created the following hand-drawn illustrations to assist with the process of internalizing Judges 4.

288 Appendix 11

Figure 6: Illustrations of Judges 4 for internalization

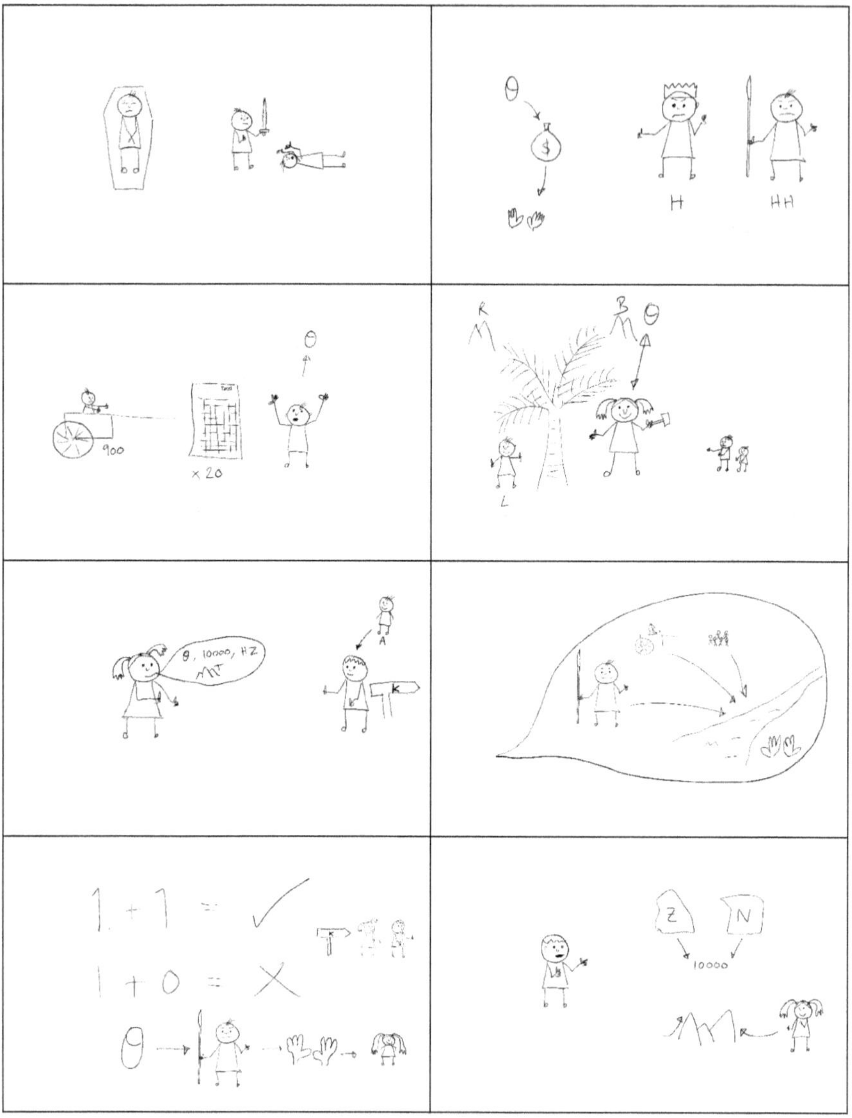

Illustrations of Judges 4 for internalization

Appendix 11

Appendix 12

Illustrations of Judges 4 by the Altai team

Figure 7: Illustrations of Judges 4 by the Altai team

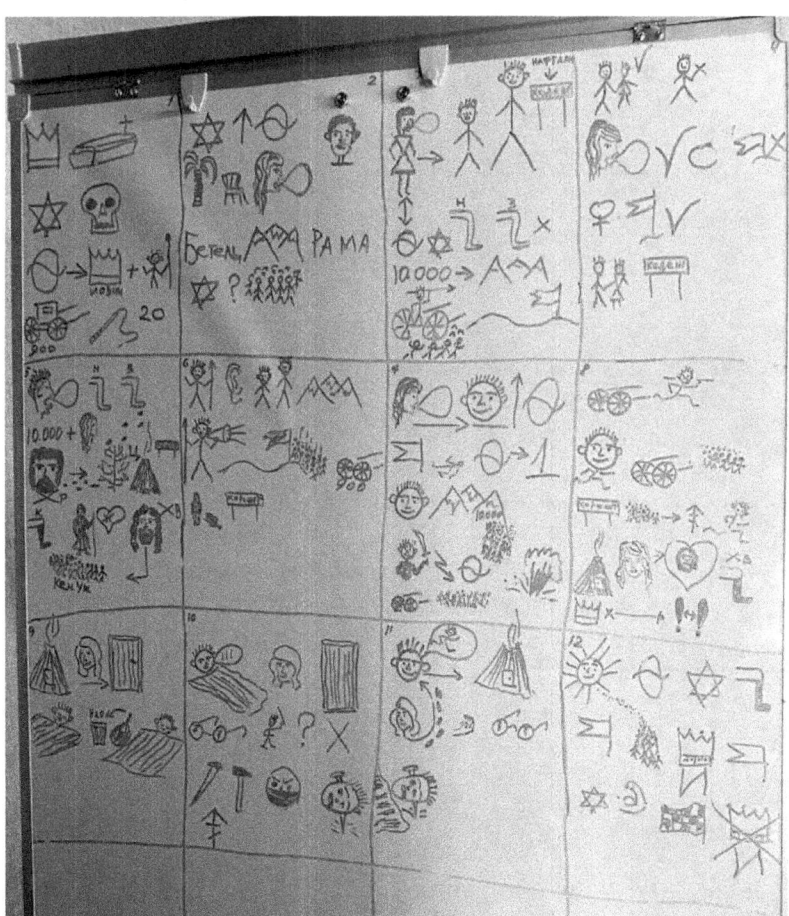

Bibliography

Adami, Elisabetta. "Multimodality." In *Oxford Handbook of Language and Society*, edited by Ofelia Garcia et al., 451–72. Oxford: Oxford University Press, 2016.

Agnew, Sarah. *Embodied Performance: Mutuality, Embrace, and the Letter to Rome*. Eugene, OR: Pickwick, 2020.

Aguiar, Daniella, and Joao Queiroz. "Towards a Model of Intersemiotic Translation." *International Journal of the Arts in Society* 4 (2009) 203–10.

Alexander, Swapna. "The Joys and Challenges of Checking Oral Bible Translation." Paper presented at the Bible Translation Conference, Dallas, TX, 2021.

———. "Oral Exegesis: Engaging Oral Translators and Leveraging the Tacit Linguistic Knowledge of MTTs." Presentation at Global OBT Gathering. Online, Aug. 2021. https://sites.google.com/tsco.org/obtgathering2021/home-obt-gathering-2021/oral-exegesis-engaging-oral-translators-and-mtts.

———. Personal email to author, Sep. 9, 2021.

Allen, Leslie C. *Psalms 101–150*. Word Biblical Commentary 21. Rev. ed. Nashville: Thomas Nelson, 2002.

Alter, Robert. *The Art of Biblical Poetry*. Rev. ed. New York: Basic, 2011.

———. *The Hebrew Bible: A Translation with Commentary*. New York: W. W. Norton, 2019.

Amzallag, Nissim. "The Meaning of Todah in the Title of Psalm 100." *Zeitschrift für die Alttestamentliche Wissenschaft* 126 (2014) 535–45.

Anderson, Bernhard W. *Out of the Depths: The Psalms Speak to Us Today*. Louisville: Westminster John Knox, 1970.

Andrews, Adam, and Missy Andrews. *Teaching the Classics: A Socratic Method for Literary Education*. 2nd ed. Center For Lit, 2017.

Armstrong, Cameron D. "Orality Reality: Implications for Theological Education in Romania and Beyond." *Transformation* 40 (2023) 16–33.

Armstrong, Ryan M. "Psalms Dwelling Together in Unity: The Placement of Psalms 133 and 134 in Two Different Psalms Collections." *Journal of Biblical Literature* 131 (2012) 487–506.

Ballarin Ducasse, Hélène B. "Developing an Oral Interpretation Translation Method." Paper presented at the Bible Translation Conference, Dallas, TX, 2015.

Barnwell, Katherine. *Bible Translation: An Introductory Course in Translation Principles*. 4th ed. Dallas: SIL International, 2020.

Bartsch, Carla. "Oral Style, Written Style and Bible Translation." *Notes on Translation* 11 (1997) 41–47.

Beck, John A. *God as Storyteller: Seeking Meaning in Biblical Narrative*. St. Louis: Chalice, 2008.

Beekman, John, and John Callow. *Translating the Word of God*. Dallas: SIL International, 1974.

Berlin, Adele. "On the Interpretation of Psalm 133." In *Directions in Biblical Hebrew Poetry*, edited by Elaine R. Follis, 141–48. Sheffield: Sheffield Academic, 1987.

Biber, Douglas. *Variation Across Speech and Writing*. Cambridge: Cambridge University Press, 1988.

Block, Daniel I. *Judges/Ruth*. New American Commentary 6. Nashville: Broadman & Holman, 1999.

Boerger, Brenda. "Freeing Biblical Poetry to Sing." *Open Theology* 2 (2016) 179–203.

———. "Poetic Oracle English Translation (POET) Psalms." Version 11b. Self-published, 2021.

Boersma, Hans. *Violence, Hospitality, and the Cross: Reappropriating the Atonement Tradition*. Grand Rapids: Baker Academic, 2006.

Boomershine, Tom. *The Messiah of Peace: A Performance Criticism Commentary on Mark's Passion-Resurrection Narrative*. Eugene, OR: Cascade, 2015.

———. *Story Journey: An Invitation to the Gospel as Storytelling*. Nashville: Abingdon, 1988.

Box, Harry. *Don't Throw the Book at Them: Communicating God's Message to People Who Don't Read*. Pasadena: William Carey Library, 2014.

Bratcher, Robert G., and William D. Reyburn. *A Handbook on the Book of Psalms*. New York: United Bible Societies, 1991.

Brown, Rick. "Communicating God's Message in an Oral Culture." *International Journal of Frontier Missions* 21 (2004) 122–28.

Brueggemann, Walter. *Israel's Praise: Doxology Against Idolatry and Ideology*. Philadelphia: Fortress, 1988.

———. "Psalm 100." *Interpretation: A Journal of Bible and Theology* 39 (1985) 65–69.

———. "Psalms in Narrative Performance." In *Performing the Psalms*, edited by Dave Bland and David Fleer, 124–343. St. Louis: Chalice, 2005.

Bunn, Stephanie. "Time as Told: Telling the Past in Kyrgyzstan." *History and Anthropology* 29 (2018) 563–83.

Butler, Trent C. *Judges*. Word Biblical Commentary 8. Nashville: Thomas Nelson, 2009.

Cambridge Dictionary. "Internalize." https://dictionary.cambridge.org/dictionary/english/internalize.

Carr, David M. *Writing on the Tablet of the Heart: Origins of Scripture and Literature*. Oxford: Oxford University Press, 2005.

Chandler, Daniel. *Semiotics: The Basics*. 3rd ed. London/New York: Routledge, 2017.

Cheung, Andy. "Functionalism and Foreignisation: Applying Skopos Theory to Bible Translation." PhD diss., University of Birmingham, 2011.

Chumakaev, A. E., ed. *The Altai-Russian Dictionary* [in Russian]. Gorno-Altaisk: Nauchno-Issledovatel'skiy Institut Altaistiki Im. S. S. Surazakova, 2018.

Cleaver, Bronwen. "A Comparison of Listeners' Responses to Two Comparative Biblical Texts Produced in the Southern Altai Language by Means of Written and the Other by Means of Oral Translation." MA thesis, Johnson University, 2020.

———. "Oral Bible Translation and its Role in the Future of Bible Translation." *Bible Translator* 74 (2023) 5–20.

Congos, Dennis. "9 Types of Mnemonics for Better Memory." https://www.ghc.edu/sites/default/files/StudentResources/documents/learningcenter/handouts/GeneralStudySkills/9_types_of_mnemonics_for_better_memory.htm.

Conquergood, Dwight. "Performance Studies: Interventions and Radical Research." *Drama Review* 46 (2002) 145–56.

———. "Rethinking Ethnography: Towards a Critical Cultural Politics." *Communication Monographs* 58 (1991) 179–94.

Coogan, M. "A Structural and Literary Analysis of the Song of Deborah." *Catholic Biblical Quarterly* 40 (1978) 143–66.

Cousins, Melinda. "Pilgrim Theology: Worldmaking Through Enactment of the Psalms of Ascents (Psalms 120–134)." PhD diss., Charles Sturt University, 2016.

Craigie, P. C. "Parallel Word Pairs in the Song of Deborah (Judges 5)." *Journal of the Evangelical Theological Society* 29 (1977) 15–22.

———. *Psalms 1–15*. Word Biblical Commentary 19. Nashville: Thomas Nelson, 2004.

Culy, Martin M. "The Top-Down Approach to Translation." *Notes on Translation* 7 (1993) 28–51.

Davidson, E. T. A. *Intricacy, Design, and Cunning in the Book of Judges*. Bloomington: Xlibris, 2008.

Davis, Kipp. "Structure, Stichometry, and Standardisation: An Analysis of Scribal Features in a Selection of the Dead Sea Psalms Scrolls." In *Functions of Psalms and Prayers in the Late Second Temple Period*, edited by Jeremy Penner and Mika S. Pajunen, 153–84. Berlin/Boston: De Gruyter, 2017.

De Vries, Lourens. "Bible Translation and Primary Orality." *Bible Translator* 51 (2000) 101–14.

———. "Local Oral-Written Interfaces and the Nature, Transmission, Performance, and Translation of Biblical Texts." In *Translating Scripture for Sound and Performance: New Directions in Biblical Studies*, edited by James A. Maxey, 69–98. Eugene: Cascade, 2012.

———. "Views of Orality and the Translation of the Bible." In *Orality and Translation*, edited by Paul F. Bandia, 17–32. London: Routledge, Taylor, and Francis Group, 2017.

DeClaissé-Walford, Nancy L., Rolf A. Jacobsen, and Beth LaNeel Tanner. *Commentary on Psalms*. New International Commentary on the Old Testament. Grand Rapids: Eerdmans, 2014.

Demchinova, Mira A. "A Collection and Study of Altai Folk Songs" [in Russian]. *Filologiya i Chelovek* 1 (2012) 1–10.

Derrida, Jacques. *Of Hospitality*. Translated by Rachel Bowlby. Stanford: Stanford University Press, 2000.

Dickie, June F. "Community Translation and Oral Performance of Some Praise Psalms Within the Zulu Community." *Bible Translator* 68 (2017) 253–68.

———. "Interacting with and Performing the Book of Ruth as a Pathway Toward Trauma Healing: An Empirical Study from Côte D'Ivoire." *Ethnodoxology* 10 (2022) 18–30.

———. "Psalm 133: Ancient Wisdom Interpreted by Contemporary South Africans." *Journal for Semitics* 29 (2020) 1–16.

———. "Using Psalms in the Church and Everyday Life." Paper presented at the Bible Translation Conference, Dallas, TX, Oct. 2021.

Dinh, Huong Q., et al. "Evaluating the Importance of Multi-Sensory Input on Memory and the Sense of Presence in Virtual Environments." 1999. https://www.semanticscholar.org/paper/Evaluating-the-importance-of-multi-sensory-input-on-Dinh-Walker/d3759e451a361779abbea1c400a253a0c40e70fa.

Doan, William, and Terry Giles. *Prophets, Performance, and Power: Performance Criticism of the Hebrew Bible*. London: T. & T. Clark, 2005.

———. *Twice Used Songs: Performance Criticism of the Songs of Ancient Israel*. Peabody, MA: Hendrickson, 2009.

———. *The Story of Naomi—The Book of Ruth: From Gender to Politics*. Eugene, OR: Cascade, 2016.

———. "Performance Criticism of the Hebrew Bible." *Religious Compass* 2 (2008) 273–86.

Dobbs-Allsopp, Frederick William. "Psalm 133: A (Close) Reading." *Journal of Hebrew Scriptures* 8 (2008) 1–30.

Doyle, Brian. "Metaphora Interrupta: Psalm 133." *Louvain Journal of Theology and Canon Law* 77 (2001) 5–22.

Dye, Wayne. "The Eight Conditions of Scripture Engagement: Social and Cultural Factors Necessary for Vernacular Bible Translation to Achieve Maximum Effect." *International Journal of Frontier Missions* 26 (2009) 89–98.

Ebbinghaus, Hermann. *Über das Gedächtnis (On Memory)*. Leipzig: Duncker & Humblot, 1885.

Ethnologue: Languages of the World. Dallas, TX: SIL International, 1999. Online version: http://www.ethnologue.com.

Farber, Neil. "The Science of Memory: Don't Forget to Remember." *Psychology Today*, Mar. 29, 2015. https://www.psychologytoday.com/us/blog/the-blame-game/201503/the-science-memory.

Fitzgerald, Danny, and Brian Schrag. "'But Is It Any Good?': The Role of Criticism in Christian Song Composition and Performance." *Global Forum on Arts and Christian Faith* 2 (2014) 1–19.

Fitzgerald, Danny. "Translating the Hebrew Psalms to be Sung: The 2010 Revised Grail Psalms, a Case Study." *Między Oryginałem a Przekładem* 3 (2021) 31–54.

Floor, Sebastian. "Reflections on the Authority and Canon of Oral Scriptures." Paper presented at the Bible Translation Conference, Dallas, TX, 2021.

Fokkelman, Jan P. "The Song of Deborah and Barak: Its Prosodic Levels and Structure." In *Pomegranates and Golden Bells: Studies in Biblical, Jewish, and Near Eastern Ritual, Law, and Literature in Honor of Jacob Milgrom*, edited by David P. Wright et al., 595–628. Winnona Lake: Eisenbrauns, 1995.

Foley, John Miles. *How to Read an Oral Poem*. Urbana/Chicago: University of Illinois Press, 2002.

———. *Immanent Art: From Structure to Meaning in Traditional Oral Epic*. Bloomington: Indiana University Press, 1991.

———. *Oral Tradition and the Internet: Pathways of the Mind*. Urbana: University of Illinois Press, 2012.

———. *The Singer of Tales in Performance*. Bloomington: Indiana University Press, 1995.

Fotso, Ervais. "Voice Synchrony in Oral Bible Translation." Paper presented at the Bible Translation Conference, Dallas, TX, 2019.

Freedman, David Noel. "Pottery, Poetry, and Prophecy: An Essay on Biblical Poetry." *Journal of Biblical Literature* 96 (1977) 5–26.

Frost, Joshua, and Heather Beal. "Leveraging Biblical Artistry for Performance and Fidelity in Luke 15." *Journal of Language, Culture and Religion* 4 (2023) 1–25.

Frost, Katie. "Basic Internalization Plan." 2018. https://www.academia.edu/104929016/Basic_Internalization_Plan.

———. "Internalization Session Lesson Plan." 2018. https://www.academia.edu/104958975/Internalization_Session_Lesson_Plan.

———. "Non-Narrative Internalization." Presentation on the Orality Landscape of Practice Online, Jul. 2021. https://sites.google.com/view/oralitylop/documents/hom/july-2021-non-narrative-internalization?authuser=0.

———. "Preparing for and Facilitating Internalization." Session for the Orality Landscape of Practice Online, 2022. https://sites.google.com/view/oralitylop/documents/hom/january-2022-preparing-for-and-facilitating-internalization.

———. "Tips for Internalizing Scripture." 2018. https://www.academia.edu/104958819/Tips_for_Internalizing_Scripture. (Login required for access.)

———. "Workshop Elements of Oral Crafting." Session taught at online OBT school, Nov. 2020. https://www.academia.edu/104959037/Workshop_Elements_of_Oral_Crafting_Nov_2020_.

Futato, Mark D. *Cornerstone Biblical Commentary: The Book of Psalms*. Carol Stream, IL: Tyndale House, 2009.

Gejin, Chao. "Mongolian Oral Epic Poetry: An Overview." *Oral Tradition* 12 (1997) 322–36.

Gerleman, Gillis. "The Song of Deborah in the Light of Stylistics." *Vetus Testamentum* 1 (1951) 168–80.

Germain, Julie. "Benefits of Performance for Translation." *GIALens* 12 (2018) 1–9.

Globe, Alexander. "The Literary Structure and Unity of the Song of Deborah." *Journal of Biblical Literature* 93 (1974) 493–512.

Gravelle, Giles. "Meaning Making and Embodiment Through Visual Interpretation." Paper presented at the 2019 Bible Translation Conference, Dallas, TX, 2019. https://www.academia.edu/42861085/Meaning_Making_and_Embodiment_Through_Visual_Interpretation.

———. "More Than Words: Linguistics, Language and Meaning." *Orality Journal* 2 (2013) 47–54.

Green, Robin. "An Orality Strategy: Translating the Bible for Oral Communicators." MA diss., Dallas International University, 2007.

Grosser, Emmylou. "What Symmetry Can Do That Parallelism Can't: Line Perception and Poetic Effects in the Song of Deborah (Judges 5:2–31)." *Vetus Testamentum* 71 (2021) 175–204.

Gunkel, Hermann. *Einleitung in die Psalmen: Die Gattungen der religiösen Lyrik Israels*. Göttingen: Vandenhoeck & Ruprecht, 1926.

———. *Introduction to Psalms: The Genres of the Religious Lyric of Israel*. Macon: Mercer University Press, 1988.

———. *The Psalms: A Form-Critical Introduction*. Reprint ed. Philadelphia: Fortress, 1967.

Harmelink, Brian. "A Narrative Approach to Translating Key Biblical Terms." Paper presented at the Oral Bible Translation Conference, Rockville, MD, 2018. https://

sites.google.com/view/obtconference2018/sessions/10-a-narrative-approach-to-translating-key-biblical-terms.

———. "Oral Bible Translation." Paper presented at the FOBAI Annual Meeting, Wycliffe Global Alliance, 2019.

Harrison, David K. "A Tuvan Hero Tale, with Commentary, Morphemic Analysis, and Translation." *Journal of the American Oriental Society* 125 (2005) 1–30.

Harvilahti, Lauri. "Altai Oral Epic." *Oral Tradition* 15 (2000) 215–29.

———. "Epos and National Identity: Transformations and Incarnations." *Oral Tradition* 11 (1996) 37–49.

Harvilahti, Lauri, and Zoya S. Kazagacheva. *The Holy Mountain: Studies on Upper Altay Oral Poetry*. Helsinki: Academia Scientiarum Fennica, 2003.

Hatim, Basil, and Ian Mason. *Discourse and the Translator*. London/New York: Longman, 1990.

Hauser, Alan J. "Judges 5: Parataxis in Hebrew Poetry." *Journal of Biblical Literature* 99 (1980) 23–41.

Hearon, Holly. "Characters in Text and Performance." In *From Text to Performance: Narrative and Performance Criticisms in Dialogue and Debate*, edited by Kelly R. Iverson, 53–79. Eugene: Cascade, 2014.

Himes, John. "Reaching the Goal: Skopos Theory in Bible Translation." Paper presented at the Bible Faculty Summit, Central Baptist Theological Seminary, Minnesota, 2015. https://www.academia.edu/14901048/Reaching_the_Goal_Skopos_Theory_in_Bible_Translation.

Holmes, James S. "The Name and Nature of Translation Studies." In *Translated! Papers on Literary Translation and Translation Studies*, edited by James S. Holmes, 67–80. Amsterdam: Rodopi, 1988.

Holz-Mänttäri, Justa, and Vermeer Hans Josef. "Entwurf für einen Studiengang Translatorik und einen Promotionsstudiengang Translatologie." *Kääntäjä/Översättaren* 3 (1985) 4–6.

Howard, David M. *The Structure of Psalms 93–100*. Winona Lake: Eisenbrauns, 1997.

Jakobson, Roman. "On Linguistic Aspects of Translation." In *The Translation Studies Reader*, edited by Lawrence Venuti, 138–43. 2nd ed. New York: Routledge, 2004.

Jakubowska, Honorata. *Skill Transmission, Sport, and Tacit Knowledge: A Sociological Perspective*. London/New York: Routledge, 2017.

Jerome (Eusebius Sophronius Hieronymus). "Letter to Pammachius." In *The Translation Studies Reader*, edited by Lawrence Venuti, 21–20. 2nd ed. New York/London: Routledge, 2004.

Katash, Sergey Sergeevich. n.d. "Altai Folk Songs and Their Didactic Motifs" [in Russian]. http://osin-music.ru/narodnaya-muzyka/altaiskaya-narodnaya-muzyka/altaiskie-narodnye-pesni-i-ix-didakticheskie-motivy.html.

Kazagacheva, Zoya S. *The Altai Heroic Epic Stories: Ochy-Bala Kan-Altyn* [in Altai]. Novosibirsk: Nauka, 1997.

Kearney, Richard. "Linguistic Hospitality: The Risk of Translation." In *Radical Hospitality: From Thought to Action*, edited by Richard Kearney and Melissa Fizpatrick, 17–23. New York: Fordham University Press, 2021.

Kelley, Robert, and Terry Whatson. "Making Long-Term Memories in Minutes." *Frontiers in Human Neuroscience* 7 (2013) 1–9.

Kelber, Werner H. *The Oral and the Written Gospel*. Bloomington: Indiana University Press, 1997.

Kenmogne, Michel. "Multilingualism, Urbanisation, and Scripture Engagement." Video presentation for participants of SIL International Conference, ICONline, May 5–6, 2020.

Kilham, Christine A. "A Written Style for Oral Communicators." *Notes on Translation Special Edition* 123 (1987) 36–52.

Klem, Herbert V. *Oral Communication of the Scripture: Insights from African Oral Art.* Pasadena: William Carey Library, 1982.

Koehler, Ludwig, et al. *The Hebrew and Aramaic Lexicon of the Old Testament.* Leiden: E. J. Brill, 1994–2000.

Kolb, David A., and Ronald E. Fry. "Toward an Applied Theory of Experiential Learning." 1974. https://www.researchgate.net/publication/238759143_Toward_an_Applied_Theory_of_Experiential_Learning.

Koller, Aaron. "Composing the Song of Deborah: Empirical Models." https://www.thetorah.com/article/composing-the-song-of-deborah-empirical-models.

Konstanski, Paul. "Digital Orality: How to Connect Your Digital Footprint to Oral Learners." *Orality Journal* 6 (2017) 13–26.

Kraus, Hans-Joachim. *Psalms 60–150: A Continental Commentary.* Minneapolis: Fortress, 1993.

Kress, Gunther, and T. Theo Van Leeuwen. *Multimodal Discourse: The Modes and Media of Contemporary Communication.* London: Hodder Education, 2001.

Kroneman, Dick. "Translation, Literacy, and Orality: Reflections from the Domain of Bible Translation." *Orality Journal* 6 (2017) 41–60.

Kuntz, John Kartje. "Reclaiming Biblical Wisdom Psalms: A Response to Crenshaw." *Currents in Biblical Research* 1 (2003) 145–54.

Larsen-Freeman, Diane, and Lynne Cameron. *Complex Systems and Applied Linguistics.* Oxford: Oxford University Press, 2008.

Larson, Mildred L. *Meaning-Based Translation: A Guide to Cross-Language Equivalence.* Lanham, MD: University Press of America, 1984/1997.

Lausanne Occasional Paper, No. 54. "Making Disciples of Oral Learners." Produced by the Issue Group at the 2004 Forum for World Evangelization, hosted by the Lausanne Committee for World Evangelization in Thailand. https://lausanne.org/occasional-paper/making-disciples-of-oral-learners-lop-54.

Le Roux, Magdel. "The Battle Against Hazor and Jael's Deadly Hospitality (Judges 4–5)." *Journal for Semitics* 27 (2018) 1–26.

Leow, Wen Pin. "Form and Experience Dwelling in Unity: A Cognitive Reading of the Metaphors of Psalm 133." *Tyndale Bulletin* 68 (2017) 185–202.

Levy, Shimon. *The Bible as Theatre.* Eastbourne: Sussex Academic, 2012.

Lindars, Barnabus. *Judges 1–5: A New Translation and Commentary.* Edinburgh: T. & T. Clark, 1995.

Longa, Victor M. "A Nonlinear Approach to Translation." *Receptor* 16 (2004) 201–26.

Lord, Albert B. *The Singer of Tales.* Cambridge, MA: Harvard University Press, 1960.

Lovejoy, Grant. "The Extent of Orality: 2012 Update." *Orality Journal* 1 (2012) 11–40.

Lovelace, Chris. "A Comparison of the Written and Oral Altai Translations of Selected Psalms." Prescience Labs, 2022. https://www.cdbr.org/_files/ugd/34917d_dca81d008eb24afba1aa33fdaa1ed448.pdf.

Lumo Project Films. https://lumoproject.com/.

Macky, Peter W. *The Centrality of Metaphors to Biblical Thought: A Method for Interpreting the Bible.* Studies in the Bible and Early Christianity. Lewiston: Lampeter, 1990.

Madinger, Charles. "A Literate's Guide to the Oral Galaxy." *Orality Journal* 2 (2013) 13–40.

Makutoane, Tshokolo J., et al. "Similarity and Alterity in Translating the Orality of the Old Testament in Oral Cultures." *Translation Studies* 8 (2015) 1–19.

———., et al. "What Do We Actually Translate in Representing Orality? A New Approach Using Complexity Theory and Semiotics." Paper presented at the Oral Bible Translation Conference, Rockville, VA, 2018.

Marais, Kobus. *A (Bio)Semiotic theory of Translation: The Emergence of Social-Cultural Reality.* London/New York: Routledge, 2019.

———. "Effects Causing Effects: Considering Constraints in Translation." In *Complexity Thinking in Translation Studies: Methodological Considerations*, edited by Kobus Marais and Reine Meylaerts, 53–72. New York: Routledge, 2019.

———. "Translation Complex Rather Than Translation Turns: Considering the Complexity of Translation." *Syn-Thèses*, 9–10 (2019) 43–55.

———. *Translation Theory and Development Studies: A Complexity Theory Approach.* London/New York: Routledge, 2014.

Marais, Kobus, and Reine Meylaerts, eds. *Complexity Thinking in Translation Studies: Methodological Considerations.* London/New York: Routledge, 2019.

Mathews, Jeanette. *Performing Habakkuk.* Eugene: Pickwick, 2012.

———. *Prophets as Performers: Biblical Performance Criticism and Israel's Prophets.* Eugene, OR: Cascade, 2020.

Maust, Drew, and Jacobus A. Naudé. "Translation Studies and Bible Translation." *Journal for Translation Studies in Africa* 2 (2021) 1–27.

Maxey, James A. "Alternative Evaluative Concepts to the Trinity of Bible Translation." In *Translating Values: Evaluative Concepts in Translation*, edited by Piotr Blumczynski and John Gillespie, 57–80. London: Palgrave Macmillan, 2016.

———. "Beyond Print/Oral Translation: A Hospitality Approach to Performance." Paper presented at the Oral Bible Translation Conference, Rockville, VA, 2018. https://sites.google.com/view/obtconference2018/sessions/12-beyond-print-oral-translation.

———. "Bible Translation as Hospitality and Counterinsurgency: Hostile Hosts and Unruly Guests." Paper presented at the Bible Translation Conference, Dallas, TX, 2013. https://map.bloomfire.com/posts/2179258-hostile-hosts-and-unruly-guests-bible-translation-as-hospitality-and-counterins.

———. "Bible Translation in the 21st Century: Missiological Paradigms." Paper presented at Bible Translation Conference, Dallas, TX, 2011.

———. "Bible Translation in the 21st Century: Translation Trajectories." Paper presented at Bible Translation Conference, Dallas, TX, 2011.

———. "Biblical Performance Criticism and Bible Translation." In *Translating Scripture for Sound and Performance: New Directions in Biblical Studies*, edited by James A. Maxey and Ernst R. Wendland, 1–21. Eugene: Cascade, 2012.

———. *From Orality to Orality: A New Paradigm for Contextual Translation of the Bible.* Eugene, OR: Cascade, 2009.

Maxwell, Kathy. "Embodying Scripture Through Performative Interpretation." In *Scripture. Christian Reflection: A Series in Faith and Ethics*, edited by Robert B. Kruschwitz, 74–77. Baylor University: Institute for Faith and Learning, 2014.

———. *Hearing Between the Lines: The Audience as Fellow-Worker in Luke-Acts and Its Literary Milieu.* London: Bloomsbury, 2010.

Mays, James Luther. "World, Worship, and Power: An Interpretation of Psalm 100." *Interpretation: A Journal of Bible and Theology* 23 (1969) 315–30.
Merriam-Webster, "Internalize." Merriam-Webster. https://www.merriam-webster.com/dictionary/internalize.
Metzger, Bruce M. "Important Early Translations of the Bible." *Bibliotheca Sacra* 150 (1993) 35–49.
Miller, Robert D. *Oral Tradition in Ancient Israel*. Eugene, OR: Cascade, 2011.
Miller, Shem. "Multiformity of Stichographic Systems in the Dead Sea Scrolls." *Revue de Qumran* 29 (2017) 219–45.
———. "The Oral-Written Textuality of Stichographic Poetry in the Dead Sea Scrolls." *Dead Sea Discoveries* 22 (2015) 162–88.
Miller-Naudé, Cynthia L., and Jacobus A. Naudé. "The Translator as an Agent of Change and Transformation: The Case of Biblical Proverbs." *Old Testament Essays* 23 (2010) 301–21.
Naudé, Jacobus A. "Equivalence." In *A Guide to Bible Translation: People, Languages, and Topics*, edited by Philip A. Noss and Charles S. Houser, 415–22. Swindon, UK: United Bible Societies, 2019.
———. "Iconicity and Developments in Translation Studies." *Signergy*, edited by Jac Conradie et al., 387–411. Iconicity in Language and Literature 9. Amsterdam/Philadelphia: John Benjamins, 2010.
———. "A Narrative Frame Analysis of the 1933 Afrikaans Bible." *Studia Historiae Ecclesiaticae* 37 (2011) 255–74.
———. "An Overview of Recent Developments in Translation Studies with Special Reference to the Implications for Bible Translation." *Acta Theologica Supplementum* 2 (2002) 44–69. https://www.researchgate.net/publication/272457168_An_overview_of_recent_developments_in_translation_studies_with_special_reference_to_the_implications_for_Bible_translation.
———. "Religious Texts and Oral Tradition." In *Handbook of Translation Studies*, vol. 5, edited by Yves Gambier and Luc van Doorslaer, 191–98. Amsterdam/Philadelphia: John Benjamins, 2021.
———. "Translation Studies and Bible Translations." *Acta Theologica* 20 (2000) 1–27.
Naudé, Jacobus. A., and Miller-Naudé, Cynthia L. "Alterity, Orality, and Performance in Bible Translation." In *Key Cultural Texts in Translation*, edited by Kirsten Malmkær et al., 299–313. Amsterdam/Philadelphia: John Benjamins, 2018.
———. "Sacred Writings." In *The Routledge Handbook of Literary Translation*, edited by Kelly Washbourne and Ben Van Wyke, 181–205. London: Routledge, 2018.
———. "Sacred Writings and Their Translations as Complex Phenomena: The Book of Ben Sira in the Septuagint as a Case in Point." In *Complexity Thinking in Translation Studies: Methodological Studies*, edited by Kobus Marais and Reine Meylaerts, 180–215. New York: Routledge, 2019.
———. "Theology and Ideology in the Metatexts of Bible Translations in Muslim Contexts: A Case Study." In *Ancient Texts and Modern Readers: Studies in Ancient Hebrew Linguistics and Bible Translation*, edited by Gideon Kotze et al., 280–99. Lieden: Brill, 2019.
———. "The Translation of Biblion and Biblos in the Light of Oral and Scribal Practice." *In die Skriflig* 50 (2016) 1–11.

Nida, Eugene A. "A Framework for the Analysis and Evaluation of Theories of Translation." In *Translation. Applications, and Research*, edited by Richard W. Brislin, 47–91. New York: Gardner, 1976.

———. "Trends in Bible Translating Within the United Bible Societies: An Historical Perspective." *Bible Translator* 42 (1991) 2–5.

Nida, Eugene Albert, and Taber Charles Russell. *The Theory and Practice of Translation.* Leiden: Brill, 1969.

Niles, John D. "Introduction to the Special Issue: Living Epics of China and Inner Asia." *Journal of American Folklore* 129 (2016) 253–69.

Nord, Christine. "Functionalist Approaches." In *Handbook of Translation Studies*, vol. 1, edited by Yves Gambier and Luc Van Doorslaer, 120–28. Amsterdam/Philadelphia: John Benjamins, 2010.

———. "Function and Loyalty: Theology Meets Skopos." *Open Theology* 2 (2016) 566–80.

———. *Text Analysis in Translation*. Amsterdam/New York: Rodopi, 2005.

———. "Text Analysis in Translator Training." In *Teaching Translation and Interpreting: Training, Talent, and Experience*, edited by Cay Dollerup and Anne Loddegaard, 39–48. Amsterdam/Philadelphia: John Benjamins, 1992.

———. *Translating as a Purposeful Activity: Functionalist Approaches Explained.* 2nd ed. Oxford: Routledge, 2018.

Oestreich, Bernhard. *Performance Criticism of the Pauline Letters.* Eugene, OR: Cascade, 2016.

Ogden, Graham S., and Lynell Zogbo. *A Handbook on Judges.* Miami: United Bible Societies, 2019.

Ong, Walter J. *Orality and Literacy.* 3rd ed. London/New York: Routledge, 2012.

Ott, Willis. "The Rationale for Orally Communicating the Scripture." *Oralities and Literacies: Implications for Communication and Education*, edited by Charles Madinger. N.p.: International Orality Network (2016) 60–64.

———. "The Literate Mind-Set." https://www.academia.edu/8298776/The_literate_mind_set.

Parry, Milman. *The Making of Homeric Verse: The Collected Papers of Milman Parry.* Edited by Adam Parry. Oxford: Oxford University Press, 2017.

Pasquale, Michael, and Nathan L. K. Bierma. *Every Tribe and Tongue: A Biblical Vision for Language in Society.* Eugene, OR: Pickwick, 2011.

Pegg, Carol. "Re-sounding the Spirits of Altai-Sayan Oral Epic Performance." Video lecture: World Oral Literature Project Workshop, 2009. https://sms.cam.ac.uk/media/756551.

———. "Re-Sounding the Spirits of Altaian Oral Epic Performance: Kai Throat-Singing and Its Repercussions." In *Language Documentation and Description 8: Special Issue on Oral Literature and Language Endangerment*, edited by Imogen Gunn and Mark Turin, 125–39. London: SOAS, 2010.

Pegg, Carol, and Yamaeva, Elizaveta. "Sensing 'Place': Performance, Oral Tradition, and Improvization in the Hidden Temples of Mountain Altai." *Oral Tradition* 27 (2021) 291–318.

Peirce, Charles Sanders. *The Collected Papers of Charles Sanders Peirce*, vols. 1–6, edited by Charles Hartshorne and Paul Weiss. Cambridge, MA: Harvard University Press, 1931–1958.

Perry, Peter S. "Biblical Performance Criticism: Survey and Prospects." *Religions* 10 (2019) 117–32.

———. *Insights from Performance Criticism*. Minneapolis: Fortress, 2016.

Pettitt, Thomas. "Before the Gutenberg Parenthesis: Elizabethan-American Compatibilities." Paper presented to plenary session of conference "Creativity, Ownership and Collaboration in the Digital Age," Media in Transition 5, Communications Forum, Massachusetts Institute of Technology, Cambridge, 2007. https://www.academia.edu/2946207/Before_the_Gutenberg_Parenthesis_Elizabethan_American_Compatibilities on January 2007.

Lau, Jessica. "How to Memorize Things Fast: 11 Memorization Techniques." 2019. https://zapier.com/blog/better-memory/.

Plueckahn, Rebekah S. "Musical Sociality: The Significant of Musical Engagement Among the Mongolian Altai Urianghai." PhD diss., Australian National University, 2013.

Pohl, Christine D. *Making Room: Recovering Hospitality as a Christian Tradition*. Grand Rapids: Eerdmans, 2011.

Polanyi, Michael. *The Tacit Dimension*. Chicago: University of Chicago Press, 1966.

Pym, Anthony. *Exploring Translation Theories*. 2nd ed. New York: Routledge, 2014.

Quak, Michel, et al. "A Multisensory Perspective of Working Memory." *Frontiers in Human Neuroscience* 9 (2015) 197.

Quakenbush, Stephen J. "Linguistic Hospitality and the Mission of God." In *God and Language: Exploring the Role of Language in the Mission of God*, edited by Michael Greed and Dawn Kruger, 285–301. Dallas: SIL International, 2022.

Radlov, Vasily Vasilyevich. *Models of Folk Literature of the Turkic Peoples of South Siberia and the Dzungar Steppe* [in Russian]. St. Petersburg: Tip. Imp. Akademii Nauk, 1866.

Rees, Robert. "Poetry: The Pnar Audio Translation Experiment." Unpublished Paper, n.d.

Reichl, Karl. *The Oral Epic: From Performance to Interpretation*. London/New York: Routledge, 2021.

———. *Turkic Oral Epic Poetry: Traditions, Forms, Poetic Structure*. Routledge Revivals. Oxford: Routledge, 1992.

———. "The Singing of Tales: The Role of Music in the Performance of Oral Epics in Turkey and Central Asia." *Classics* 14 (2016) 1–23.

———. *Singing the Past: Turkic and Medieval Heroic Poetry*. Myth and Poetics. New York: Cornell University Press, 2000.

Reiss, Katharina, and Vermeer, Hans J. *Towards a General Theory of Translational Action*. Routledge Tübingen: Niemeyer, 1984/2013.

Reiss, Katharina. "Adequacy and Equivalence in Translation." *Bible Translator* 34 (1983) 301–8.

———. *Translation Criticism—The Potentials and Limitations*. Manchester: St. Jerome, 1971/2000.

———. "Type, Kind, and Individuality of Text: Decision Making in Translation." In *The Translation Studies Reader*, 2nd ed., edited by Lawrence Venuti, 168–79. New York: Routledge, 1971/2004.

Reynolds, Chase. "The Shape of Communities Along the Communication Continuum: Considerations for BT and SE Strategies." Mar 3, 2020. https://map.bloomfire.

com/posts/3767692-the-shape-of-communities-along-the-communication-continuum-considerations-for-b.

Rhoads, David. "From Narrative in Print to Narrative in Performance." *Oral History Journal of South Africa* 5 (2017) 1–24.

———. *Mark as Story: An Introduction to the Narrative of a Gospel*. 3rd ed. Minneapolis: Fortress, 2012.

———. "The New Testament as Oral Performance." Mar. 23, 2015. https://vimeo.com/160142546.

———. "Performance Criticism: An Emerging Methodology in Second Testament Studies—Part I." *Biblical Theology Bulletin* 36 (2006) 118–33.

Ricoeur, Paul. *On Translation (Thinking in Action)*. Oxford: Routledge, 2004.

Robar, Elizabeth. "Discourse 101d: Discourse Layer Overview." Oct. 2, 2021. https://www.youtube.com/watch?v=0EWt40a1B_M.

Robbins, Vernon K. *Exploring the Texture of Texts: A Guide in Socio-Rhetorical Interpretation*. Valley Forge, PA: Trinity, 1996.

Ruge-Jones, Philip. "The Word Heard: How Hearing a Text Differs from Reading One." In *The Bible in Ancient and Modern Media: Story and Performance*, edited by Holly E. Hearon and Philip Ruge Jones, 101–13. Eugene, OR: Cascade, 2009.

———. "Those Sitting Around Jesus." In *From Text to Performance: Narrative and Performance Criticisms in Dialogue and Debate*, edited by Kelly R. Iverson, 27–52. Eugene, OR: Cascade, 2014.

Rushing, Daniel. "God's Women and God's Peasants: The Song of Deborah as Heroic Poetry for Marginalised Peoples." 2015. https://www.academia.edu/11058884/Gods_Women_and_Gods_Peasants_The_Song_of_Deborah_as_Heroic_Poetry_for_Marginalized_Peoples.

Russell, David Syme. *Between the Testaments*. Philadelphia: Fortress, 1960.

Salisbury, Murray. "Praise Psalms." Video for JCBT, Jerusalem, 2020.

———. "Psalm 133." Presentation for Altai Translation team, Jan. 2022, online.

———. "Translating and Performing Biblical Poems." Presentation for EMDC, Nov. 2023, online.

———. *Translating the Psalms by Singing Them: Promoting Heart-Engagement and Poetic Power*. Unpublished paper presented at the Bible Translation Conference, Dallas, TX, 2015.

Sammut-Bonnici, Tanya. "Complex Adaptive Systems." In *Wiley Encyclopedia of Management* 12, edited by C. L. Cooper et al., 1–2. Hoboken: John Wiley & Sons, 2015.

Saurman, Todd, and Saurman, Mary Beth. "Song Checking." In *All the World Will Worship: Helps for Developing Indigenous Hymns*, edited by Brian Schrag and Paul Neeley, 179–85. Duncanville, TX: Ethnodoxology Publications, 2005.

Schaefer, Konrad. *Psalms*. Berit Olam: Studies in Hebrew Narrative and Poetry. Collegeville, MN: Liturgical, 1993.

Schaff, Philip, ed. *St. Augustine: Exposition on the Book of Psalms*. Naples, FL: Grace Works Multimedia, 2010.

Schechner, Richard. *Performance Studies: An Introduction*. 3rd ed. New York: Routledge, 2013.

Schneider, Tammi J. *Judges*. Berit Olam: Studies in Hebrew Narratives and Poetry. Collegeville, MN: Liturgical, 1985.

Schrag, Brian. *Creating Local Arts Together: A Manual to Help Communities Reach Their Kingdom Goals*. Pasadena: William Carey Library, 2013.

Schubert, Eva. "Research About the Altayn Magtaal (Ode to the Altay Mountains)." Research paper from Hovd University, Mongolia, 2007.

Seed Company. "OBT Projects Translation Advisor Internalization Notes Template." Unpublished manuscript, 2019.

Segal, Benjamin. *A New Psalm: The Psalms as Literature*. Jerusalem: Gefen, 2013.

Seow, Choon-Leong. "An Exquisitely Poetic Introduction to the Psalter." *Journal of Biblical Literature* 134 (2013) 275–93.

Shiner, Whitney. *Proclaiming the Gospel: First-Century Performance of Mark*. Harrisburg, PA: Trinity Press International, 2003.

Shreve, Gregory M. "Levels of Explanation and Translation Expertise." In *Hermes— Journal of Language and Communication in Business* 57 (2018) 97–108.

———. "Translation as a Complex Adaptive System: A Framework for Theory Building in Cognitive Translatology." In *The Routledge Handbook of Translation and Cognition*, edited by Fabio Alves and Arnt Jacobsen, 69–87. London/New York: Routledge, 2021.

Stahl, Janet. "Internalizing in Storytelling: An Argument for Using Storytelling to Train for Bible Translation." Unpublished Paper. 2020.

Stahl, Jim. "We Tell to Remember: Bible Storying and Collective Memory." Paper presented at the Bible Translation Conference, Dallas, TX, 2013.

Stahl, Jim, and Stahl, Janet. "Oral Bible Storytelling as Shaped by On-the-Job Competency-Based Training and Group Experiential Learning." Paper presented at the Bible Translation Conference Online, 2021. https://www.btconference.org/proceedings-2021/oral-bible-storytelling-as-shaped-by-on-the-job-competency-based-training-and-group-experiential-learning.

———. "Sermon on the Mount OBS." Paper presented at the Orality Landscape of Practice, Sep. 2022. https://sites.google.com/view/oralitylop/documents/hom/september-2022-sermon-on-the-mount-obs.

Scriptura. "Psalm 1: Overview." Aug 3, 2022. https://www.youtube.com/watch?v=CrRZwy8MoFw&list=PLnbf64RXbjCl1VWhJ8bvUSlA2ikoIWGjd&index=2.

Stangor, Charles, and Jennifer Walinga. *Introduction to Psychology*. 1st Canadian ed. Victoria, BC: BCampus, 2021.

Stecconi, Ubaldo. "Peirce's Semiotics for Translation: Fidelity and Translation." In *Communicating the Bible in New Media*, edited by Paul A. Soukop and Robert Hodgson, 249–80. New York: American Bible Society, 1999.

———. "The Foundation of a General Theory of Translation Built on the Semiotics of C. S. Peirce." PhD diss., University College London, 2006.

Steffen, Tom. *Worldview-Based Storying: The Integration of Symbol, Story, and Ritual in the Orality Movement*. Richmond, VA: Orality Resources International, Centre for Oral Scriptures, 2018.

Steffen, Tom, and William Bjoraker. *The Return of Oral Hermeneutics: As Good Today as It Was for the Hebrew Bible and First-Century Christianity*. Eugene, OR: Wipf & Stock, 2020.

Sternberg, Meir. *Poetics of Biblical Narrative*. Bloomington: Indiana University Press, 1987.

Sul'gin, B. *About the Altai Edge. Maadai-Kara, Altai Heroic Epics [in Russian]*. Moskva: Nauka, 1973.

Sundersingh, Julian. *Audio-Based Translation: Communicating Biblical Scriptures to Non-Literate People*. Bangalore, India: SAIACS; Reading, UK: United Bible Societies, 2001.

Surazakov. S. S., and Shinzhin K. V., eds. *Altai Heroes in 15 vol.* [in Altai]. Tuulu Altaidyng bichik chygarar izdatel'stvozy: Gorno-Altaysk, 1958–95.

Swanson, Richard W. *Provoking the Gospel: Methods to Embody Biblical Storytelling Through Drama*. Cleveland: Pilgrim, 2004.

———. *Provoking the Gospel of Mark: A Storyteller's Commentary, Year B*. Cleveland: Pilgrim, 2005.

Swarr, David, et al. *Master Storyteller: God's Oral Communication in the Bible and Hebrew Tradition*. Richmond, VA: Center for Oral Scriptures, 2017.

Tarasova, Zoya. "The Role of Women in the Sakha Epic Olngkho 'N'urgun Bootur the Swift' by Planton Oiunskii." *Sibirica*, 12 (2013) 28–55.

Tate, Marvin E. *Psalms 51–100*. Word Biblical Commentary 19. Nashville: Thomas Nelson, 1998.

Toler, Kris. *A Key Ingredient in Achieving Naturalness in an Oral Translation*. MA diss., Dallas International University, 2020. https://www.researchgate.net/publication/346967413_Internalization_A_Key_Ingredient_in_Achieving_Naturalness_in_an_Oral_Translation.

Toler, Kris, and Toler, Susan. "A Shift in Understanding: Internalization as a Tool for Understanding." Paper presented at the Bible Translation Conference, online, Oct. 2021. https://www.btconference.org/speakers-2021.

Tov, Emanuel. *Scribal Practices and Approaches Reflected in the Texts Found in the Judean Desert*. Leiden: Brill, 2004.

Towner, Philip H. "Translation from the Other Side: Process Before Product or 'In Defense of Lost Causes.'" *Bible Translator* 69 (2018) 150–65.

Toy, Crawford Howell. *A Critical and Exegetical Commentary on the Book of Proverbs*. International Critical Commentary Series. Edinburgh: T. & T. Clark, 1899.

Tsumura, David Toshio. "Sorites in Psalm 133, 2–3a." *Biblica* 61 (1980) 416–17.

Turino, Thomas. "Signs of Imagination, Identity, and Experience: A Peircian Semiotic Theory for Music." *Ethnomusicology* 43 (1999) 221–55.

Turner, John R., and Baker, Rose M. "Complexity Theory: An Overview with Potential Applications for the Social Sciences." *Systems* 7 (2019) 1–23.

Tymoczko, Maria. *Enlarging Translation, Empowering Translators*. 2nd ed. London/New York: Routledge, 2010.

———. "Translation as Organized Complexity: Implications for Translation Theory." In *Complexity Thinking in Translation Studies: Methodological Studies*, edited by Kobus Marais and Reine Meylaerts, 138–58. New York: Routledge, 2019.

———. "Reconceptualizing Translation Theory: Integrating Non-Western Thought About Translation." In *Translating Others*, vol. 1, edited by Theo Hermans, 13–32. London/New York: Routledge, 2006.

Tyukhtenev, T. S. *The Songs of the Altai People* [in Russian]. Gorno-Altaysk: Gorno-Altaysk Altayskiye Knigi Isdatelstvo, 1972.

Van Aswegen, Kobus, and Regine Koroma. *Understanding Oral Bible Translation*. Chicago Heights, IL: Word for the World, 2021.

Van Deusen, Kira. *Singing Story Healing Drum: Shamans and Storytellers of Turkic Siberia*. Seattle: University of Washington Press, 2004.

Van Doorslaer, Luc. "Risking Conceptual Maps: Mapping as a Keywords-Related Tool Underlying the Online Translation Studies Bibliography." *International Journal of Translation Studies* 19 (2007) 217–33.

Van Rooyen, Marlie, and Naudé, Jacobus A. "Media and Translation." In *A Guide to Bible Translation: People, Languages, and Topics*, edited by Philip A. Noss and Christine S. Houser, 586–90. Swindon, UK: United Bible Societies, 2019.

Verbitskiy, Vasily I. *"The Jangar Song": A Collection of Ethnographic Articles and Studies* [in Russian]. Gorno-Altaysk: Ak Chechek, 1893.

Vermeer, Hans. "What Does It Mean to Translate?" *Indian Journal of Applied Linguistics* 13 (1987) 25–33.

Voinov, Vitaly. "Politeness Devices in the Tuvan Language." 2014. https://www.academia.edu/9815884/Politeness_Devices_in_the_Tuvan_Language.

Walton, John H., and D. Brent Sandy, D. *The Lost World of Scripture: Ancient Literary Culture and Biblical Authority*. Downers Grove, IL: InterVarsity, 2014.

Ward, Richard F., and Trobisch, David J. *Bringing the Word to Life: Engaging the New Testament through Performing it*. Grand Rapids: Eerdmans, 2013.

Wendland, Ernst R. *Analyzing the Psalms*. 2nd ed. Dallas: SIL International, 2002.

———. *Finding and Translating the Oral-aural elements in Written Language: The Case of the New Testament epistles*. New York: Edwin Mellen Press, 2008.

West, Travis M. "The Art of Biblical Performance: Biblical Performance Criticism and the Genre of the Biblical Narratives." Ph.D. diss., Vrije Universiteit Amsterdam, 2018.

Wood, Gallina. "Wisdom of the Altai in Epic Poetry." MA diss,. Masaryk University, 2007.

Yagmur, Kutlay, and Kroon, Sjaak. "Objective and Subjective Data on Altai and Kazakh Ethnolinguistic Vitality in the Russian Federation Republic of Altai." *Journal of Multilingual and Multicultural Development* 27, no. 3 (2006) 241–58.

Yenchinov, E. V. "'The Jangar Song'—The Ritualistic Songs of the Altai Peoples" [in Russian]. 2002. http://ethnography.omsu.ru/page.php?id=480.

Younghans, Holly M., et al. "A Time to Reflect: Initial Responses on Oral Bible Translation from Translation Consultants." Paper presented at the Bible Translation Conference, Dallas, TX, 2019.

Zenger, Erich, and Frank-Lothar Hossfeld. *A Commentary on Psalms 51–100*. Hermeneia. Minneapolis: Fortress, 2005.

Zogbo, Lynell. "From Scripture to Song: On Organizing a Poetic, Music-Oriented Bible Translation Workshop." Paper presented at the Bible Translation Conference, Dallas, TX, 2013.

———., and Wendland Ernst R. *Hebrew Poetry in the Bible: A Guide for Understanding and for Translating*. New York: UBS, 2000.

Zucker, David J. and Reiss, Moshe. "Subverting Sexuality: Manly Women; Womanly Men in Judges 4–5." *Biblical Theology Bulletin: Journal of Bible and Culture* 45 (2015) 32–37.

VIDEOS

Play link to all the recordings: https://www.youtube.com/playlist?list=PL7n-aftH4CS3ECHZA97ckjtnlF__OKMTK

Video 1 - https://www.youtube.com/watch?v=EAGZvxbpSSQ
Video 2 - https://www.youtube.com/watch?v=_ob4HoobHFA
Video 3 - https://www.youtube.com/watch?v=JMty4xrYZxo
Video 4 - https://www.youtube.com/watch?v=92dAgQ8At4A
Video 5 - https://www.youtube.com/watch?v=HD7Kc5CgFCo
Video 6 - https://www.youtube.com/watch?v=YGGsRKkA3L4
Video 7 - https://www.youtube.com/watch?v=qsqfHcI_PJw
Video 8 - https://www.youtube.com/watch?v=tngISYjPzAY
Video 9 - https://www.youtube.com/watch?v=XDXgupSVIE8
Video 10 - https://www.youtube.com/watch?v=MoufSu7daBk
Video 11 - https://www.youtube.com/watch?v=8ZrNNzosEDc

INTERVIEWS

Interview with Swapna Alexander, Sep. 9, 2021
Interview with OBT team 11 in India, Dec. 11, 2019
Interview with OBT team 10 in India, Apr., 2021
Personal interview with Aidin Kurmanov, Jun., 2022
Personal interview with Anatoli Turulanov, Jun., 2022
Personal interview with Bair Turulanov, Jul., 2022
Personal interview with Bolot Bairshev, Jun., 2022
Personal interview with Daniel Danzheev, Jul., 2022
Personal interview with Emil Terkishev, Jul., 2022
Personal interview with Kidrash Shumarov, Jun., 2022
Personal interview with Natalya Enchinova, Jul., 2022
Personal interview with Nikolay Sergetkishov, Jun., 2022
Personal interview with Nogon Shumarov, Jun., 2022
Personal interview with Yuri Chendeyev, Jul., 2022

www.ingramcontent.com/pod-product-compliance
Lightning Source LLC
Chambersburg PA
CBHW070232230426
43664CB00014B/2269